ROUTLEDGE LIBRARY EDITIONS: PSYCHIATRY

Volume 14

DRAMATHERAPY AND PSYCHIATRY

DRAMATHERAPY AND PSYCHIATRY

DOROTHY M. LANGLEY AND
GORDON E. LANGLEY

Routledge
Taylor & Francis Group

LONDON AND NEW YORK

First published in 1983 by Croom Helm

This edition first published in 2019
by Routledge
2 Park Square, Milton Park, Abingdon, Oxon OX14 4RN

and by Routledge
711 Third Avenue, New York, NY 10017

Routledge is an imprint of the Taylor & Francis Group, an informa business

British Library Cataloguing in Publication Data
A catalogue record for this book is available from the British Library

ISBN: 978-1-138-60492-6 (Set)
ISBN: 978-0-429-43807-3 (Set) (ebk)
ISBN: 978-1-138-62481-8 (Volume 14) (hbk)
ISBN: 978-1-138-62492-4 (Volume 14) (pbk)
ISBN: 978-0-429-46037-1 (Volume 14) (ebk)

Publisher's Note
The publisher has gone to great lengths to ensure the quality of this reprint but points out that some imperfections in the original copies may be apparent.

Disclaimer
The publisher has made every effort to trace copyright holders and would welcome correspondence from those they have been unable to trace.

Dramatherapy and Psychiatry

DOROTHY M. LANGLEY
with Gordon E. Langley

CROOM HELM
London • New York • Sydney

© 1983 Dorothy M. Langley and Gordon E. Langley
Croom Helm Ltd, Provident House, Burrell Row,
Beckenham, Kent, BR3 1AT
Croom Helm Australia, 44-50 Waterloo Road,
North Ryde, 2113, New South Wales

Published in the USA by
Croom Helm
in association with Methuen, Inc.
29 West 35th Street
New York, NY 10001
Reprinted 1987

British Library Cataloguing in Publication Data

Langley, Dorothy M.
    Dramatherapy and psychiatry.
    1. Psychodrama
    I. Title II. Langley, Gordon E.
    616.89'1523   RC489.P7

ISBN 0-7099-1624-8 (pbk.)

Printed and bound in Great Britain
by Billing & Sons Limited, Worcester.

CONTENTS

Acknowledgements

1. What is Dramatherapy?   9
2. Games   23
   Appendix I: Some Useful Games   27
3. The Elderly   39
4. Schizophrenia   54
5. Personality Disorders   75
6. Rehabilitation   88
7. Role Play   96
8. Social Skills   112
9. Theatre   133
10. Reminiscence *Gordon E. Langley*   142
11. Audio-visual Aids   156
    Appendix II: Some Useful Music   167
12. Looking Both Ways: A Psychiatrist's Guide to Dramatherapy *Gordon E. Langley*   171
13. The Patient, the Therapist and the Goal *Gordon E. Langley*   179
14. The Role of the Dramatherapist   189
15. Some Other Considerations   202
    Appendix III: Some Useful Addresses   216
Bibliography   218
Index   223

ACKNOWLEDGEMENTS

I would like to thank the following people:

My husband	for his love which helped me to grow, his support and encouragement in my professional development and the writing of this book, for allowing the use of his diagrams and teaching aids, and for contributing three chapters from his own experience of dramatherapy.
My children	for tolerating my frequent absences and preoccupations, and for their interest in my work and bringing home ideas from their own drama lessons!
Gwen Williams	for keeping the household on an even keel.
Gill Meredith	for hours of typing and the way in which she has organised me!
Baz Kershaw	for permission to use his material in the chapter on reminiscence.
Vivienne Furze	for allowing me to use her invented games in the chapter on the elderly and photographs of them in action.
Ivy Broom	for sharing an afternoon of simple games to be used as a photographic model.
Exe Vale Hospital Drama Enthusiasts	for permission to publish photographs of a training session.
Leon Winston	from whom I have learned so much. For his own enthusiasm for drama which never fails to stimulate me.
Linda Crosby	for her patience and help in compiling the index.

My many friends among the patients and staff of Exe Vale Hospital with whom I have had the privilege of sharing experiences over the last twelve years. Without them, this book would never have been written.

DML

1 WHAT IS DRAMATHERAPY?

Drama

For many people the term 'drama' is synonymous with 'theatre'. Misconceptions have arisen from this which create expectations and unnecessary anxiety about its use in therapy. There is a difference in that drama is a personal experience in a group and theatre is communicating the experience to others. Baz Kershaw (personal communication) puts it succinctly: 'Drama is primarily concerned with the personal growth of the individual as part of a group; theatre raises the results of that growth to public significance through metaphorical presentation'. Of particular interest to those involved in the psychology of personal adjustment is the fact that drama came into being from the time that man first began to explore himself in relation to his environment, and goes far beyond the confines of theatre. This exploration stems from man's desire to create and drama has creativity as part of its being. It engages the imagination to look at and explore attitudes rather than characters. Drama is about extending boundaries of time and place as far as they can go and our emotional responses to them. It poses the question – 'What if?' – allowing us to look at the possibilities of where a situation could lead if allowed to go to its limits, and alternative ways of getting there. The process is one of exploration through interaction and it happens in the present although we may be concerned with events of the past or future. It seeks to answer the question – 'What if?' – through action and interaction, sharing that experience both with other people and our environment. In the process, drama can make use of other art forms: music, painting, dance, sculpture, etc.

Theatre

The conventional idea of theatre is that of a stage and auditorium with tiered seats, an idea which most of us have experienced. In recent years there has been a loosening of the concept to admit that theatre can take place without a stage and that props, lighting and costume are not necessary. As Peter Brook (1968) says – 'I can take any empty space and call it a bare stage. A man walks across this empty space while someone else is watching him, and this is all that is needed for an act of theatre to be engaged.'

Theatre has its roots in religion. The early rituals in which people participated taught them about the gods. The dramatic experience of these rituals was a way of coming to terms with the environment and its problems. The myths with which we are familiar were developed and became part of the whole experience. It was the Greeks who created theatre as we know it. They built theatres with a stage and auditorium and encouraged writers to produce scripts for actors to present to the audience. In medieval times Mystery Plays were produced by the church to teach bible stories to the congregation, most of whom could not read. The actors were members of the congregation and the plays were performed in church. Later, Morality Plays came into being in order to teach the ethics which stemmed from bible stories. As these became more earthly in content, they also became more bawdy, until finally the church could not tolerate them and the players took to the streets and acted there. It was the rise of the Guilds who supplied actors for traditional parts in plays that finally produced acting as a profession. One member from each Guild was sent to take part in the local pageant. As it became the custom for one person to be selected more than others, he gradually became the actor for his Guild until, by Shakespeare's time, acting had become recognised as a profession in its own right. Actors were usually itinerant, travelling with a cart which served both as transport and stage. Plays were still a means of teaching, not only about church doctrines, but also about life in general and were a way of presenting topical issues to the people. They were 'a mirror held up to nature' (*Hamlet*).

Today we think of actors as highly skilled professionals or amateurs with varying skills developed as a hobby. In either case the standard to which they perform dictates the enjoyment and insight which the audience gains from it. The higher the standard of production, the more (usually!) the enjoyment. So whether the performance is professional or amateur, it is a play, mime or sequence of events presented to the audience who enjoy it or not depending on standards of writing and acting. The higher the standard the more likely it is that theatre will teach us something about ourselves and give us an increased sensitivity to the issues portrayed. The audience, however, are not passive recipients but react among themselves by laughter, applause, silence, coughing, etc., and so communicate their feelings to the actors. This actor/audience relationship becomes a shared experience in which a sympathetic understanding can be created. Unlike drama, theatre must have an end-product and the final presentation is the result of a period of rehearsal. However, each performance is unique in that it happens at one particular time, is shared by the people present (both actors and audience) and because their varied experience and personalities are peculiar to that moment.

Therapy

A visit to the theatre, a game of golf, painting, playing the piano and many other activities, we frequently say 'lifts us out of ourselves', makes us 'feel better', 'forget our problems', 'feel more relaxed' or 'feel more refreshed'. All these terms imply change in some way. We are probably all dissatisfied with some part of our lives and our ability to effect a change to a more desirable state depends on our intelligence, personality and experience in life. We are motivated towards a set of goals which can be variously described, but one useful way of looking at this is that of Maslow (1943). He says that 'There are at least five sets of goals, which we may call basic needs. These are briefly physiological, safety, love, esteem, and self-actualisation. In addition, we are motivated by the desire to achieve or maintain the various conditions upon which these basic satisfactions rest and by certain more intellectual desires.' He goes on to say that we have a hierarchy of our basic needs which may change from time to time, but one always emerges as more dominant than the others. As soon as that need is gratified it no longer becomes an active motivator, so we are always striving for something else (see also Chapter 3). If we are unhappy, creative activities can lift us out of ourselves, thus effecting a change. Treatment (or therapy) in a strict medical sense of healing is also bringing about change — changing symptoms in the direction of health. Creativity can produce emotional change in healthy people. Changing people with emotional disorders to a primarily creative experience can, therefore, be regarded as treatment. The treatment of emotional disorders involves changing emotions and attitudes in the direction of health. Creative activity, i.e. drama, produces change in a similar direction.

It is easier to accept change at some times than at others. While some people may become paralysed into rigid inactivity, Kaplan (1961, 1964) postulates that the crisis of illness heightens some people's willingness to consider change. If we consider a state of equilibrium (i.e. health) to be the most desirable state, then we can see how a crisis such as illness or anxiety is a stimulus to change and so upsets the balance. In order to restore this balance, we resort to either adaptive (constructive/creative) behaviour or maladaptive (neurotic) behaviour. The latter, although producing short-term gain is, in the end, self-defeating. For if we choose the latter, we find ourselves in a vicious, maladaptive circle which, if treatment is to be effective, has to be broken at the point of contact with the adaptive circle and emerge constructively redirected to get on the path to equilibrium again (Figure 1.1).

Figure 1.1: Maladaptive Behaviour Will Not Restore Stability

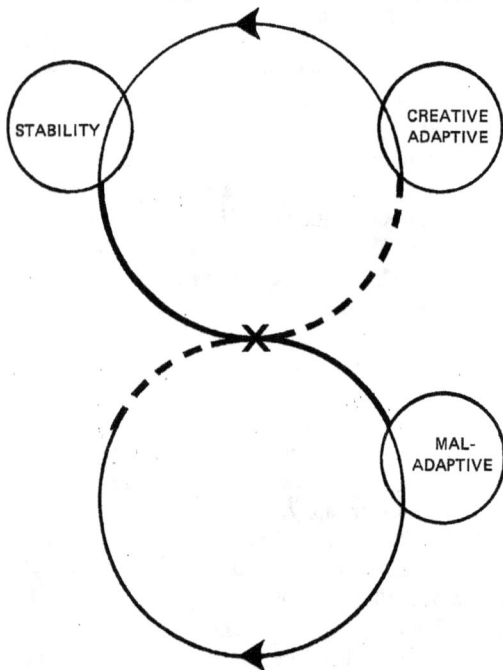

Therapy, in my definition, involves creating an environment in which healing can take place, so anything that facilitates a move from the maladaptive behaviour towards the adaptive and personal equilibrium can be described as therapeutic. Although we all hope to reach the goal of equilibrium, therapy does not discount temporary or incomplete change as being valuable. Therefore, if someone 'feels better' following some activity, the temporary change is no less valid than a permanent one. A number of such changes could be additive and become more enduring. However, the creation of an environment conducive to change does not necessarily mean that the recipient will take advantage of it. We create the environment and use certain therapeutic tools, but it is ultimately a matter of whether the client will allow the change to take place. It is as well to remember that the client does not owe the therapist a change, so the therapist must not be continually expecting it. If change takes place it is because the client has allowed it to happen and not because the therapist has done something for him. Sometimes the 'therapy' has to be geared towards motivation. Then the first goal is that of changing from a complacent acceptance of his present state to a desire for change. This is a decision only the client can make and cannot be forced upon him.

The Therapist

People come into training as therapists for varying reasons. Such reasons are personal to us and our desires to give/receive, be accepted/rejected, be of value, or in authority, or to compensate for something we feel lacking, or to relate to other people, are all involved. Whatever our motivation, both conscious or unconscious, we come into training to acquire skills in order to help others change. Training will vary according to our professional discipline and the school at which we learn it. But if we are facilitating change in others, we must be aware of aspects of our own personalities which need to change. If we do not deal with our own major conflicts and prejudices they are likely to influence our attitude towards our client's conflicts. This personal development does not cease on qualification as a therapist. As we continue to change we discover new areas of ourselves of which we may have been unaware. We may see ourselves reflected in our clients and need to come to terms with our own neurotic traits and behaviour. If we are not open to such change ourselves, we may be depriving our clients of the opportunity of maximum growth in a professional relationship. As the therapist broadens his own experience and develops as a person as well as in terms of professional skills, he will also grow in confidence and be able to modify his own ideas as the client unfolds his personal conflicts and problems. We need to be flexible both in our skills and our attitude towards the client. We need to be sensitive to a loose concept of what a patient's illness/behaviour is about. As we know him better we maybe need to change our ideas about him. Therefore we need to be free in ourselves and able to modify our views.

Dramatherapy

The use of the arts in therapy is not new. When David played and sang to Saul it was to soothe the rages of his epileptic temperament. The creative experience was a tool which helped bring about a change of mood.

I would define dramatherapy as the use of drama as a therapeutic tool. It is not, as in theatre, an acquired skill which people can or cannot do, but a medium in which each person can participate *at his own level.* It is an extension of the natural play that we all know as children that gives people the means to become more creative and spontaneous beings. For the client there is no *standard of performance* in the theatrical sense. *The therapy is in the doing.* It is concerned with all the arts and overlaps with many other activities. By the use of games and improvisation (spontaneous scene) we help the promotion of personal growth. The main ways in which we do this can be listed as follows.

Trust: We need to promote trust within all our group members. Usually patients will trust staff members easily, but we need to work harder to develop trust with their fellow clients. A simple exercise like allowing another person to lead you around the room with your eyes closed invites trust from the one and responsibility for another person from the other.

Group Cohesion: Simple games can become a shared experience. Touching games, working and talking in close physical proximity, and games requiring group decisions help to form a sense of group identity.

Imagination: Can be stimulated by guessing games and mime. It is important that adults retain and use their imagination. We often see this as something belonging to childhood, but in fact we need to use our imaginations in problem-solving. If we cannot imagine where a situation can lead, we may find ourselves in trouble. Likewise, if we cannot imagine the limits of an action, we may also find ourselves in a situation with which we cannot cope. Derek Bowskill (1973) writes 'Imagination enables us to cut through the probable, achieve the possible and glimpse the unattainable.'

Memory: Can be stimulated and exercised by music and games.

Projection Techniques: Can be fun if presented as games.

Sensory Perception and Physical Awareness: Games can be used to develop all the senses. Physical contact allows people to learn to become aware of the feel and sounds of their own and other people's bodies without feeling anxious (Figures 1.2 and 1.3). The image people have of their own bodies is sometimes relevant to their behaviour. *Movement:* This is important to us all. If we do not use our muscles they cease to function properly. Movement can be enjoyed for its own sake or as a means to achieving an end. The way we move is also an important non-verbal communication in body language. Long-stay patients with few activities and depressed people who are concerned only with their problems have little motivation for movement. In drama we can give some kind of stimulation and motivation for movement.

Figure 1.2: Physical Proximity — Group Tangle

Figure 1.3: Physical Proximity — Warmth and Pressure

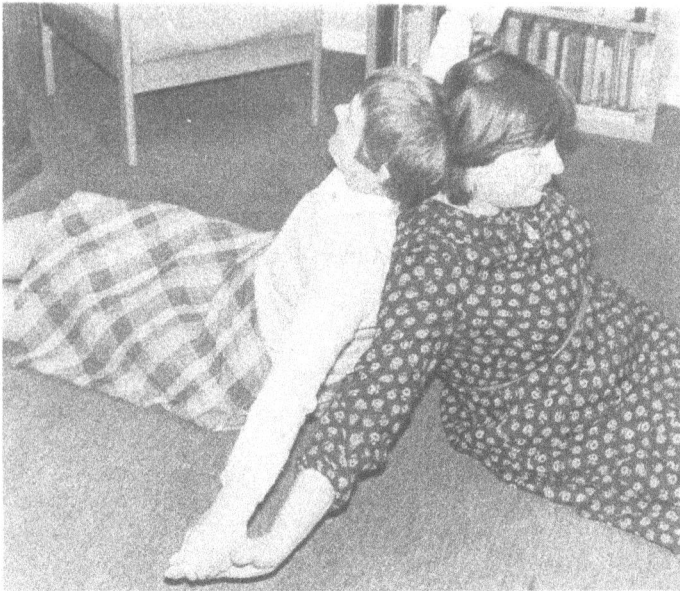

Relaxation: This goes hand-in-hand with movement. The greater the tension we put on our muscles, the greater the relaxation when we let it go. Relaxed bodies lead to relaxed minds, and tension, both physical and mental, is common with our clients. They need to learn not only how to relax to sleep at night but also how to move in a relaxed way and so ease tense muscles.

Concentration: Can be encouraged by simple games and activities.

Communication: Both verbal and non-verbal communication can be explored and if necessary learned in drama sessions. Sometimes people are inhibited in a social situation because they do not have a good vocabulary. Word games can become a learning situation. Sometimes people are giving the wrong non-verbal cues to the world and so creating more problems for themselves. Drama is a valuable way of looking at this.

Social Rehearsal and Role Play: We can look for different ways of coping with a situation by playing impromptu scenes, rehearsing a difficult interview, or learn something of interview techniques and how to converse with strangers.

Motivation: Above all, we aim to encourage people to widen their horizons, desire new experiences, and have the confidence to reach out for them.

Drama can be used in three ways in therapy.

(1) Enrichment

Anyone, no matter what age, abilities or intelligence, can enjoy drama. The play element of drama should make it fun. If it is not enjoyable, the therapist needs to ask herself 'why?'. We seem to be bound to the idea that medicine must be unpleasant to be any good and the thought of having *fun* presupposes that dramatherapy is not an 'in-depth' therapy but an activity simply to pass the time. Long-stay patients are generally deprived of fun. Either the treatment is expected to 'do you good' in the sense that it is unpleasant or there is nothing to do but watch the television. The skills of interaction are soon lost and with it frequently the ability to have fun. This aspect of dramatherapy is often neglected or passed by as irrelevant, but I think it is as important as the other uses of drama.

(2) Towards a Specific Goal

Such goals might include rehabilitation, social skills, overcoming phobias, role exploration, etc. The dramatherapist uses the powerful tool of drama, which we have seen takes experiences, situations, conflicts, and looks at them in detail, to explore alternative ways of dealing with them and possible outcomes. By working through defences dramatically it is possible to uncover the problems involved. The client may have a vague idea about his illness/behaviour but the insight gained through drama can help him to see more clearly. Time, however, is limited and the dramatherapist has to find efficient methods by which the development can be speeded up. In training, he learns about the patterns of behaviour and unsatisfactory ways of coping with problems that motivate people to seek therapy. He also learns ways in which to use his skills to deal with specific problems. If one is treating any kind of illness, either physical or mental with drugs, then it would be illogical to give the patient all the drugs on the market in the hope that one would cure him. This kind of 'blanket' treatment may achieve some results or may even be harmful. Similarly, the dramatherapist does not present his client with the 'blanket' of drama but channels his dramatic activities in the manner most appropriate to his circumstances. He learns to match the therapy to the illness/behaviour problem. By selecting the groups carefully, the

dramatherapist can work at the same time with a few people whose
needs are similar and who can reach their goals more quickly if their
dramatic experience is directed along certain lines. So careful selection
is the first way of achieving efficiency. Then comes the channelling of
dramatic activities. For example:

Group A: A group dealing with role exploration may spend a long
time looking at fantasy roles. The group could look at the role of
holidaymaker — Where could I go? What could I do? They could
have, in fantasy, the holiday of a lifetime and by extending the role
have some idea of what might happen and how they might behave.
This experience could be stored up for use when they actually went on
holiday. It could be a trip abroad or simply the ward outing.

Group B: A group which has gathered to overcome phobias would not
spend time on a fantasy holiday, creative and enjoyable as that may
be. Their activities would be directed towards exploring space and
movement within it, physical awareness of one's own body and
proximity to others, the anxiety these things arouse and
experimentation of ways of dealing with it.

The selection of group goals is important and the therapist has to
know sufficient about the needs and abilities of the group to ensure
that:

(1) The overall goal is achievable.
(2) The group does not continually set unattainable goals.
(3) The goals the therapist sets for himself, within that group (which
    may not be the same), are not beyond his reach. For example:
    (a) A therapist has a long-stay group of patients and the goal set
        by the ward team is rehabilitation.
    (b) The group may not understand the full implication of this and
        may simply set their goal as 'having fun'.
    These two are compatible provided the group is capable of entering
    into the 'games' spirit and the dramatic material is fun at their level
    (e.g. an improvisation about ghouls and ghosts would be great fun
    for children but long-term schizophrenic patients may become so
    involved in a morbid fantasy that they are unable to cut off from it
    and the experience becomes prolonged and threatening and no
    longer fun. Their need is reality).
    (c) The therapist may set for himself a personal goal of relating
        at a certain level to all members of the group. If he continually
        pitches that level too high and never achieves the relationship
        goals he set for himself, he will become disheartened and

disillusioned no matter what goals the group attain.

(3) Psychodrama

Psychodrama is a form of psychotherapy which was devised by J. L. Moreno in the 1920s and 1930s. He was impressed by the way in which children were able to play out stories and express quite deep emotions when he led them in impromptu activity groups. First he formed a 'theatre of spontaneity' in which actors performed unscripted scenes and were encouraged to draw on their own experiences. Later his use of trained actors as auxiliaries was replaced by group members as he developed his technique. He produced a whole new process of psychotherapy which he termed psychodrama and which was the basis for a new wave of group psychotherapies. He defined it as an exploration of truth through dramatic methods.

Psychodrama is a group process with the problems of one person, the protagonist, as the centre of activity. Moreno observed that in life we have a script and role to which we adhere, but psychodrama gives us an opportunity to try out new scripts and perhaps find a new role or a new approach to an old one. This is done by spontaneous scenes set up by the protagonist to look at himself and his relationships, and for the acting out of painful or desired situations. These situations are played for real, and the protagonist is supported by a 'double' who helps him to say and do things he finds impossible alone. He is helped both to feel and to express his emotions through a catharsis of feeling, thus ridding himself of emotions which may have built up over years. This flood of emotion can be a creative and extremely important experience, and is not what is commonly called 'acting out'.

Psychodrama uses many of the exercises of dramatherapy to develop trust and group cohesion. Games and relaxation are frequently used as 'warm ups' to sessions to help group members prepare their minds and bodies for the group sessions. Psychodrama, as we know it today, did not come into being overnight. The structure evolved as Moreno became aware of needs and of new ways of working. As one trains in psychodrama and experiences the power of it repeatedly, a trust of the method develops. I have found this to be true both of staff in training, and clients in groups. They learn to trust not only the therapist but also the process being used. Initially, the anxieties of both staff and clients seem to centre around 'What will happen if I (they) let go of emotions?' I never cease to wonder at the power of psychodrama and the mind that created it. All the safeguards one needs are there within the structure if you look for them. There are three phases to psychodrama, first the warm up in which the group prepares for action and a protagonist is selected. Second is the action, when the protagonist works through a series of scenes from the periphery of the problem to the heart of the matter. Finally comes the sharing when all group members share from their own experience and feelings with the protagonist.

Training is not so much a learning of technique, but a continual exposure to this structured role play until it is absorbed and becomes part of one's way of thinking. The time it takes for this to happen varies with the individual, but it cannot happen quickly as there is so much to experience and assimilate. This is why adequate training is imperative. Until the structure has become a part of us, we cannot use it to maximum effect.

Psychodrama and dramatherapy have much in common, but whilst psychodrama is directed towards emotional catharsis, dramatherapy does not necessarily demand deep emotional involvement. In my experience, psychodrama requires a certain level of intelligence and verbal capacity and is a powerful method of psychotherapy for selected patients. As I see it, at the moment, it has a limited application but as my own experience increases I find I am working psychodramatically with people I previously considered unsuitable. So, I may change my opinion as time goes on and I develop professionally. However, dramatherapy is of value to everyone, no matter what age, intelligence, physical or verbal abilities, provided it is presented at the appropriate level. In the confines of this book I intend to discuss only dramatherapy and not psychodrama, particularly in the context of psychiatric patients.

Mental Disability

There are three main categories of psychiatric disability:

(1) Psychosis. The schizophrenias and some depressive illnesses come under this heading. Acute symptoms may be incomprehensible to anyone but the client and may be dramatic in nature. Bizarre behaviour may result and these are the illnesses which can sometimes fit the popular conception of 'madness'. The application of dramatherapy here will be dealt with in Chapter 4.

(2) Neurosis. We all have some neurotic traits — fear of heights, spiders, feelings of inadequacy, lack of self-confidence, behaviour that is too

aggressive or passive, etc. This is part of the 'normal' personality. In some people (usually as a result of conflict or anxiety) these feelings become so important that the neurotic traits dominate their waking life and maybe interfere with their sleep. It is this distortion of normality that is termed neurosis. The drama therapist spends much of his or her time with these clients. I have not considered the application in a separate chapter, preferring to write under headings of specific needs rather than diagnostic categories.

(3) Organic Brain Disorders. These are mainly the dementias and psychiatric problems of ageing and epilepsy. The application of dramatherapy is discussed particularly in Chapter 3. Epilepsy is not considered separately but long-stay clients are included in Chapter 6. Short-stay clients will be incorporated into groups according to their special needs.

These psychiatric handicaps have nothing to do with physical or intellectual ability and are not related to intelligence.

Mental handicap is impaired intellect which can be present from birth or the result of physical illness or injury which either arrests mental development or, if the brain damage is very severe, causes regression to an earlier stage of development. Mental handicap is irreversible and the damage cannot be repaired. Therapy is directed towards development, rehabilitation and enrichment. I do not propose to deal with mental handicap as I cannot do it justice here; it requires a book in itself. However, mentally handicapped people are prone to the same psychiatric, behavioural and emotional problems as all of us and dramatherapy can therefore be applied in that context.

Aims of this Book

I am writing this book in an attempt to answer the questions continually put to me by family, friends, colleagues and students alike. 'What is dramatherapy? What do you do? How do you set about it?' I hope this will be a simple and practical answer to the questions asked by various people:

(1) Colleagues in other disciplines who would like to refer patients to groups but are not sure what dramatherapy is.

(2) Members of staff whose patients attend dramatherapy sessions and

who would like to know what it involves.

(3) Those who think they might like to train in dramatherapy but are not sure what they will be letting themselves in for.

(4) People who work in other areas of drama and who would like to know of its application in therapy.

(5) Dramatherapy students who would like to read about their subject.

(6) Dramatherapists with whom I would like to share my ideas and ways of working. We often work in isolation and unsupported and I would like to think that this book could help others to feel that they are not alone in the field and perhaps give them the stimulation that we all need at some time.

(7) All professionals working with the mentally ill and who wish to know what dramatherapy can offer their patients or clients.

(8) Those who are just curious.

These are the people for whom I am writing. Yet, although the information is here in this book, drama is a dynamic experience and written information can be flat and lifeless. No amount of writing can be a substitute for real experience. So if what you read interests or stimulates you, I hope you will complement your reading by going out and experiencing the power of drama for yourself.

2 GAMES

Since Eric Berne (1964) published his book *Games People Play*, therapists have tended to use the word 'game' in his sense. Consequently, whenever I talk about drama games I have to explain that these are non-competitive learning games and not ways of 'getting one over' another person. For a long time dramatherapy meant games to me and it is only in the last few years that I have recognised other theatre skills used in therapy. Games are still very important and when working with long-term patients I frequently plan a whole project on games played to a purpose.

All new groups, no matter what final level of work will be achieved, begin with group cohesive games, trust games and relaxation together. Without these preliminaries I find it impossible for a group to reach a stage of personal commitment and self-revelation before its closing after eight or ten sessions. Short-stay clients are rarely together for longer than this and it is important to get a group working as soon as possible. Long-stay clients are usually more withdrawn and take longer to form relationships, so that one can spend months on basic trust and cohesive games. It is important in all therapy to work at the pace the group sets for itself, but drama games are a valuable short cut.
This is becoming obvious in all kinds of group training and activities, not just dramatherapy. Games are even used on management courses.

Drama has its roots in creative games and basic skills of hand and eye are needed. My favourite introduction to a new group is:

(1) The ball/name game — as you catch the ball call your name. Progress to throwing the ball to a named person in the circle.
(2) Divide into groups of three or four with balls or hoops. Ask the group just to experiment with the apparatus and discover how many different ways they can find to use it.
(3) In the same groups, devise a game using your apparatus and composing rules.
(4) Then meet together to discuss how people are feeling.

So, in the first twenty minutes or so of a session, a new group has achieved:
(a) Knowing a few names and so 'personalising' people.

(b) Relating to an object (i.e. ball) before being asked to relate to people. This is a less threatening approach than relating directly to another human being.

(c) Looking at another person to throw a ball but not being required to have eye contact directly.

(d) Leaving their chairs (and safety) in order to play.

(e) Being in close proximity and possibly physical contact with three others in the group.

(f) Using imagination and ingenuity and possibly previous experience in games with objects.

(g) Being involved in group decision-making.

(h) Familiarity with others in groups, often with laughter in making the decision.

(i) Disciplining themselves to accept the rules of the game.

(j) Entry into sharing of feelings with a large group.

For some groups this is enough for the first session. Others go on to work in diads and triads, relating to more people with each game. This is always my opening with new staff groups and introductory workshops, a tactic which immediately gives cause for discussion and further interaction. Not only basic games are useful. Depending on the group, one can progress through a whole series of games to role play games and finally, role play itself. Here are a few:

Trust Exercises. Commencing with just closing eyes, which requires a lot of effort from some patients, progressing to blind walk and variations, falling into the arms of the group, lying on backs, allowing oneself to be lifted by groups, working in diads, triads and large groups.

Eye Contact Games. Finding partners, cat and mouse, communicating by gaze, looking at everyone in the room, trying to say something by gaze.

Physical Contact Games. Bumping into people, hopping and putting people off balance. Sculpting in diads or groups. Any game requiring linked hands. Walking in mazes, tying groups in knots, balancing with partners, etc.

Sensory Perception and Body Awareness Games. Any game which concentrates on parts of the body, clapping, stamping, jumping. Miming the removal of heavy objects, listening, looking, tactile games.

Emotional Awareness Games. Miming an emotion, moving to represent feelings, creating roles/characters from feelings.

Memory Games. Cueing games of all kinds. Shopping lists. Name games and reminiscence games all help to sharpen views and retain memory.

Role Play Games. I went to market . . . I packed a suitcase . . ., etc. Shopping games and simulation, guessing games about prices and products. Fantasy games and improvisations.

Group Cohesion. Almost any kind of game where people are asked to co-operate with others helps to make a cohesive group, particularly physical contact games that bring people closer both physically and emotionally. Sharing games like telling a partner about a favourite place, describing a favourite room, etc. Building games, both physical and mental, help group decision-making and cohesion.

Concentration. Mirror work is particularly good for developing concentration. Some groups can only manage this for brief periods at first because of the high degree of concentration required. Listening games, awareness games, such games as walking with eyes closed and listening to partners' instructions against a background of noise. Trying to read against incessant interruptions from a partner.

Communication Games (Verbal and Non-verbal). Tell a partner how to get from this room to the dining room. Show someone how you feel about him without using words. Pass a 'touch' feeling around the room. Mime an emotion or colour. Make a machine as a group for others to guess its purpose.

Energising Games. If a group is becoming low in energy or concentration, a short, sharp game such as run and touch four walls, a door, a window and back to your place, or touch named colours or textures, etc. Movement as a means of energising a situation is valuable both in psychodrama and dramatherapy.

Aggressive Games. These are useful both to allay anxiety and to control aggression. Bumping into people, finger fencing, shadow boxing, allow people to turn anxiety into aggression and release it in a controlled manner. The rules of the game are the safety valve.

The essence of games is that they have rules. These are explained at the outset, and the players know exactly what will be asked of them. This allays the anxiety and insecurity of the unknown. For someone who finds physical contact difficult, it can be a relief to know the limits of contact one will have to face. To create one's own rules not only causes interaction but also enables people to take risks and extend their boundaries.

APPENDIX I: SOME USEFUL GAMES

Trust Games

Blind Walk

In partners — A closes eyes and B leads him/her around the room.
Variations:

(a) Holding hands.
(b) Guiding with one finger in small of back.
(c) Touching fingertips only.
(d) No physical contact — just giving directions.
(e) Call directions from other side of room.

Circle of Trust

Groups stands in circle. One member in centre with eyes closed. He/she
relaxes and allows group to hand him round the circle from one person
to another. Variations:

(a) Stand in line and pass person along it (less protected than in a circle).
(b) In circle, person stands with feet in centre of circle and allows
    himself to fall into hands of rest of the group.
(c) In threes, A, with B and C either side, falls backwards and forwards
    between them.

Robots

In pairs, A is robot and B is inventor. A can only walk in straight lines
and respond to commands — start, stop, turn left, turn right, etc. A
cannot stop unless commanded even if he is faced with an obstacle.
Variations:

(a) As above but robot has eyes closed.
(b) A is a puppet and cannot move limbs unless B moves them for him.
(c) A is a puppet with invisible strings which B manipulates (no
    physical contact).

Tweetie
Group closes eyes. Leader touches one person who becomes 'tweetie'.

27

Group mills around and each time one person touches another he asks 'Tweetie?' The reply is 'Tweetie'. The person who is in fact 'tweetie' does not reply but joins hands with the person who has asked him; thus a chain of 'tweeties' is formed, none of whom replies to the question. Continue until whole group is in chain.

Still Pond

One person closes eyes and stands still. The others mill around until he says 'Still pond'. He moves until he touches someone. He explores the face with his fingers until he guesses the identity. He can move to other people until he guesses correctly.

Sitting Circle

Group forms closed circle, each touching the person in front and behind him and holding the waist of the person in front. On command 'Knees bend' everyone bends knees until sitting on knees of person behind.

Conveyor Belt

Two lines of people facing each other. One person lies on his back between the first few couples. They lift him to head height. He relaxes, closes eyes and is passed down the whole length of the line at head height and gently lowered to the floor at the end.

Balancing

Partners face each other and see how far off balance they can move without falling. Variations:

(a) Same as above but sitting on the floor facing each other.
(b) Partners back-to-back link arms. A bends forward until B's feet leave the floor and he is balanced on A's back.
(c) In a group, stand as wide as possible, feet firm, hands held and extended — whole group leans backwards balancing each other.

Cohesive Games

Tangle

Group forms circle holding hands. One pair drops hands and one of them becomes leader. He weaves in and out of group, under arms, around them (while still holding hands) until group is in a knot. Group untangles without breaking hands. Group decides how it can be done. (See also

Figure 1.2.)

Machine

One person stands in centre and starts a simple movement as part of a machine. Others in turn join in co-ordinating movement until the whole group is working together.

Noughts and Crosses

Place nine chairs in three rows. Divide group into two teams – noughts and crosses. Play game as for written O's and X's but using people from each team alternately to sit in chairs.

Adverb Game

One person, A, leaves room. Others choose an adverb, e.g. 'happily'. A then instructs group to perform actions in the manner of the adverb for him to guess.

Group Pictures

Divide into two groups. Each group forms a tableau or picture, i.e. wedding group, family outing, etc. Each group guesses title of the other group's picture.

Group Hum

In circle, each member hums on one note. Together, group takes deep breath and each hums own note until breath is finished.Variations:

(a) Loud and soft hum, leader orchestrates it bringing in members humming louder, softer, etc., as leader of a choir.
(b) Ding dong – each member sings 'ding' or 'dong' alternatively on own note.
(c) A sings 'ding', holding it until B has sung 'dong' and C has sung 'ding'. Meanwhile, B sings 'ding' until C has sung 'dong' and D has sung 'ding' and so on, making a continuous bell sound.

Group Yell

Group in a circle, crouch down, take a deep breath and as everyone stands up start yell softly, but getting louder as they stand up until standing on tiptoe with arms outstretched.

Circle Story

Each person in turn adds a sentence to a story Variations:

(a) Each person brings something from outside (stone, flower, etc.) and includes it in his part of the story.
(b) Each member says a word of well-known quotation, e.g. 'To be or not to be, that is the question', as if said by one person.
(c) As above but add emotion — sadly, happily, laughingly, etc.

Introduction Games

Names

Each person gives his own name with an adjective, occupation and place beginning with the same letter, e.g. Dorothy the dainty dancer from Dagenham. Variations:

(a) Give name and say how you are feeling today.
(b) Give name and a movement to go with it.
(c) Give name and tell the group members something you would like them to know about you.

Two-minute Autobiography

In pairs, A tells B about himself for two minutes. Reverse with B reciprocating to A. A then tells group as much as he can remember about B, who also does likewise.

What Have We in Common?

In pairs, each finds three (or five) things that pairs have in common, e.g. both ride bicycles, enjoy swimming, have blue eyes, etc. Return to large group and see who else shares the same things.

If I Weren't Me

Each person introduces self by name and says — 'If I weren't me I'd like to be (names person in history, public eye, etc.) because . . . (and finishes with the reason why)'. Answers can be as serious, funny or unlikely as individual wants.

Active Games

Finger Fencing

In pairs, have a fencing match using right forefinger as foil and left arm held behind back. To score you must touch partner between shoulder blades with right forefinger.

Clumps

When leader calls a number each person has that number of parts of his body touching the floor, e.g. five — two feet, two hands and forehead touch floor. Variations:

(a) As above but in groups. Given number of parts of body from group, e.g. if group has five people, each stands on one leg.
(b) As above but mobile. Move whole group across the room with given number of parts of body still touching floor.

Fishes in the Sea

A group in each corner of the room with name of a fish, e.g. herring, cod, plaice, mackerel. One person in centre of room. Leader calls a fish name, e.g. herring, and says go out for a swim. Herring runs and touch opposite wall and return to corner. Person in centre tries to catch a fish. If successful they change places. Variations:

(a) As above but add command 'Sea is rough'. All fish leave 'home' and touch opposite wall and go back to place.
(b) Play the game in a circle of chairs facing outward. Fish names are given in rotation. On command group run round the outside of the circle and back to place. Last person to own chair is out. On command, 'Sea is rough', everyone runs round until command 'Sea is calm', then returns to chair.

Empty Chair

Circle of chairs close together. A chair for each person. One person leaves his chair and stands in the centre. Group keeps moving clockwise to next chair. Person in middle tries to sit in empty chair. If he succeeds, person who should have moved into it takes his place in centre of circle. Variation: Group sits in chairs around the room. All have to keep changing places with others by silent signals. As soon as seated look for another person with whom to exchange. One person has back to group, when he turns to face group anyone not sitting in a chair is out and must remain seated until end of game.

Man the Ship

Group stands in line in centre of the room. On hearing the command, 'Man the starboard', run to make line by right-hand wall. 'Man the post' means run to the left. 'Man the ship' means return to centre. Variation: As above but eliminate last person to get in line until winner remains.

Tag (Figure 2.1)

One person is 'It'. Group runs around the room. If touched by 'It' join hands with him until whole group join chain. Variations:

Figure AI.1: Tag

(a) When touched by 'It', individual has to keep moving the part that has been touched, e.g. if touched on arm keep moving it until touched elsewhere (perhaps head) when head movement takes over.
(b) Individual holds the part that has been touched, e.g. knee if that is the part of the body touched by 'It'.

Quiet Games

Good News – Bad News

Individual tells partner of two events in the past week. 'Good news' is something positive that has happened and 'bad news' something negative. Share in large group.

Pass the Buck

Silence in group. Leader holds 'buck' (ball), throws it to person who attracts his attention and may then speak. As soon as he returns it to leader he must be silent again. Variation: Give group a subject for discussion. All silent. Leader throws 'buck' to someone who must speak all the time he is holding it on the subject given.

Rule of the Game

One person leaves room. Others decide on the rule, e.g. you must cough at the end of each sentence. When person returns he tries to discover rule by asking members questions about themselves.

Pass the Object

Leader holds an imaginary object and passes it to his neighbour miming carefully to show size, weight, delicacy, etc., of object. Pass it round the circle. Variations:

(a) Each person changes the object before he passes it on.
(b) Take a piece of material and use it as an object, e.g. hat, broom, bandage, etc.

Word Wizard

Leader is 'Word Wizard' who takes away all but four words each. Individuals choose their own four words and have conversations using only those four words. Variations:

(a) Leader gives group same four words.
(b) Four common words are forbidden. Hold conversations without using them.

Eye Contact Games

Wink Murder

One person leaves the room — he is the detective. Rest of group selects a murderer. On return, detective tries to discover murderer who kills by winking at others who 'die' dramatically.

Don't Make me Laugh

In pairs, A tries to make B laugh. B has to keep a straight face as long as possible.

What's Different?

In pairs, A turns his back whilst B alters something about his appearance, e.g. removes watch, undoes a button, etc. A has to find out what's different. Variations:

(a) One person leaves room and someone changes appearance. On return he has to guess who has changed.
(b) As above but whole group changes appearance.

Mirror

In pairs, A faces B. A starts a movement and B follows as if in a mirror. Variations:

(a) Group in a circle. Leader starts a movement which all follow.
(b) As above but change leadership.
(c) As above but one person leaves room whilst leader elected. On return has to discover who is leader.
(d) In pairs, face partner who is your reflection in mirror. Perform action, e.g. comb hair, tie a tie, etc.

Leader of the Orchestra

One person leaves room. Group chooses a leader who starts actions of playing an instrument. Rest of the group follows. He changes instrument at will, e.g. violin, trumpet, drum, double bass. When person returns to room he has to guess who is the leader of the orchestra.

Children's Games

Musical Chairs

Chairs placed in a line facing alternate directions. One less chair than number of people. All walk to music. When music stops each person has to sit on a chair. Person without chair is out. Remove another chair and so on until winner is left. Variations:

(a) Instead of removing chair, person who is 'out' remains seated, occupying a chair permanently.
(b) As above, but also remove chair so that people have to sit on each other's knees (maybe three or four per chair!).
(c) A circle of chairs, one per person. Each person marks his own chair. Group walks round to music. When music stops each person must return to his own chair. Last one to sit down remains seated throughout the game.

Grandma's Footsteps (or Peep Behind the Curtain)

One person stands with back to group. Others creep forward towards him. Anyone found moving when he turns has to go back to start (Figure AI.2).

Figure AI.2: Grandmother's Footsteps

Witches Cauldron

Make a circle of chairs for 'cauldron'. One person is witch. He chases others and whoever he catches he puts into the 'cauldron'. Continue until all in 'cauldron'. Variations:

(a) Captive can be released from 'cauldron' when another person enters.
(b) Captive can be released by another member of group rescuing him.

Musical Statues

Group walk to music. When music stops all must freeze and hold position. Anyone moving is out. Variations:

(a) As above, but when music stops everyone must sit on floor. Last one down is out.
(b) As above, but use one movement, e.g. walk, skip, run, jump. When music stops change to another movement.

Simon Says

Leader gives instructions which group must follow. If instruction is not preceded by 'Simon says' anyone moving is out.

Pork and Beans

In pairs, A asks questions and B can only answer 'pork and beans'. If he says anything else he is eliminated. Variation: Two groups, one asking questions the other answering 'pork and beans'. Mill around conversing.

Yes/No

Each person has ten beans. Mill around having conversations without using the words 'yes' or 'no'. Anyone who does must give a bean to person with whom he is speaking. Person with most beans at the end wins.

Sense-training Games

Kim's Game

Put several articles on a tray and give group time to see them. Remove one (or more) articles and ask group to name missing object.

I Went to Market . . .

In circle, group makes shopping list. First person says — 'I went to market and in my basket I put . . .' (naming object). Next person repeats this and adds another item. So on round the circle with the last person remembering the whole list. Variation:

(a) I packed my suitcase . . .
(b) I went to the beach . . .
(c) I went into the garden . . .

Shops

One person leaves room. Group decides on shop with each member of the group being a commodity sold in that shop, e.g. bread, cake, roll, biscuit, etc. On person's return, group shouts their commodity in unison and he has to guess the kind of shop (exclude a supermarket!).

What Can You Hear?

Complete silence. Each individual makes a list of sounds he can hear. Share in group. Variations:

(a) What can you see through the window?

(b) What can you feel? Identify objects by touch.

Chinese Whispers

Group sits in circle. One person whispers into the ear of person on his right who passes it on until it comes back to the originator. Variations:

(a) Group closes eyes and passes a non-verbal message by touch only.
(b) Try passing message by eye contact only.

Personal Assessment Games

I am a Shoe

Each person is asked to add three qualities which an object possesses, e.g. 'I am a shoe' — 'warm, soft and comfortable'. Mill around repeating sentence to whole group. Then ask individuals to think of the qualities they used and see what these says about them as people. Share in pairs or group. Variations:

(a) I am a chair.
(b) I am a tree.
(c) I am a coat.

If She Were a Flower

One person, A, leaves the room and group selects another person, B, to be a mystery person. On return, A asks questions of group members in turn, beginning — 'If she were a . . .', e.g. If she were a flower which would she be? If she were a car, what make? What kind of chair? What article of clothing? What country? What tree? Variation: One person selects another but does not tell group. All the group ask him questions as above.

Self-advertisements

Each person writes an advertisement describing and selling himself as a friend (no more than 20 words). Variations:

(a) Group writes advertisement for named group member.
(b) Individuals write advertisements for other members. Read them out for group to guess who they are.

Road Map

Draw a road map of your life marking events, e.g. crossroads, shady spots, town, country, sunny areas, etc.

Lifeboat

Group is in a lifeboat which is too full and sinking. Three people must be thrown overboard. Give good reasons why you should remain in boat. Variation: Group decides who should go. (Only use in very trusting groups.)

Who Said It?

One person leaves room. Others each make a statement about him. On return he is told statements and asked to guess who said them.

Difficult Problems

Each person writes a problem he finds difficult to talk about. Papers are shuffled and each person selects one. Each then talks about it as if it were his own problem. It can then be discussed by the whole group with the author remaining anonymous.

Group Body

Each person decides which part of the body he would be if the group were a person, e.g. head, heart, index finger, hand, foot, etc. Group then lies in position as if body is lying on floor. Each makes a statement of what it feels like.

This is Your Life

One person agrees to be director. He then recounts an incident from his own life. He allocates roles and the group acts it under his direction.

3 THE ELDERLY

The Ageing Process

As people grow older there is a natural physical slowing down. It takes longer to do things and reactions are slower. The more complicated the action or choice, the slower the response. This is something each has to recognise. Some find acceptance and adjustment difficult. Short-term memory frequently becomes blunted and can be a source of anxiety. It can lead to crises in relationships when people fail to do things or forget where they have put articles (usually valuables). Sleep patterns alter, people need less sleep at night and take more 'cat naps' during the day.

Physical disabilities become more common. Stiff joints, healed fractures, and disused muscles make movement difficult and sometimes painful. Hearing and eyesight are often less sharp, so noise and bright lights can be physically painful or uncomfortable. There is frequently an embarrassment over deafness and sometimes a tendency to social withdrawal. Some people feel dizziness on sudden movement, difficulty in balancing is common and with it a fear of falling over.

These are all a part of the normal ageing process and something we should bear in mind when working with elderly people in any situation.

Nature of Disability

(1) Physical

When working with elderly people in a psychiatric setting we need to acknowledge the normal physical ageing process mentioned above. There may well be severe physical difficulties which confine people to wheelchairs or to the use of walking aids. Elderly people tend to tire easily, have a limited concentration period, and, in varying degrees, impaired memory, those with dementia being the worst in all respects. Therefore, frequent brief sessions are more effective than a long session once a week. Some have a tendency to giddiness, so head movements, stooping and swaying should be kept to a minimum. Balance is affected, so physical support should always be available and group members encouraged to do whatever activities they feel happy doing. They should not be pressed into any situation in which they feel physically insecure.

Communication is a most important factor in work with the elderly. Deafness and impaired vision and memory all tend to hinder communication and cause people to be wary of contact with others. It is important to be seen when talking to a group; stand where others can see who is speaking and whom is being addressed. Deaf persons will not always be able to locate the position of a sound by hearing alone, so do not approach people from behind and always speak to them by name, or touch them gently to see if they have dozed off to sleep! Touch can be reassuring but, sometimes, frightening, especially if it is unheralded, and so should be used with care. Do not try to move people without ensuring that they are aware of what you are doing. Anything that startles people can make them feel insecure and trust is as important in this group as in any other. If these few basic rules are kept in mind, then communication and trust can be established within the group.

(2) Mental

There are three main groups of mental disability in psychiatric work with the elderly:

(1) Disorders of mood — usually depressive illnesses — many of which can be successfully treated. People with this kind of disorder tend to be short-stay or day patients, sometimes being readmitted as the need arises.

(2) Disorders of memory — usually dementias which can vary from mild forgetfulness to severe memory loss, disorientation and impaired awareness.

(3) Chronicity and institutionalisation cause a large number of elderly people to remain in hospital. These are people who have had severe mental illness (usually schizophrenia) and been in hospital for years before modern treatments were in use. Their acute illness has passed but they are left with a slow, unemotional personality and difficulty in relating to others. On top of this they have been in hospital for so long that there is a lack of individuality and and motivation to do anything. They have grown old in hospital and so have become part of the elderly hospital population but do not have diseases specific to ageing.

Grouping

There is a wide range of both physical and mental abilities in any group of elderly people. Most start with a large degree of independence and as their illness progresses, the amount of help they require increases. For some, there is a sudden change from complete independence to great dependence on others, for example the physical and mental after-effects of a stroke. Dependence, however, is not the only criterion for admission to hospital. Some people who are fairly independent but have no relatives or friends to help and are beyond the help that the Social Services can offer, may be admitted to hospital. Others, who are very dependent on friends or relatives, may remain at home with those caring for them. Day centres help relatives to do this, and the amount of time spent at such centres again varies with the resources available at home. So when we start dramatherapy sessions we are usually presented with a very mixed group. Diagnosis is not very helpful as the range of abilities of people with any particular illness can be very wide. Long-stay psychiatric patients scarred by psychoses, those recovering from depression and people whose initiative has been repressed by institutionalisation may well have more in common than those who suffer from organic degenerative disorders.

It seems more practical, therefore, to form groups using dependency as a criterion. The tendency is for the low-dependency group to contain depressed and mildly demented people and long-term schizophrenics, while the high-dependency group contains mostly people with moderate or severe dementia. The level of physical dependency of course will vary in each group. On the whole it is better to group on mental capacity rather than on physical. In this way the anxiety that drama activity may be regarded as childish and members not co-operate can be overcome by careful grouping and explanation before the group starts *at a level each can appreciate.*

There are occasionally younger people who fit into groups for the elderly. I have been asked to include group members sometimes as young as 40 who have a pre-senile dementia. They are usually very active physically but deteriorate rapidly mentally. I have taken them into the group but usually tried to give a little extra individual time to encourage them to use their physical powers as much as possible. However careful the selection, there always seem to be people at either end of the ability range who could fit into another group! So I frequently subdivide the group, even if this means dividing the time as well. It is better to spend half a session with two separate groups of differing abilities than one whole session with a mixed-ability group. The time and energy wasted in trying to reach everyone at once can be used much more productively in two smaller groups. This grouping is essential to ensure that all members are stretched a little and none is under-rated or overtaxed.

Music

Music is an instant means of gaining people's attention (see also Chapter 11). Most elderly folk love a sing-song and a few bars of a familiar tune, played or sung, will soon arouse interest and participation. Radio and television are often used as continual background for the day-room activities. People may listen or not, according to how they feel, so it is necessary to establish group-time music as something different. Live music is the most effective, but not always available. Some day rooms have a piano, but there is usually a shortage of pianists and central heating is not kind to the piano. Anyone who can play a tune on a recorder or guitar is invaluable to work with the elderly. Likewise, anyone with a good, strong voice, who can involve the whole group in a song, has a useful contribution to make.

Most people of 70 or over will remember the days of their youth when the whole family gathered for a sing-song. Each will have his 'party piece' which he would sing or recite solo. Recall of distant memories, possibly even in some persons with brain damage, remains long after recent memories cease to be retained. So, it is not unusual for people with such impairment to be able to remember their 'party piece' even though they cannot remember which day of the week it is. There is often a desire to perform in front of the group and if this is encouraged, one can use the family ritual established in childhood as a group ritual to end the session on a 'party' note. On Sundays family hymn-singing sessions used to be common and the place of hymns in the family life of older people should not be forgotten. Hymns are as valuable a source of community singing as music-hall songs. There are some good tunes and rhythms to use, and if there is an opportunity to talk about the verbal content of a hymn, it can lead to valuable exchange of ideas and expression of emotions.

Singing is not the only form of music one can use. Listening to records and talking about the mood of the music or the fantasies it evokes can be a creative group experience which helps to bring people closer together. Percussion can be fun and so can making your own instruments either in a formal session from a variety of tins, boxes, etc., or spontaneously by beating rhythms on bodies, chairs, tables, etc. Memories of school days are often pleasant, so don't be afraid of using activities that may have been used in school. As long as it is presented as an adult activity, from one adult to others, and *not* as a childish activity from an adult to children, there is no fear that people will feel insulted by it.

Movement

Movement is an integral part of drama, and where can it be better applied than with people who sit in wheelchairs all day, or whose ability and motivation to move anywhere is limited? As soon as one starts singing music with a good rhythm, feet start tapping and hands start clapping. Upon these spontaneous movements, one can build up a pattern to exercise the whole body. By holding the hands of someone who is seated, it is possible for the therapist to enable the patient to move arms and waist, hold hands above the head which encourages deeper breathing, sway gently as part of the song and dance without leaving the chair. It is equally possible to encourage kicking movements, gripping movements of hands and toes, and relaxation whilst sitting in a chair. More active people can be encouraged to walk to the music. Depending on the physical and mental abilities within the group, one can develop a pattern of movement to create dances based on walking. More able groups can manage ballroom or country dancing, but in my experience this is rare. There may be one or two people capable of complicated movement and it is possible to allow them to develop alongside the less able by giving some time during the session for individual activity.

When working with a group whose physical abilities vary, it is important for the group to accept the variations so that no spirit of competition or inability creeps in. Use walking aids and wheelchairs as part of people's personal space and make allowances for extra time required by their owners. If the therapist sees appliances as a positive aid to accomplishing things rather than an obstacle to be overcome, so will the client.

Games

Drama is based on play and the non-competitive games which form basic drama are ideal for use with the elderly (see Chapter 2). Critics who feel that we are treating the elderly as children should be reminded that retirement is frequently a time for involvement in games. How many people spend more time on the golf course or playing bridge during their retirement? Senior citizens frequently have whist drives and scrabble games. Retirement is a time for increased leisure and leisure brings with it games. Just as children develop skills of memory, balance, dexterity, verbal ability, sensory experience, etc., by simple games — so at the other end of the scale we aim to preserve and possibly develop skills that are declining. Ball games are fun at any age, and the skills required in throwing and catching must be used if they are not to be forgotten. Games can be played which help to keep fingers nimble and which require concentration and co-ordination. If these are graded to the abilities within the group, and attention is given to individual progress, they can become a useful method of preserving skills and, consequently, pride in one's abilities. Word and memory games are of value only if they are of the appropriate level and do not make the group anxious about mistakes.

Repetition is important in groups where memory is impaired. The more something is repeated, the more likely it is to be remembered, and there is security in remembering 'what comes next'. This does not mean that the group should not progress, but progression should be slow in order to allow for maximum memory retention. Consequently, one has to guard against the boredom which could arise amongst staff members. They need continual reassurance that what they are doing is important and that the slow progress shows awareness of needs, not inability to lead a group. Above all, staff should not be demanding or embarrass the patient by criticism of an unduly prolonged silence. It is better, after a brief pause, to fill the gap with your own answer or statement which then becomes a cue for learning.

Games which involve sensory perception are particularly valuable to the elderly, but must be played with regard to visual and auditory disabilities. There is a need to use the remaining hearing, sight, etc., and games which practise these can be included in the dramatherapy sessions. Touch is a sense we tend to forget and when people come into hospital they are often cut off from the sensuous contact of home. If sight and hearing are failing, the senses of smell and touch need to be encouraged and not ignored as so often happens. For example, an elderly person may compensate for lack of sight or hearing at home by getting pleasure in stroking the cat, kissing a grandchild, touching familiar china and furniture, smelling the scent of flowers, soap, polish or house in general. In hospital, where everything is unfamiliar, there should be encouragement to explore and begin to enjoy the environment sensuously. Maybe nurses have to wear uniform, but the therapist is usually able to choose what she wears. I have found that patients often comment on the colour and style of my clothes and have therefore made a habit of wearing a variety of styles, colours and textures and allowing them to feel velvet, silk, etc., as well as see them.

Reality Orientation

Most people are familiar with the process of reality orientation (see also Chapter 10). It is a method of helping disturbed people to orientate themselves in time and place and reality (see Holden and Woods, 1982). It can be practised in group sessions and also by an ongoing process of continually reminding people of the environment. Games of time, place and space can be part of the dramatherapy session, but the therapist could invent games to be used at other times. Simple things like 'What kind of trees can you see from the window?', 'Are there any leaves on them?', 'What does this tell us about the time of the year?' This can be personalised by 'What trees do you have in your garden?' ' . . . see from your window at home?'. In the low-dependency group you could ask members in pairs to take their partners on an imaginary walk round their own house/garden/shopping centre; or in pairs ask members to tell their partner how to get from here to the dining room/ dormitory/library, etc. This could be extended to a description of what is seen on that journey. It could be checked by a walk to that room and extended even further by one partner leading the other, whose eyes are closed, on that journey and feeling the surfaces to experience the things which have been described. Once the therapist has freed her own imagination to think in terms of simple games like this, the possibilities are endless. It is less a matter of technique and more a way of looking at relationships and people, places and events.

Role Play (see also Chapter 7)

Ageing is a period of major role change. Retirement is perhaps the most obvious of these. The role of wage-earner and all the subsidiary roles that go with it no longer exist. Hopefully these can be replaced by other satisfying roles, but the transition period may not be easy. New roles may bring about other changes, e.g. widowhood may mean that a woman goes to live with her daughter and so gives up the role of housekeeper too. The expectations for the role of grandmother who lives in the next town may differ from those of grandmother who lives in the same house. When people come to visit her in her daughter's house, grandmother may no longer be hostess, as the house does not belong to her. When people become sick and very dependent on others, then roles can be reversed. It is the daughter who washes, cares for, placates and makes decisions for the parent.

In a low-dependency, verbally skilled group one could do a lot of role playing to help people to adjust to these changes, but the chances of having a hospital group capable of doing so, are rare. However, I can see opportunities for such groups on pre-retirement courses and out-patient or day-patient groups. Although I have been able to work like this with individuals in other groups, the opportunity for a programme entirely centred round role changes in the elderly has not arisen.

My experience of work with the elderly has been entirely within the confines of a psychiatric hospital. Consequently, my work has been mainly basic drama, and role play has been limited to dressing-up games, stories created round pictures shown to the group, and talk about roles rather than actually playing them. The step from 'talking about' to 'becoming' is a difficult one for people who are already confused or disorientated and I can see no value in role play if it is not used for a purpose. If this purpose is to have fun, then we have to be sure that is what it is, and not confusion or embarrassment. Nevertheless, not all elderly mentally ill patients are 'confused'. They may be depressed, grieving or anxious. It is possible to use role play with these people and draw on their past experience, e.g. if you were a farmer's wife, what would you see from the kitchen window? What would you be doing at this time of the day? This kind of simple role play activity can often lead to recall and communication of past experiences and interaction within the group.

Reminiscence Therapy (see also Chapter 10)

It has always been recognised that elderly people like to recall the days gone by. Sometimes the past seems closer and more real than the present. Familiar stories are repeated until families can become bored with them. It is now being recognised that there is a value in reminiscence and a place for it in therapy. Recalling past experiences, communicating them to others, having them appreciated by others and sharing common experiences can help to integrate personality. If the reminiscence is then evaluated in the present situation it can become a means of learning. Past experience and position help to establish identity in the present, and the communicating of events is a social experience shared with others. We frequently need to draw on past experiences to solve present problems, so there is a value in remembering them.

Reminiscence therapy started in America as a form of individual therapy in the 1960s. It has been developed in Britain using audio-visual aids by M. Kemp. Whilst working with the Architects' Department of the DHSS designing hospital accommodation for the elderly, he became interested in reminiscence therapy and has produced tapes and slides which can be used in a group setting or on an individual basis.

Medium Fair Charitable Trust, a community theatre company in Devon, England, became interested and developed reminiscence theatre. This was so successful that, with the help of the Manpower Services Commission, they formed the Fair Old Times Company. They experimented with different styles of performance and audience participation, at first presenting short scenes from different periods within memory, bringing along articles from that period (flat irons, washing boards, etc.) and involving the audience with explanations and experiences of their use. Finally the company devised the process of meeting a group of people, listening to their experience and returning, at a later date, to enact scenes created from these discussions. This would be followed by a further social visit and advice given to staff about extending the experience by use of tapes, slides and museum articles.

It is unfortunate that at a time when reminiscence theatre was emerging as a practical proposition, the Fair Old Times Company had to disband through lack of funds. However, a body of knowledge and experience now exists and will hopefully be put to good use when the financial situation is improved.

Low-dependency Groups

Before starting a new group I usually meet the ward staff and discuss the purpose of the group. This is sometimes a surprise because staff do not always associate dramatherapy with elderly patients with any particular goal. It may be that a goal emerges during this discussion. If not, I agree on a group 'just for fun'. After the first session I have some idea of the ability of the group and sometimes the goal becomes obvious. It may be relearning or reinforcement of the role of shopper, and then I gear the games towards that end. If no other goal becomes obvious, I am quite happy to have a group which simply enriches the lives of its members. That is the ultimate aim of all therapy.

It is important when starting a new group that the members are prepared in advance and are not suddenly plunged into playing games which may seem childish. It is quite easy to say something like — 'We are going to meet regularly for x number of sessions and while we hope to have fun together, there is a purpose behind everything we do'. Most people readily accept the need for physical exercise, so I talk about that first; this leads to exercise of the mind, memory and senses. As we play each game I usually say 'Did you enjoy that?' or 'How was that?' and then comment on what we have achieved: learning people's names, interaction, group decisions, etc. In much the same way I use games and discuss their uses when training other members of staff. This shows from the outset that there is a purpose to the activities and gives people a chance to say how they feel about it.

A typical programme for the role of shopper would be:

Session One: Getting to Know Each Other

(1) The ball-name game.
(2) Find three things in common with your partner.
(3) Join with another pair and find a place you all know, come back to the group, tell the first letter and see if others can guess.

These should each lead to some general discussion and interaction and be enough for the first session. Finish with singing some favourite songs if it seems appropriate in order to bring the group together on a happy final note.

Session Two:

(1) The ball game calling the person to whom you are throwing.
(2) I went shopping and in my basket I put . . .
(3) Tell your partner which are your favourite shops.
(4) Have some pictures from advertisements and ask small groups to say which shops they would buy them in.
(5) In a large group share views on shops: supermarkets, local stores, multiple stores. Which are better for shopping?
(6) Finish with singing or possibly a dance.

Session Three:
(1) Each person has the name of a commodity on his back and asks questions until he finds out what it is.
(2) Back in the group, discuss where you would buy these things.
(3) Show pictures from advertisements and, in pairs, decide how much you think each article would cost.
(4) Discuss in group, finishing with the cost of tea or coffee available in the hospital shop.
(5) Finish by making tea together in the group.

By this time the group should be fairly cohesive and changing from fantasy games to reality games (see Chapter 7). I would work in this way until finally setting up a simulated shop, first using advertisement pictures, then real commodities. Group members each take turns to be shopkeeper and customers. The final sessions should be reality-testing ones; the whole group could go to the hospital shop for tea. During one week individuals could be taken shopping outside the hospital. The final week would be to take the whole group to a local café outside the hospital for a cup of tea and if staff allowed it to shop in town as well. The whole group experience would then range from simple, secure games and fantasy role play to an actual experience of the real role.

High-dependency Groups

These groups are likely to consist of people who will probably remain in hospital. It may be that some could be rehabilitated to another ward or possibly care in some other kind of institution. If this were so, I would see their membership of the present group as preparatory to joining another group, maybe more than one until ready for removal to another ward. The activities in this group would be limited, and aimed initially at goals which each member could attain in order to gain confidence. It is possible that group members will not remember what happened from one session to another and the measure of success may well be that the group members recognise the therapist as a familiar face after several sessions. If staffing allows, a one-to-one relationship of staff and group members is desirable. Memory games of any length would be inappropriate and I would concentrate on physical movement, skill preservation and development, sensory experiences, singing and general involvement.

I would select the group carefully to have three or four people of similar dependency. A co-therapist would be an advantage and if the group were any larger, a necessity. It would not be necessary to prepare the group beforehand as they would probably forget before the first session. It is better to commence the first group by saying something like 'Hello, I'm Dorothy and I hope to be meeting you every day at this time for the next ten days. I will bring some equipment along and we can do some things together which are designed to help keep your fingers nimble and your mind active.' I doubt whether the kind of people I have in mind would be able to assimilate all this but I feel that it has to be said just in case someone has been underestimated. People who do not communicate may still be able to understand. There is so little known about organic brain disorders that I feel it is certainly worth trying direct communication.

Touch is a very powerful means of communication and so needs to be used carefully with people who do not respond to words. We can handle people roughly when in a hurry or angry ourselves. These feelings are quickly communicated to others who may think it is directed at them and that they have done something wrong. Any sudden movement or touch can be startling so it is as well to approach people both verbally and physically in order to orientate them when there are disabilities of hearing, vision and mental confusion. Some elderly psychiatric patients are confused as part of their illness, some are preoccupied with the thoughts induced by their illness, some are confused because of sensory disabilities (failing hearing, sight), and some are not confused at all despite loss of memory or depressive illness. As the therapist gets to know the individuals in a group it is important to assess the amount and type of confusion. She can then adjust her own behaviour by speaking louder, being seen, etc., and so facilitate communication.

In this chapter I have talked about dramatherapy groups. As my experience widens and I am asked to work with increasingly more severely disabled people, I see a need to work on an individual basis with some people. Daily or even more frequent sessions of games geared to the individual need could be an interesting way of working. It would be time-consuming and require the help and co-operation of ward staff, but may be a way to help retain skills and physical abilities.

I cannot emphasise too much the value of really long-term work with the elderly. It is slow, but not boring, because personalities can never be boring. It can be threatening if one is of an age that one sees more working years in retrospect for oneself than in the future and has not come to terms with the problem. Anxieties felt by participants are best talked out with trained staff.

The rewards are great if one is prepared to look for small successes rather than impressive changes. Group members are usually enthusiastic and willing because they are pleased to see different people. There is a tendency to exclude very sick people from hospital social events as they are usually unable to participate because of their physical or mental state. So activities that are designed for the group and held on the ward, which is secure, help confused people to participate in a familiar setting. Work with the elderly is an excellent point to begin dramatherapy. I worked with two similar groups, one for five years and another for two years. During this time I learned more about accepting limited goals, adapting material, finding suitable levels for group work and the need to adapt the pace of progress, than with any other area I have worked in psychiatric hospitals. One can experiment with non-verbal means of communication, and not worry about failures as they will not be remembered! Above all, pleasure expressed by people whose life is limited by physical and mental illness when they are involved in the creative experience, is a great incentive to the therapist to seek new ideas and spheres of activity. Also the gratitude and co-operation of ward staff finding people interested in their patients who tend to be forgotten is a source of stimulation and an opportunity to form a team.

A suggested programme for work with a high-dependency group might be:

Session One:
(1) Introduce self by name.
(2) Find out names of group members (if they are unable to tell, ask staff).
(3) Throw a large coloured ball around the circle.
(4) Play some old-time music and encourage singing and clapping.
This would probably be enough for the first session.
Session Two:
(1) Give my name.
(2) Greet each individual by name.
(3) Throw and bounce large ball around circle.
(4) Play music encouraging singing, clapping, stamping.
Session Three:
(1) Give my name.
(2) Greet each individual by name.

(3) Throw, bounce and kick ball in circle.
(4) Play music, sing and aim to get people on their feet or moving in wheelchairs.

It is possible to make simple games which require skill and help preserve sensual and manual dexterity. A voluntary helper who worked with me for several years was very inventive in this way. Here are a few of her ideas. Perhaps you can add to them yourself.

(1) Apple trays can be used to catch tennis balls.
(2) Egg cartons can catch ping-pong balls. The trays can be on the floor, table or held by the partner or therapist who catches the ball. It then becomes a game of shared skills.
(3) Plastic balls can be attached to bats by a length of string to allow chairbound people to play without constantly losing the ball (Figure 3.1).
(4) Skittles made of boxes can be played in a large circle on the floor or, in smaller groups, on a table.
(5) Blowing bubbles encourages deep breathing.

Figure 3.1: Home-made Games for the Less Able — Shared Activity

(6) Blow table tennis table balls across the table with drinking straws (Figure 3.2).
(7) Playing in pairs, each pair holds drinking straw in mouths. Put a plastic cup on the drinking straw and pass the cup onto partner's or therapist's straw without using hands.

Figure 3.2: Home-made Games for the Less Able — Deep Breathing

(8) Play 'conkers' by tying corks onto pieces of string. The skills are the same as in the conventional game but without the risk of damage from hard or split conkers.
(9) Percussion instruments can be used individually for sensory games or in a group to music.
(10) Flowers, leaves, conkers, etc., can be used for the group to handle and smell as a guessing game.

This same lady always arrived with a flower, twig or fruit from her garden or that she had picked on her journey. She brought simple things that stimulated senses and memories and was a tangible link with the outside world.

These are a few ideas and no doubt you will find more. Care has to be taken that clients do not eat whatever you bring in, so be sure it isn't harmful! I am always prepared to try any activity but find that the simpler, more direct the activity, the more likely it is to succeed.

4 SCHIZOPHRENIA

It is estimated that over half the patients in Britain's mental hospitals are suffering from schizophrenia (Pringle, 1973), so it is likely that the dramatherapist will, at some time, find herself dealing with problems caused by this condition. The word schizophrenia is derived from two group words, 'schiz' (split) and 'phrenia' (mind). It is characterised by emotional flatness or incongruity, a withdrawal from reality, blunting of drive, poverty of ideation, misperceptions such as hearing voices and idiosyncratic symbolism and false beliefs in the form of delusions. There is an inability to see things as a whole. The schizophrenic has difficulty forming gestalts. For example, instead of looking at a face and recognising it as a whole, he perceives eyes, nose, mouth, etc., and has to make a mental effort before he can put them together as belonging to a known person. This response takes time and consequently the schizophrenic is often slow to react. This fragmentation of perception mirrors the fragmentation of personality that is indicative of schizophrenia.

There have been many theories concerned with the cause or explanation of schizophrenia and a few that may be useful to a practising dramatherapist will now be described.

Explanations

Delusional Mood Theory

It is accepted that schizophrenia causes the client to feel differently about people and objects. One theory (Jaspers, 1963) maintains that the mood is the origin of the behaviour and everything else stems from it. The schizophrenic cannot understand his mood change and tries to explain it to himself by projecting it onto people or objects outside himself as the cause, e.g. he feels out of touch with people, so says that they are in love with someone else or trying to ignore him, or that it is all the effect of electrical wires.

Loss of Ego Boundaries

The schizophrenic person has difficulties in separating himself from the rest of the world. He is not sure what belongs to his own body

and mind and what belongs to other people or objects. This leads to
a passivity of feeling which he projects onto a third party in order to try
and explain it. He feels he is a passive agent for some external force —
the television, electrical wires, etc. He attributes things wrongly — his
own thoughts to hearing voices. He disowns his inner impulses and
attributes them to the influence of external sources (Schneider, 1957).

Selective Inattention

The mind (ego) takes in cues through the five sensory channels. These
stimuli put in a total impression of what is happening to us and together
give one meaning in our minds which results in action. Memory and
thought are involved in the present moment; for example, a child burnt
by fire is wary of fire. We are living in the here and now, but it is given
meaning by comparison with past experiences. We are aware of various
stimuli — noises in the garden, heat from the fire, people talking,
smoking, etc. — and respond appropriately to whichever is the most
important stimulus of the moment. A schizophrenic person, however,
finds all the stimuli of equal importance and therefore does not know
which to respond to first, and so becomes overwhelmed by them. He
cannot shut off the stimuli nor separate them individually, so he reacts
by signs of psychosis — hallucinations, delusions, etc. (Chapman and
McGhie, 1963).

Stress

Several studies have shown that the schizophrenic is particularly sensitive
to stress. Rahe *et al.* (1967) found that a change in lifestyle in the
weeks before a schizophrenic breakdown was common. The reactions of
a schizophrenic person and those of his family in the early stages of the
illness perpetuate the stress. Venables (1966) has shown that
schizophrenic people have a heightened physiological arousal; in the face
of this they withdraw to try to restore the balance.

Causes

Dopamine Theory

There are a number of theories linking schizophrenia with brain chemistry
of which the current popular one is the dopamine theory. This postulates
that there is a faulty mechanism in the dopamine channels. Receptors on
certain nerve cells become hypersensitive to dopamine and this results in
abnormal functioning of the cells.

Heredity Factor

There appears to be evidence for genetic factors in the cause of
schizophrenia and considerable research has been done in this field,
notably the studies of twins by Gottesman and Shields (1966). Studies
of the genetics of schizophrenia in families, twins and adopted children
show that there is a genetic predisposition and yet also suggest that
this is not a total explanation.

Family Conflict

R. D. Laing (1965) does not see schizophrenia as an illness but as a
reaction to impossible family conflict. He says that this is the only way
the client can cope with an intolerable situation.

Psychoanalytic

Melanie Klein (1952) (see also Segal (1975)) holds that schizophrenia
is a regression to an infantile stage of personality development. The
child builds defence mechanisms to cope with its anxiety and, under
pressure, the schizophrenic regresses to these or, in some cases, never
really develops beyond them. This seems to suggest that there is a
fundamental difference between the way neurotic and psychotic
people handle relationships in that the schizophrenic will split off
unwanted aspects and attribute them to other objects or people.

Double Bind

This theory demonstrates the difficulties families of schizophrenics
have in communication. A parent may say 'yes' in a tone that infers
'no' or say 'I love you' while giving non-verbal cues of hate. The child
becomes so confused by this that he grows up with severe problems
in both giving and receiving communications which result, under stress,
in schizophrenia (Bateson *et al.*, 1956).

This is just a brief synopsis of some of the many theories concerning
schizophrenia. If we take them all into account, we get a pattern which
might be expressed as: genetics loads the gun, neurochemistry is the
powder with which it is loaded, microsocial factors (stress, family
influences) pull the trigger, while macrosocial (unemployment, poverty,
poor housing and relationships) are the consequences.

The Pattern of Disability

Whatever we may or may not accept of the many theories about schizophrenia, we are left with a pattern of disability containing all or some of the following elements:

(1) Difficulties in relating to other people.
(2) Confusion when presented with more than one stimulus at a time.
(3) The need to project feelings, sounds or thoughts which are unacceptable onto a third party. This is often manifested in paranoia, hallucinations and delusions.
(4) Difficulty in seeing things as a whole which leads to delayed responses.
(5) In the motor sense, (4) results in awkward and jerky physical movement.
(6) Confusion about the peripheries of self — body and mind, including sexual identity.
(7) Inability to accept ambivalence in relationships. It is difficult to accept good and bad in the same person or situation, so it is necessary to see one as all good and another as all bad.
(8) A need to be right to assure oneself of sanity. This results in family frictions. The client has to prove himself right and others wrong to reassure himself; the family has to prove itself right and the client wrong in order to establish its own sanity.
(9) Regression to childlike behaviour.
(10) Withdrawal to an inner world of fantasy which is not necessarily a pleasant one and can make life a waking nightmare.
(11) The difficulties that have to be overcome and the inner life led by the schizophrenic make it very difficult for him to concentrate on the present. Our reality is unreal to him but his fantasies are not. Consequently, he is unable to work at a high intellectual level and may need to accept less demanding occupations, although intelligence is not grossly disturbed.
(12) His own inner world occupies his emotional energies, so that he is likely to respond to emotional situations with psychotic episodes. Research has shown that schizophrenics in families who show little anxiety about their symptoms are hospitalised less and adjust more easily than those whose families react with high emotion and criticism (Vaughan and Leff, 1976).
(13) Delusions and hallucinations may cause the schizophrenic to act impossibly and in a manner which is incomprehensible to us. This is particularly disturbing if he has involved another real person in his unreal world.
(14) All these lead to a lack of trust in other people, yet there is a need

for reassurance. This creates a conflict which is difficult to resolve.

Schizophrenia has two modes of onset. One is a slow, insidious one in which relatives see a gradual change in the client. He manages to live with his symptoms and not present a drastic change to the outside world. It is usually some crisis like a family row, unemployment or maybe simply family anxiety about his umkempt appearance or apparent laziness that prompts the client (or his family) to seek help. By this time the schizophrenia has become almost a way of life and a chronic disability. The other mode of onset is rapid, florid and sometimes dramatic in nature – a suicide attempt or some bizarre or violent action as a result of hallucinations or paranoia. The client is frequently young and intelligent with perhaps a history of being a solitary and quiet person. Urgent treatment is required to prevent a chronic condition.

What Has Dramatherapy to Offer in the Management of Schizophrenia?

In practice there are three groups of schizophrenics to be considered.

(1) Recent Onset

These clients come to the psychiatric services following a recent onset of schizophrenia and show florid symptoms, may be withdrawn, confused, depressed or even violent. The range of intensity of the symptoms can vary considerably from extreme passivity to bizarre and antisocial behaviour. The effect of this unexpected experience and behaviour can be a great shock to both the client and relatives. Neither can understand what is happening and conflicts arise as each tries to make sense of the situation. The fear of behaviour that appears 'mad' has its effect on them both as they seek to justify and explain their own feelings and attitudes. The client's mental, physical and emotional confusion and withdrawal from reality make it essential that he is not involved in any situation that would cause him further unnecessary stress.

Needs. These include:

(1) Active pharmacological treatment if it is indicated.
(2) Stability and reassurance at a non-threatening level.
(3) A structured secure environment in which the client can begin to relax and assimilate what is happening to him.

At this stage I think that dramatherapy has nothing to offer except maybe more stimuli and further confusion. Personally, I do not work with acutely schizophrenic clients or those who are 'borderline' and may be precipitated into a psychotic episode by stress or an emotional atmosphere. There are some psychiatrists who would advocate risking a psychotic breakdown with clients who are precariously balanced but I have not worked with them myself. I would need very convincing evidence to be party to anything that would plunge another human being into the disturbing state of psychosis. Clients I have known have described the horror of these episodes and there are some very vivid descriptions in a booklet entitled *Schizophrenia from Within* (1975) published by MIND. My rule is to exclude a client from a group and any possible benefits rather than risk doing him harm. This is my opinion and a strong one but there may be others who would disagree with me. However, sometimes a client, whose schizophrenia has not been diagnosed, will be sent to a role play group. His difficulties in adapting to the group can reveal the true nature of his disability. Dramatherapy then becomes a diagnostic tool.

(2) New Chronic

Given prompt treatment, many people recover from a psychotic episode completely and may never have another breakdown. Others recover but later have a recurrence. Others, despite treatment, do not recover completely and are unable to live the full life they had previously. They may require supervision and assistance of varying degrees for a long time, maybe for the rest of their lives. For some there is a residual disability which requires adjustment, and for them and others there may be intermittent recurrence.

Needs. These include:

(1) Coming to terms with the disability and learning to live with it.
(2) Finding ways of relating to others.
(3) A return of family if that is desirable, *or*
(4) A sheltered environment, lodging, group home, etc.

It is at this point that dramatherapy can play an important part in rehabilitation. The client will not suddenly be pushed into a stressful situation, so there is time and opportunity to introduce him to drama techniques and for him to learn to gain in confidence by them. When a schizophrenic client has recovered from his acute phase, the residual disabilities may be incapacitating. It may be unwise for him to return to his previous occupation or family situation. Stress could cause further breakdown and preoccupation or confusion will make it impossible for him to work at a high intellectual level. It may be necessary therefore to accept a lesser role. Women may not be able to cope with children and household, so they must be prepared to accept help. This could be anything from placing children in a foster home to the services of a home help. Role play is a valuable medium for exploring new roles and coming to terms with role change.

(3) Long-stay

There is a large group of clients who have had schizophrenic episodes before the use of modern treatments. Some of these have learned to live with their disabilities through adaptation to life in an institution. They have become dependent on that institution and cannot adapt to a new way without help. If they are to be enabled to live in other settings, they will need new forms of adaptation and modes of behaviour which are more appropriate to their new surroundings.

Needs. These include:

(1) Discarding the enveloping 'patient' role acquired over the years.
(2) Creation of new roles and recreation of old ones (see Chapter 7).
(3) To be given responsibility and learn to accept it.
(4) To find individuality and learn to express it.
(5) If possible, to move out of hospital to a sheltered environment.

The rehabilitation of long-stay clients is described in detail in Chapter 6, so I will not make further comment here.

Bearing in mind the fourteen difficulties I mentioned that form a pattern of disability (you may think of even more), we can look at the contribution of the dramatherapist under a number of separate headings.

Trust (Figure 4.1)

Having survived the trauma of a psychotic episode, the client emerges very bewildered. He is still not sure what has happened to him and how far he can be understood by others. The effect his breakdown has had on family and friends may determine his ability to come to terms with it himself. If he has been rejected or feels let down he will be unsure how far he can trust other people. He may have a recollection of disturbing scenes both at home and in hospital which affect his relationships in therapy.

The first thing we can do to help to develop trust is to accept him into the group as he is now without expectations from his past achievements. We need to create a non-threatening environment which does not present stress. There should be no pressure on group members to participate or even stay in the room for the whole session. The group should not be too large – six to eight people in all. There should be no attempt to work at a personal level until trust is established. Many trust exercises (Figure 4.1) are performed with the eyes closed. This is very threatening and not something to do in the initial stages as one would with the neurotic client. The dramatherapist needs to devise other trust exercises based on balance or helping others to achieve things physically, e.g. cross a barrier of chairs together. Physical contact with others is often difficult so this should be restricted to activities which allow plenty of personal space yet encourage dependence on others. Eye contact is difficult, often because of the client's preoccupation with the supernatural or guilt over fantasies. He could be afraid that another might read his thoughts or fantasies by eye contact, so this should be avoided at first. Simplicity, time, patience, reassurance and a clearly defined structure will be rewarded eventually. Progress should be slow, gentle and reassuring. Repetition is comforting and secure, so do not be afraid to use exercises that are popular. Sometimes a dance or game can become a ritual that a group likes to repeat at the conclusion of each session or when there is a need for reassurance.

Groups vary with the disabilities of their members, but I have worked with some groups for long periods. When the members feel free to talk about their psychotic fantasies there is often a sense of relief at having shared a terrible burden but this stage is only reached by careful preparation and mutual respect. There is one group with whom I have had contact for three years. The members have come to trust each other and can admit that a crisis is imminent. Some will ask to be excused from a group session and both they and the staff realise that further help is required. Others will leave the group during a remission and ask to join it when the need arises. I always have a sense of privilege in working with this particular group. The simple things of life – cooking, shopping, collecting children from school, even watching television – are achieved by continual efforts of will. The manner in which they support each other in crises and the open way in which they share the private agony of their psychotic experience fills me with humility.

Body Awareness

It is common for the schizophrenic client to be unsure of the peripheries of his own body, sometimes to the extent of being unsure of his own sexual identity. Anything we do in drama that involves the senses can help to retrain and reassure him. The mind takes in cues from all five senses which are formed into a total impression of events. Sight, touch, smell, hearing and taste have equal value to the schizophrenic client and cause him to be unable to respond when presented with multiple stimuli. By concentrating on one sense at a time we can encourage a reaction to individual stimuli, so games that use the senses separately are valuable whereas those presenting more than one stimulus at a time are less so. Equally, it is not helpful to work to a background of music or talking.

Anything that relaxes or emphasises the peripheries of the body is useful. To lie down on the floor and trust your whole body to it can be threatening to some people, so it is better to start by relaxing in a chair. This can be linked with body awareness by asking the group to concentrate on parts of the body they can feel touching the chair and the ground. Ask them to name the areas that are in contact with other things — clothing, watches, rings, etc. Ask them to concentrate on sounds only outside the room, then those in the room, then finally those in their own bodies (e.g breathing). If it is getting near to lunchtime and people hear rumbling stomachs, the group usually concludes with laughter. In another session one can spend time just concentrating on one part of the body, e.g. tap a tune on your knee, your neighbour's knee, touch your forehead with your knee, walk on your knees, etc. If this is planned and presented carefully there can be laughter when people get into awkward positions. Ask group members for ideas about using knees. The session should be kept simple and instructions clear. It could be patronising to ask intelligent adults to concentrate on their knees, so ample explanation and discussion time must be used. Encourage people to talk about the exercises and their feelings about them. It often leads to a sharing of distorted perceptions which, if accepted by the therapist and acknowledged by other group members, can be a reassuring experience.

Movement

If the schizophrenic inability to see things as a whole is also present in a motor sense, the result is often jerky, uncoordinated movements. Added to this, movements or patterns of movements are sometimes involved as a superstitious safeguard against threatening hallucinations, or maybe

Figure 4.1: Group Trust through Tension and Relaxation. A. Leaning Back on Floor

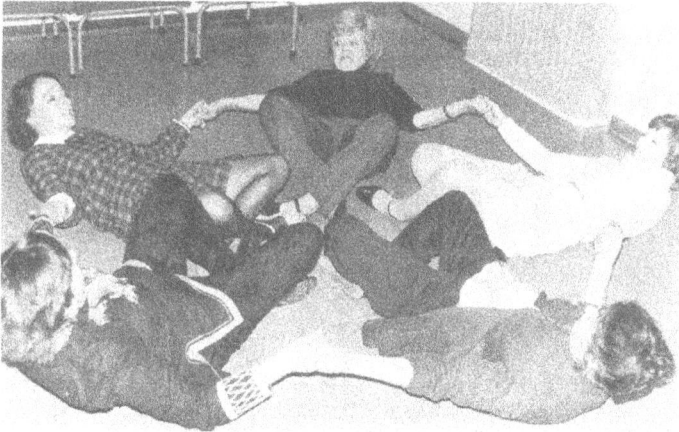

B. Sitting up Together

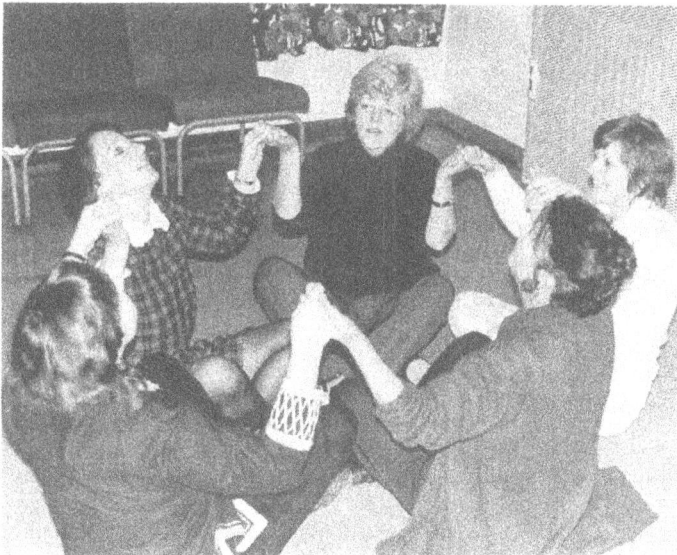

C. Standing and Stretching

D. Handing Round a Circle

voices tell the client to move in a particular way. So the dramatherapy skills of movement can be valuable. Try to encourage flowing continuous movements; even an awareness of movement itself and a rational approach to it can help. Again it is necessary to have only one stimulus, so don't use music with movement at an early stage. Later, when the group has learned to cope with movement alone, it can be useful to produce fluidity by working to rhythm and perhaps music. Movement can be another way of body awareness and concentration on where the hands, feet, legs, heads, etc., are in space is useful.

Concentration

Difficulty in concentration must be acknowledged. It is better to have frequent short sessions rather than one long one. Allowance should be made for individual variations so that people feel free to stop when concentration flags. Sense-training games require considerable concentration and many activities which the therapist can do easily require much more effort for a schizophrenic client. We should respect this and give plenty of praise and encouragement. Games should be short at first but when repeated can gradually take longer in order to build up gradually in concentration. Word games are good for concentration but do remember that schizophrenic thought and understanding can be distorted, so it is preferable to work towards word games at a later date. Mirror work is useful both in concentration, co-ordination and working with others but again facing another person and looking at him can be threatening, so it should be used with care in the early stages.

When starting a new group on a ward I like to be in a room that is open for people to come and go as they please. I found this was ideal for a group in a disturbed ward. Clients could come for a few minutes, leave and return when ready. Some would stay the whole session, others only a short time. No one was asked to remain longer than he wanted. This worked well and I found that some people could gradually increase their group time as their ability to concentrate improved.

Relating

Constant, inanimate objects are less threatening than people. The object fulfils the role projected onto it, unlike people who do not always accept projections and behave at times in an unexpected way. I find it useful to start new groups by asking clients to relate to objects rather than a person. Balloons, a ball, a hoop, a rope, percussion instruments all have their uses. Even an established group finds it necessary to play a ball

game after a break in group work. One can imagine the anxieties
produced by putting a schizophrenic client in a group at all. The
expectation of relating to all these people could be overwhelming.
Equally, the intensity of relating to one other person can be just as
taxing, so I like to start working with sub-groups of three or four
people, keeping them constant at least for the first half of the
session, then either coming into a large group for a few minutes at
closing or changing the structure of the sub-group for a short period.
I prefer to work from small groups to pairs, back to small groups and
finally working as a whole as the group progresses.

Any games which encourage interaction are useful but keep them
low key and impersonal at first. It is difficult to say how you move
on because each group is individual and moves at its own pace. It is
important to be in touch with group members and allow them to
progress individually. By setting up a system of groups it is possible
to cater for all needs. One such project was devised by a charge nurse on
a ward for schizophrenic people. He started with a group of about ten
people in a rehabilitation scheme. With the aid of some drama
students and another member of staff he worked for ten weeks with
this group (A). He then closed it and started another group (B) with
those who were ready to move on leaving the basic group (A) to
work at its own pace. The second group then developed and closed
and another small group (C) started at an advanced level. By this
time groups (A) and (B) were able to merge. He took his final group
of three clients through to a social skills and role play group.
Provided the therapist is working for stated periods it is possible
to keep reforming groups to allow people to move at their own
pace without feeling rejected or inadequate. If it is possible to involve
people from outside the client's usual environment (i.e. other staff,
volunteers, etc.) it gives initial help to a large proportion of people
who relate easily in a group. Done sympathetically this gives the group
confidence to risk more.

Compromise and Decision-making

I link these two because they seem to be two sides of the same coin.
The client may appear very rigid and uncompromising in his need to
be right in order to reassure himself of his sanity. He can also find it
very difficult to make even simple decisions because he cannot risk
making mistakes. It would make him even more vulnerable and unsure
of himself. Drama is ideal for this because there is no right or wrong
way of doing it, only the experience matters. It takes time for clients

to assimilate the fact that it does not matter which decision they make or how they perform, only that they do it. Having established this the decisions can gradually become more complicated and meaningful so that the group finishes with a permissive environment in which it is possible to make mistakes or decisions which could have been wiser. When this stage is reached and the client finds that the world won't fall around his ears, he can gradually gain confidence to accept that he could be wrong or at least to make a compromise.

So games that encourage individual and group decisions are valuable. In the making of the group decisions, no matter how small, someone usually has to compromise. This can lead finally to role play in which the client can practise the kind of behaviour he will meet and have to cope with outside the group.

Some Points to Remember

(1) Fantasy Life. Some people with schizophrenia have a vivid fantasy life. If the therapist challenges this, the client is immediately faced with his own sanity problems. However, it is possible to collude with this, remain his friend but not help him towards reality. This is illustrated in Ibsen's play *Peer Gynt*. In Act IV when Peer is taken to the asylum he attempts to enter into the delusions of the people there and succeeds only in helping them to destroy themselves.

I always accept fantasy without comment at first, building up a calm, accepting atmosphere which encourages trust. I don't enquire about fantasies or question them, but just accept that they are part of the individual. When we have built up sufficient trust (and this may take a very long time, perhaps years) I can voice my perceptions without loading them with a moral value of right or wrong; for example, the client might see a particular chair as a grotesque creature and I would just accept this silently at first. If I contradict him and say 'Nonsense, it's just a brown chair', I challenge any sense of security he may have. If I agree with him and say 'So it is a horrible creature', I am not helping him to discriminate between fantasy and reality, which is our ultimate goal. Later, when trust is established I could say 'Oh, it's interesting that you see it as a monster, but I see it as a brown chair', in a matter of fact way. However, I have to be very sure of a trusting relationship before I would even attempt this.

Clients are understandably reluctant to talk about their fantasies until they begin to have some insight. Then it is sometimes reassuring to talk about them in a group where it is a common experience. However well I know someone, I would not ask direct questions or press him to talk. It is not part of the role of the dramatherapist to pry (see Chapter 14) but to accept what the client offers and use it in a dramatic setting to help him towards reality. This is always the goal with schizophrenia, so, unlike role-play groups, I do not work with fantasy (see Chapter 7) but work on practical situations geared towards reality, e.g. a role-play group works on fantasies of a traveller, etc. With a schizophrenic group I would enter the role play perhaps by asking them in pairs to shift an imaginary piano. It is a fantasy situation which requires co-operation but also practical ideas. The fantasy is in imagining the proportions of the instrument and representing them in space. It causes laughter, sometimes reminiscence of real furniture moving and can start a discussion on roles and an entry into role play, but does not give much space for schizophrenic fantasy.

(2) Stimuli. The fact that schizophrenic clients cannot cope with multiple stimuli has only just been recognised in psychiatric hospitals. It has been a common practice to leave radios, televisions and record players on as a background. Even when group work has been in progress on a ward there have been complaints about the noise being stopped because there was no entertainment for non-group members! This is important knowledge for the dramatherapist. If we do not want our schizophrenic clients to 'shut off', then we must keep sensory input as simple as possible. When speaking try not to gesticulate. Use music as a single stimulus, not as a background or for added effect. If there is noise in the corridor that the therapist cannot control, incorporate it if possible into what you are doing. For example, a cleaning team with machines could be the basis for games about cleaning. If it is a noisy client or short-lived voices, stop the session and acknowledge that the noise has come from outside. It is part of awareness as well and so should not be ignored.

(3) Slowness. Do not confuse a slow reaction with stupidity, deafness or inattention. We need to allow time for words to be heard individually and then put into a sentence instead of a whole ('Gestalt') being received. There was one client I knew who had to repeat each word to herself as it was said. Even with a very supportive group this became too much of a strain for her. She was still repeating one person's statement when another was saying something else and if two people talked at once, even for a few seconds, she was lost. Group therapy was not appropriate for her, but the experience of being with supportive, sharing people helped and she began to form relationships with group members

outside the group situation. That was a few years ago, but now I am more experienced I would probably suggest she join a movement group where there is less talking but still support.

Confusion of reality and fantasy also causes a slow reaction, so do not give a whole stream of instructions. Take each part of an exercise separately and individually. Give the instructions clearly, ascertain that they are understood, then allow the group to perform them before giving them the next step, e.g. 'Decide who is A and B (wait for this to be achieved). Have you all done that? (wait for slow ones to answer). A is the master and B is the servant. Find a position which shows this (wait until you can see that everybody is ready). A gives the orders and B has to do everything he is told (wait). Everyone know what to do? (Wait) Right? Go! (wait until ready for changeover). Bring your scene to a conclusion (wait for this to be done). Everyone ready? (wait). Don't discuss what you feel yet, we will do that afterwards. Now change over. A is the servant and B is the master (wait). Everyone know what to do? (wait). Take up body positions (wait until they have done so). B now tells A what to do and he has to perform it (wait). Ready? Then go!' This should be delivered in a matter-of-fact, clear voice, not shouted as if to deaf people or in a manner to undervalue them or undermine their status. We are dealing with intelligent adults with disabling thought disorders, not the mentally handicapped or children.

(4) Ambivalence. The tendency to see people as all good or all bad colours all relationships. In therapy we aim to help clients to come to terms with their ambivalence by accepting the bad with the good. One can model this by accepting the clients at all times. Extremes of behaviour may have to be controlled and the therapist needs to ask the question 'Am I overtaxing this client?' We all have our 'off days' and the schizophrenic client may express this by antisocial behaviour. Whilst we cannot encourage disruptive incidents or allow others to be upset by them, it is not a moral issue and we must be careful not to use judgemental tones if we have to intervene. It is better, if possible, to compromise or distract in some way. For example, if a client is restless and is disturbing the group by continual movement, acknowledge it and say 'Mary is keen to be up and doing today, let's do something active'. This may fulfil the need if it is a transient one. If the restlessness continues, say something like 'We are trying to concentrate here, perhaps you would like to do something active over there?' and detail a member of staff to set up an activity in a

corner of the room.

My experience is that disturbance is usually self-limiting because clients will leave the room, if given that freedom, to seek some other outlet or support. It is only when people are compelled to remain in the group that disturbance is prolonged. I like to work with the maximum number of staff or voluntary helpers in these groups, partly for modelling and partly for allowing individual needs to be met in this way. The therapist needs to have a good liaison with ward staff who will be aware of the clients who may act impulsively. The ward staff know the clients well and are used to handling them, so if a problem arises it is better to let them deal with it. Nevertheless, careful planning and thought about the group session and the relationships within it can possibly prevent ugly scenes. If there is an aggressive outburst, the therapist should see that the client is cared for by a member of the ward staff and then return immediately to her group. The group leader is responsible for the entire group, not individual actions (see Chapter 14). There should be sufficient staff for somebody to deal with the individual while the leader cares for the group. A calm approach at all times is imperative.

It is threatening for the schizophrenic client to admit that other people see things differently. He likes to see things in terms of black or white because shades of grey are confusing, belonging to neither one extreme nor the other. In therapy, we need to communicate to the client that he is reacting to the same reality as others, help him to find ways of understanding why he is doing this and give the security to be able to admit it and withdraw from situations at times. It is sometimes better to withdraw temporarily from a difficult immediate situation than risk protracted breakdown.

We need to create a clear structure within which we can work without ambiguity. The client cannot cope with roles with undefined boundaries, so when working on roles we need to explore what the role entails, help him learn the skills needed to meet them and motivate him to use them.

This means that the therapist needs to be very clear of her own aims and objectives and to deal with one thing at a time. It would be confusing to plan the first session with a few trust exercises, some body awareness, decision-making, etc. It is better to spend half a session or even a whole one on each activity until the group is thoroughly familiar with what they are doing and the reasons behind it. There is no need to dwell on lengthy explanations that could embarrass the client by expecting him to expose his schizophrenic disabilities. When starting body awareness, for example, simply say 'It is sometimes difficult to understand ourselves in relation to the rest of the world, so let's concentrate on our bodies for a bit. Just relax in a chair and become aware of the parts of your body that are touching it.' This does not give the client the impression that his guilty secret has been discovered or that there is something very unusual or wrong about the experience — just that it happens. At a later stage games of compromise can help cope with compromise in reality. A good one is:

A and B volunteer to perform separate tasks. They leave the room while the group decides for them. Each knows only his partner's task — perhaps A has to switch on the light and B touch the curtain. A asks B to do something towards his goal and B will do it if he thinks it is reasonable and A does an equally reasonable move like this:

A: 'Stand up'.   B: 'I will if you will too'.
A: 'Take two steps right'.   B: 'I will if you face the wall'.
A: 'Walk to the door'.   B: 'I will if you walk to the window'.

There are variants on the game and possibilities of making it more complicated.

(5) Emotional Stress. An atmosphere of high emotion is very threatening for schizophrenic clients so it is important to keep a feeling of calm acceptance and security in the group. Intensive role play and psychodrama should not be undertaken at first and later only with full medical co-operation and nursing support. I would not work at any depth with schizophrenic outpatients unless they attended a day centre with a supportive environment. With these groups I plan sessions for mornings and possibly on the first day of the weekly attendance, so that the clients have the full advantage of nursing care and counselling after the session. It is only after a long period of low-key preliminary group work that I attempt any form of depth.

I have already mentioned the double bind theory and it is important that the therapist does not fall into the trap. Our cues must be clear and honest. This sounds easy but when we are closing a group and have to hurry to a meeting, we are sometimes impatient with the slow clearing of the room. If someone is lingering in putting on her coat and apologises for keeping you it is easy to say 'Don't hurry there is plenty of time' in a tone that reveals your desire to hurry. It is better to say 'I'll help you on with your coat because I have to be at a meeting by mid-day'.

Not only must the therapist be honest about her own emotions but she should try to help the clients express theirs. Miming an emotion is a good way into discussion of them. It is difficult for the client to admit to his own emotions or to own them. This is why he needs to project them onto others in his paranoid state. Discussion of things that cause emotions – anger, sadness, etc. – in an unemotional manner can help people to own them. In trusting groups it can lead to verbal acceptance of projection – 'I used to think that it was the TV making me feel restless'. Sometimes a re-enactment of an emotional situation helps to clarify it. Usually this is a family row or angry verbal conflict, but the act of replaying the scene without the emotion can give insight. I find it is more successful to have another group member mirror behaviour rather than using the role reversal technique (see Chapter 7) because of the schizophrenic confusion about personal identity. Some clients find it not only threatening but also impossible to do.

(6) Group Selection. The pattern of disabilities which we term schizophrenia indicates the need to work with clients who all have them or are tolerant of them. Sometimes a person whose mood is low and reactions slowed because of chronic depression will fit into the group, but the general rule is to group those clients who can work at the same level and pace. This ensures that no one feels the strain in keeping up with others. It is important, however, to allow for growth within the group and try new and challenging things.

The suggested sessions at the end of Chapter 6 are suitable for the long-term schizophrenic client, so I will at this point describe only sessions suitable for the 'new chronic' group. These clients are usually in the younger age group, so they can be physically active sessions. It is important to prepare group members beforehand so that they know that they are attending a group, that it will involve games and actions and they are free to leave if they find it difficult.

Session One
(1) Have a number of balloons ready inflated. Greet the group and suggest keeping the balloons in the air as a warm-up.
(2) Remove all balloons except one, hit it across a circle calling own name as you do it.
(3) Divide into sub-groups of three or four, each with a balloon. Call name of person you pass balloon to.

(4) Each group discuss how many different ways they can pass the balloon to each other.

(5) Discuss in large group.

(6) Each group devises a game with a set of four rules.

(7) In large group discuss this and the whole session.

Session Two:

(1) Warm up with general balloon game.

(2) Form sub-groups and each demonstrate game and rules created in the last session. Discuss.

(3) Each group has a skipping rope. Skip in small groups.

(4) Half small group at each end of the rope. Keeping it taut, gradually move hands down the rope until both parts of the group meet and touch hands.

(5) Repeat exercise (4) but in pairs. Discuss.

(6) In pairs, arms outstretched, fingers just touching, A leads B round the room. Reverse and discuss.

(7) Relax and stretch in the group. Discuss the session with reference to the space used.

Session Three:

(1) Warm up with balloons/balls/ropes/hoops.

(2) In small groups find different ways of using them. Discuss.

(3) In pairs, have a tug of war with ropes or if group is ready just by holding hands.

(4) Discuss in terms of tension and relaxation.

(5) Sit on a chair and relax (the therapist talking through).

(6) Be aware of parts touching the chair (clothing touching, feet touching floor).

(7) Stand up, keeping relaxed, and walk being aware of feet. Try walking on other surfaces — carpets, step on chair, etc.

(8) Concentrate on feet. What would it feel like if walking on stones? How would you walk? In cold water? Hot pebbles? Soft grass? How would you walk?

(9) Walk into a circle. Hold hands at arms' length. Walk into the centre, lowering arms as you do. This brings you physically closer. Keep going until feet are touching neighbours on both sides. Discuss this and the whole session.

You have now introduced to the group trust, body awareness, movement, concentration, relating to objects and others, and group decision-making which involves compromise. Continue in this way involving the senses, gradually introducing more complicated actions and getting physically closer. When the group is comfortable relating in pairs, gradually increase the size of sub-groups until working in one large group together.

5 PERSONALITY DISORDERS

Another group of people who find their way to dramatherapy groups are those suffering from personality disorders. These are not a range of symptoms with a defined onset but part of the total personality and are present from early adult life. Some people with personality disorders manage to cope and live their lives without seeking help. It is usually a social crisis or their antisocial behaviour that brings them to seek psychiatric treatment. They may also become clinically ill, usually with depression.

Psychopathic Personality

This is a term frequently used and abused by the layman. Blair (1975) states that the term 'psychopath', 'psychopathic personality' and 'psychopathic disorder' are synonymous, which might help to relieve the confusion — but not much! He gives the origin of the term from two Greek words — 'psychos' which means mind and 'pathos' which means derangement. So it is a derangement of the mind not amounting to insanity. The first reference in England was by a Bristol psychiatrist, Dr Prichard (1835) who referred to moral imbeciles whose intelligence was unaffected but whose condition was 'manifested in feelings, temper or habits'. It was Henderson in 1939 who first outlined a commonly used classification (Batchelor, 1969). He divided them into three categories:

(1) Predominantly Aggressive. These are people who habitually react with violence. Their behaviour is impulsive and without insight. They lack both emotions and conscience and show no guilt or regret for their acts. They often end up in prison and come to the psychiatrist as a result of antisocial behaviour.

(2) Predominantly Inadequate or Passive. Lacking in love, these people cannot form long-term relationships, are irresponsible and unable to cope with situations in an adult manner. They tend to be the petty delinquent, shoplifter, etc. There are also those who develop 'invalidism closely allied to neurotic and psychotic states' (Henderson, 1962).

75

Included in this latter category are pathological liars and people who lie constantly and without need (some turn this to their advantage and become confidence tricksters). He also includes eccentrics, who do not usually find their way into psychiatric clinics.

(3) Predominantly Creative. These are unstable, bizarre people who may be very intelligent to the extent of genius. They may have great qualities of leadership, coupled with immaturity and emotional instability. Of these, Napoleon and Lawrence of Arabia are typical examples.

Unlike most diagnosable psychiatric disorders, there is however a legal definition of the condition. The Mental Health Act, 1959 (United Kingdom) states:

> In this Act 'psychopathic disorder' means a persistent disorder or disability of mind (whether or not including subnormality of intelligence) which results in abnormally aggressive or seriously irresponsible conduct on the part of the patient and requires or is susceptible to medical treatment.

It is important to remember that a psychopathic personality is not diagnosed by one or even two antisocial acts but by a habitual pattern of behaviour, perhaps dating from childhood and adolescence although not diagnosable until adult life. It may start in youth, reach its zenith in early adulthood and then tend to diminish, so that the behaviour may have become more socially controlled by the time the client is in his mid-forties.

Causes

There is some evidence that psychopathic personalities are the result of some cerebral organic malfunction. Some show immature or abnormal patterns when the electrical activity of their brain is recorded. Henderson (1962) says that their impulsive conduct is similar to the trigger-like reaction of the epileptic. West (1974) points out that there is a significant excess of XYY ('super male') chromosomes in males in special hospitals, but the significance of this finding has been challenged. He goes on to say that too much attention to personal peculiarities and defects may divert attention from the economic and social problems surrounding them. Sociologists attribute the condition to social conditions and Scott (1966) points out that it is the attitude of relatives as much as the behaviour of the clients that causes admission to institutions. Flew (1973) asserts that it is a result of faulty social learning.

Whatever the causes, we are faced with people who:

(1) Act impulsively and antisocially and have a low tolerance of frustration.
(2) Show no evidence of conscience, feel no guilt or remorse.
(3) Fail to learn by experience and punishment.
(4) Lack deep emotions, cannot feel for others and have difficulty maintaining relationships.
(5) Are manipulative and deceitful.
(6) Tend to need a large amount of personal body space.

Other Personality Disorders

A psychopathic personality is perhaps the best known label, but in spite of attempts by lawyers it is not precisely defined. Perhaps because of this and the fact that in the United Kingdom there are potential legal implications for compulsory detention in a mental hospital, it is common practice to use the term 'personality disorder' in a broader sense to describe those whose inadequacy or socially disruptive behaviour is less severe and pervasive. These are people whose neurotic traits or depression may appear to be part of their personality. Their inability to communicate adequately may be so frustrating that they may commit irresponsible or antisocial acts or perhaps resort to self-mutilation. Whilst legal classification is important, it is unwise to label everyone who has some of the psychopathic characteristics a 'psychopath'. This is particularly important in adolescence, when irresponsible, rebellious and aggressive behaviour may come within the bounds of normality.

Scott (1977) sees a logic in antisocial behaviour which at first is inexplicable or even insane. The behaviour seeks to allay basic anxieties. Aggressive acts are perpetrated or threatened in order to improve the client's own self-image. Habitual lies stem from untrusting parents and many dangerous offences are based on the client's inability to cope with the problems of human relationships. All these themes are familiar to the dramatherapist.

The difficulties of diagnosis and treatment are emphasised by Thorley and Stern (Hill, Murray and Thorley, 1979) who point out that the forensic or prison psychiatrists may see many personality disorders in their work and are probably the least likely to diagnose specific personality types with any degree of confidence. They point out that by treating personality disorders in hospitals, clients are forced to take on the sick role. This gives an expectation that something can be done *to* him. In fact there is no magic, little can be done in this sense and that puts the onus back on the client to make a contribution. While in the sick role, he must be encouraged to develop personal responsibility and do things for himself. This causes a role conflict between the passive sick role and the active responsible role. Many of the clients are lacking in social skills and are behaviourally handicapped.

Thorley and Stern suggest two areas of treatment: that of feeling, the intrapsychic world and that of doing, the external world of action. There is inevitably some overlapping of the two areas and it may be that more than one approach is needed. A clear conceptual framework is necessary but consistency is more important than the model used. Although some therapists believe it is not impossible to treat these people in a psychiatric hospital, other prefer to treat them in special units within prison or forensic units. Some clients will still find their way into other psychiatric establishments.

To include one aggressive psychopath in a group with other diagnostic categories is to seek disaster. His manipulative or aggressive behaviour can cause hostility, anxiety and disruption. However, the passive, inadequate personality-disordered client can sometimes be helped in a supportive group. As there are rarely sufficient numbers in hospital at one time to form a separate group, the dramatherapist needs to assess individual clients before accepting them for therapy.

I worked for some years in a local forensic unit with groups of young men, most of whom were detained by Court order. A few of these have subsequently been admitted to a psychiatric hospital and been referred to my groups where their behaviour has been not disruptive but rather more manipulative and attention-seeking, as if in competition with the rest of the group for my interest.

Aims of Therapy

Acceptance as a Person

I found working in the forensic unit very different from the psychiatric hospital. The group members were young, active and often highly intelligent, but usually immature. Group dynamics as described by Bion (1961) were more pronounced and the initial behaviour of most clients was designed to test me in all ways. As it was a psychodrama group, certain unit rules were relaxed. It was the only place where the residents were allowed to swear in front of a lady, they were allowed time off work to attend, there was no compulsion to stay until the end of the session, there were no written notes and I had a clear contract that nothing personal was ever disclosed outside the group. Newcomers swore excessively, would leave the group to show disapproval and relate events which could not possibly be the truth during the first few sessions. Later, when it was possible to work at a personal level, a common need to be accepted as they were, without any judgement on their behaviour, was frequently expressed. This was usually a need for parental acceptance, but it coloured all their relationships with authoritative figures. Until I could show that I valued them as people, although I did not agree with their behaviour, I could not establish a working relationship.

Trust

People who habitually lie and steal and behave antisocially are not those who are usually trusted. A vicious circle is created — the client wants to be trusted and lies to get out of trouble, but relatives react by becoming less trusting when they discover the deception. Many clients have been rejected at an early age by parents and friends and later by society. It is sometimes difficult to know which came first, the rejection or the unacceptable behaviour. Some of the clients in the group mentioned above had a long history of foster homes, institutional care, detention centre, Borstal and prison. Their dislike of any form of discipline and mistrust of authority resulted in even more rejection. There is a great need and, sometimes, a real desire to break the chain.

Responsibility in a Group

Whenever difficulties arise in groups, a common way to handle it is projection. 'He made me angry' is the common cry, not 'I was angry with him'. Clients who are always in trouble find it difficult to accept their own feelings, which may appear too powerful to control. Special units are designed to give opportunities to learn responsibility for themselves in and responses to group situations. The group frequently sets its own limits by making decisions for dealing with disruptive clients. The censure of the rest of the members helps to build up a pattern of more acceptable behaviour. Behaviour modification programmes work towards this same end.

Discipline

A firm, sympathetic discipline is required which gives a framework for action and allows for maturation. Most children object to an imposed discipline, but it is necessary until they learn self-discipline. Our clients' immaturity is akin to that of the child in this respect. If we are going to provide an environment in which self-discipline can be learned, it must involve setting limits. An explicit set of rules, kept to the minimum and clearly set out, allows the client to see what is expected of him.

Employment

Many clients arrive with erratic work records. The lack of self-discipline, poor relationships and disruptive behaviour frequently result in termination of employment. It is important to establish a constant work pattern. Consequently, special units concentrate on employment, usually within the grounds of the institution, in kitchens, gardens and domestic work on the wards. The times for work, meals and recreation are closely adhered to and a pattern is set which will hopefully become a habit in the future.

Where does dramatherapy fit into this pattern? I personally did not wish to have evening sessions. Drama as recreation is commendable, but I did not want it confused with dramatherapy. Recreation takes place outside worktime. Clients were released from work to attend therapy sessions and it had to be established that they were expected to put effort into it. Finding the right balance between this expectation and the freedom of dramatic experience was not easy. The group was considered by some members of staff to be a matter of 'skiving' off work, particularly if music and laughter could be heard coming from the room. I was glad of any opportunity to talk about dramatherapy in staff meetings.

Control of Impulsive Behaviour

This is not easy to establish and it grows with self-discipline. Sometimes, however, behaviour that seems impulsive has a logic to it. I discovered in one group (average intelligence in the 60–90 range) that some of their actions were the result of educational problems and of lack of knowledge of alternative ways to behave (Langley, D.M., 1979b). Among these was a deficit of social skills as well as poor educational attainment.

Aversion therapy is sometimes used, particularly with sexual offenders. Again, it is only as successful as the client will allow. One young man described how he cheated by conjuring up images that allowed him to disregard the pictures presented to him in aversion sessions!

It is important to be realistic as to how much can be achieved for people with personality disorders. Sometimes one can only work towards motivation. Until the client sees a need to change and has a desire to do so, no one can hope for maturity. Even when motivated, he will improve very slowly and maybe with frequent relapses. These should be accepted with sympathetic understanding but not ignored. The aims should be towards improvement rather than cure. If the therapist invests the therapy with personal achievement or gratification she will not be able to work for long without disillusion. We can only present a framework and offer tolerant support. The client must do the rest for himself. However, even if the client cannot be cured, he can sometimes be guarded and helped to guard himself from the worst excesses of his behaviour. Scott's (1977) analogy of the psychopath as a hoop rolling unstably downhill and requiring occasional taps to help it keep upright and on course is a good one.

What has Dramatherapy to Offer

(1) Conceptual Framework

Drama is an excellent conceptual framework in which to view behaviour. Working from fantasy of what we would like to be, we can look at reality (and hopefully) see ourselves as we are. Then we can begin to build and develop the areas of our personality we find lacking.

(2) Trust

I must continually emphasise the need to build a trusting relationship in groups (e.g. Figure 5.1). This is of paramount importance for people with personality disorders because of the need to break the chain of mistrust. The therapist must be a model for trusting behaviour, and should be prepared to enter into all trust exercises herself as well as sharing a general trust in individuals and the group. For this reason it is sometimes better to delay 'blind' exercises until the group has learned not to take advantage of the therapist's closed eyes! Working with a member of staff or co-therapist can ensure that this does not happen. It is also important to emphasise responsibility in trust exercises. There is a need to explain that the object is to prevent your partner coming to harm and insist on the seriousness of this responsibility. If we allow clients to disregard this without comment in the early stages, it is more difficult for it to be taken seriously later.

Figure 5.1: Group Trust through Touch. A. Feeling Faces

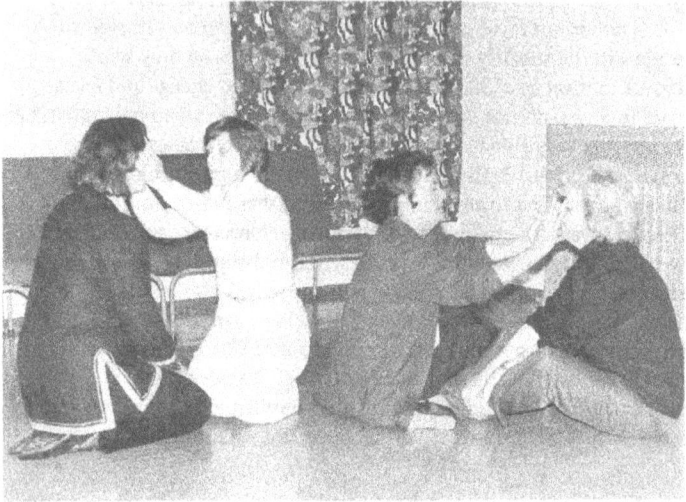

B. Feeling Hands

(3) Cohesion in the Group

Working in a group is an important skill to learn. These clients have usually been 'outsiders' for most of their lives and they have no idea how to begin relating appropriately. The making of group decisions and the need for compromise are useful ways of exploration. Careful selection of group members is essential and there is a need to be clear about the aims of the group. Sexual offenders can be rejected unless dealt with in a separate group. Less intelligent clients can become a butt for ridicule and scapegoating, so it is as well to have separate groups for high, average and low intelligence. I found that the less intelligent groups were, on the whole, unable to make use of the insight gained by psychodrama, so would suggest concentrating on drama-based exercises until the therapist has been able to assess the potential of the group.

(4) Social Skills

This is a very important subject (see also Chapter 8). The forming and maintaining of relationships and behaviour in different situations do not come easily to these clients. They often need plenty of personal space and tend to give confused body cues — looking aggressive as a defence does not help gain others' confidence in forming relationships. Misinterpretation of others' body language also leads to difficulties. There was one memorable session in which the group members had voiced a desire to form long-term sexual relationships rather than 'just have sex with anyone who offers'. We had a visiting drama student who very expertly portrayed the girl who wanted sex, the one who wanted a sexual relationship and the one who wanted companionship. In a series of role plays the group practised dealing with each kind of girl and looked at their own responses. To some it was a revelation that behaviour differed according to the needs of the person involved. This was a group of low intellect and maybe needed the explanation that there were different approaches to relationships with women.

This group also worked well at interviewing techniques and dealing with aggressive behaviour in others. Another thing that came to light was that the clients often had no idea of their own strength. What was designed simply to push people out of the way in a game could, in fact, knock them over. We had one session in which we tried to explore this by going into a cricket field and throwing balls of various weights in order to see how much force was needed and how much effort was required to send them a certain distance. Although the group enjoyed this I felt that I learnt more from the session than they did. It really required a programme designed by the physical training instructor who had more expertise than I in this sphere. It is important in any kind of physical activity or role play practice to be sure that the client understands what he is doing and is not just repeating a series of words and actions which have been modelled for him.

(5) Role Exploration

The ability to look at roles objectively and learn role expectation is vital. These clients need to relinquish the 'sick' role or 'bad' role and find satisfaction in other roles. The methods of doing this are described in Chapter 7.

(6) Personal Development

Drama is an excellent medium for personal development (Way, 1967). When we are at ease with dramatic methods, we sometimes get moments of insight which come when least expected. If we allow ourselves to look at each experience we have in the sessions, we will see how we are continually projecting ourselves, our needs, problems and feelings into our creative activities. The self-knowledge thus acquired can be used to strengthen our self-concept and bring about desired changes. The fact that drama is a group activity means that we can use the group to reflect and observe our own behaviour. If guided skilfully, the group will highlight our errors of judgement and help us gain insight in a supportive environment.

(7) Relaxation

Tension is common to all of us. The immature and antisocial behaviour shown in personality disorders sometimes causes us to miss the inner tension, which is often the root of that behaviour. This is particularly so of people who mutilate themselves — cut their wrists, swallow foreign bodies or violently abuse their bodies in some way. It is not a matter of lying down to relax. There is a need to learn to relax at will and move in a relaxed fashion. Relaxation in anger helps to disperse it. Relaxation in fear can help to overcome authority problems. If the client gets tense when he is interviewed by an authoritative figure he is likely to react by being abusive or difficult in order to release that tension. By learning to relax at will he can come to the situation with a new approach.

(8) Honesty

In drama the therapy is in the experience. The more we give ourselves over to that experience, the deeper it is. This becomes more easy with practice and the veteran will emerge from each session knowing more of himself. No one, and certainly not the therapist, is going to question his experience; it is unique and private to him. If he is prepared to share it with the rest of the group, he may gain even more insight and the others may benefit too. If he is not honest with himself, he will not gain much from the experience. In this way dramatherapy can offer an alternative to lies and fantasies. It is very personal and cannot be challenged, so the client is free from any pressure to perform to a pattern. This gives him an opportunity to be honest with himself and gain the rewards of such honesty, perhaps for the first time in his life.

When planning sessions it is important to have our aims and objectives clear. However, the mistrust and behaviour problems that go with personality disorders indicate a careful introduction to drama. There is usually defensiveness, scepticism and a fear of being made to look a fool, so adequate explanation is necessary at all times. I found that I had to work through a pattern of resistance before work could begin in earnest. This usually involved:

(1) 'Why are we here?' 'What is expected of us?' 'Are we being treated as children?'
(2) Expressions of hostility against the institution in general.
(3) Expressions of hostility against authoritative personnel.
(4) 'Why should we change anyway?'

It would take half the sessions to work through this by which time about half of the ten members would have dropped out. The final five sessions would produce intensive work from the remaining group members. However, in the low-intelligence group this was not so. Having become familiar with drama and trusting it, the group remained intact and enthusiastic. I would suggest when starting groups with such clients that you have a period in which the aim is simply to introduce drama as a method of development.

Session One:
(1) Introduce yourself by name and state two things you would like the group to know about you.
(2) In pairs, find three things you have in common. Report back to the large group. After each pair has spoken, ask if anyone else in the group shares these things.
(3) If this has not brought a sharing of interest, repeat the exercise

specifically to find common interests.

(4) The discussion of common interests may continue until the end of the session. This does not matter. Allow plenty of verbal expression during the early groups to establish that this is allowed and use it as an outlet for anxiety. Also the therapist can use this time to become conversant with the interests, attitudes and feelings of the group.

(5) Tense and relax in a large circle. Discuss relaxation and the ways of doing it. If possible conclude the group by relaxing on the floor or chairs together. This is probably sufficient for the first session with these voluble clients.

Session Two:

(1) Tug of war in pairs. Discuss in terms of relaxation and personal strength.

(2) Tell a story in a circle, each member contributing a sentence. Discuss the importance of words and/or imagination.

(3) In pairs, describe to your partner a place where you feel at ease. Share in the large group.

(4) Ask for a volunteer to create his place by using people, furniture, etc., from the room. One or two clients may be prepared to do this. Indicate how the use of props can add another dimension to the original description.

(5) In a large group discuss whom you would invite to the place described. This may bring a discussion on trust and will indicate how the clients feel about named individuals.

(6) Concentrate on the people who are present in the room and admit to yourself whom you would like to know better. Do not express it to anyone.

Session Three:

(1) Wink murder.

(2) In pairs, A is given the title of a book, play or film to represent non-verbally to B, who guesses what it is. (As there is a fear of being made to look foolish. I prefer to do this in pairs rather than groups. I also avoid the word 'mime' as this infers skill.)

(3) Discuss this and what it feels like to use actions without words.

(4) If the group is ready, perform a blind walk. If not, relaxation on the floor and encourage people to close their eyes. Discuss.

(5) Tell your partner (or the group) of someone you have met whom you feel you could trust. There may well be people who say they have never been able to trust anyone. Allow plenty of time for discussion and sharing.

(6) Mirror work in a large group. The therapist starts movements which all follow. Ask for volunteers to lead.

You have now introduced games, trust, relaxation, non-verbal communication and a structure for role play. Working in pairs or a large group cuts down the possibility of disturbance. Relating to only one other person is less embarrassing and more likely to encourage serious involvement when the therapist is not supervising. Unattended sub-groups have a habit of getting out of hand! A large group is open, and everyone knows what is happening so that there is no hidden fear that a rival group is laughing at you. Continue with games, exercises and discussion until the group is ready for fantasy role play. After eight or ten sessions the therapist should review the group's progress with the ward staff. It may be that the group is ready to work towards a specific goal. If it is not, continue with the introduction of drama as your aim for a little longer.

6 REHABILITATION

After any kind of illness or crisis which has affected a person's ability to function within his usual roles, there is a period when he needs to learn how to regain his former position in society (or social networks). The objectives are clear when a patient has had a physically disabling illness, and both occupational therapy (OT) and physiotherapy can offer appropriate physical aids (Bennett, 1978). This can be true of any illness, even such a common one as a lengthy pneumonia. There is a period when the person concerned has to readjust from the role of patient needing care and physical assistance to his normal role of father or wage-earner or whatever, as well as perhaps coping with a residual physical or psychological disability. Similarly it is also true of a major crisis such as bereavement when there has to be a change of role from chief mourner to an entirely new role of widow, whilst retaining some old roles such as mother.

Physical aids can offer nothing in these situations. If the illness is a psychiatric one and mental symptoms have resulted in long or short periods in hospital, then the rehabilitation period is most important and needs to be carefully planned. The need to return to work has long been appreciated and industrial therapy is now an accepted part of a rehabilitation programme. The need to join clubs and socialise is also met to some degree, but before a patient can reach the stage of joining a club, a lot of barriers need to be overcome (Bennett 1977:1978).

The change from the dependent role of patient to that of an independent social being can be a very threatening experience (see Chapter 7). As a patient, physical needs are met without question, but the thought, skill and physical effort required to prepare a meal for oneself or a family may need considerable practice before the role is successfully changed into that of cook. Without constant encouragement to learn new, or re-learn old skills, the effort required may seem too great and the role of patient more desirable than that of cook. On a social level, the role of depressed patient may require less effort than that of mother or hostess. So, the first need to be met is motivation. The simple games and 'party' atmosphere of a drama group enable a patient literally to get up from his chair and become involved in social activities, without the threat of being in an obviously social situation. As he gradually comes to trust other group members, he will gain the confidence to try new activities.

It is customary in our society for adults to confine physical contact to people very close to them, yet the usual method of helping an unhappy or sick child is to cuddle, rock or physically soothe him. On admission to hospital the patient is deprived of contact with close relations and put in the dependent child role with substitute parents. So, it is the nurse who touches whilst bathing or giving an injection, the doctor whilst examining, and possibly the occupational therapist whilst teaching some skill, or the social worker/psychologist to comfort in distress. These are all within the context of dependency which puts the staff on a different emotional level from the patient. In order to change his role to be on equal terms with staff, the patient has to learn to initiate physical contact in a manner that does not ask for help or sympathy or transgress professional taboos. He needs, also, to touch people who are not playing a supportive role to him, i.e. other patients, voluntary helpers, etc. Some people find physical contact with others difficult as part of their illness, or have always found it threatening and this is reinforced by illness. The patient role does not usually demand one to initiate physical contact and so the ability to do so becomes weaker. After a long period as a patient, this can be threatening and confusing. It is necessary to re-learn the code of physical contact in social situations. This can be gently introduced into drama sessions by games that involve touch in a 'safe' way because limits are set by the rules of each game. There is no compulsion to play games, the the patient can go as far as he desires in touch and no further. By allowing him to regulate the speed at which he proceeds, he can gain confidence to repeat the contact.

In normal conversation we are, at times, expected to engage in eye contact with others. Sometimes this becomes very difficult, particularly if we are anxious, self-conscious, or feel we have something we do not want other people to know. The less confident we feel about handling a situation, the less likely we are to meet someone else's gaze. The very nature of a psychiatric illness reduces self-confidence. To be placed in the role of patient implies seeking skilled help. In the psychiatric field it means seeking skilled help just to cope with living. This reinforces the lack of confidence. Any fantasies or distortion of perspective brought about by the illness can contribute to the desire to hide thoughts and a reluctance to meet another person's gaze. Games which require looking at another group member, not necessarily with eye contact, can allow a patient gradually to look and be looked at within the limits of the game until he can progress to eye contact.

Words can become very important in psychiatric illness. Meanings can become distorted, while obsessional repetitions, hallucinating voices, confusion and memory impairment can be an embarrassment when leaving the sheltered environment of a hospital and entering a less understanding and, possibly, hostile society. So it is useful to introduce word games to the drama group. At first, these can be very simple ones, like each person thinking of an object beginning with a certain letter. It can progress through a whole range of memory and verbal games into role-play improvisations where a patient can rehearse scenes and experiment with the words he can use in a certain situation.

The acceptance of the patient role reduces the need to make many personal decisions – when, where and what to eat for example. Although the stated philosophy is to leave as much decision-making as possible to the patient, it is still part of the dependent role to look for help and possibly relief from making decisions both on a personal and group level. Before one can move effectively from the role of patient to that of parent, for example, there must be the ability to decide how to spend the income and how to come to a family decision of what to do at the weekend. Drama asks us to make decisions – Who shall I be in this improvisation? What emotion can I mime? – at a personal level, and also at the group level – What are the rules of this game? What kind of family are we representing in role play? This sharing of decisions leads to a sharing of responsibility within the group. One person's decision to act a role becomes part of the group's decision to present a family scene and the responsibility for portraying it falls on the group and their ability to express their meaning rather than on an individual. This shared responsibility in a simulated situation can be a learning process for reality.

A psychotic illness or one in which the patient retreats into fantasy can leave a confusion as to the boundaries between reality and fantasy, even the physical limits of one's own body. Games which require the recognition of named parts of the body help to make the image clear. If the drama sessions always work towards reality, defining the boundaries, this will clarify the situation and help the patient to leave his fantasies with the role of 'sick me' rather than take them into that of 'healthy me'.

Having developed slowly through all these processes, the patient should be in a position to try out different roles. This involves an appreciation of emotional responses and sufficient control to show emotions in a socially acceptable fashion and at appropriate times but without undue inhibition. This can be effected by rehearsing the roles that will be expected of him by society. Improvised scenes can be set up and he can practise being father, worker, husband, member of the darts team or whatever roles he is insecure with. This role rehearsal is frequently considered the main function of drama in therapy, but in fact it should be the climax to a carefully planned programme of gradual rehabilitation. It is at this point that the patient should begin to relate to staff in a less dependent fashion, gradually emerging as an emotional equal rather than looking for help. It is this final step that makes staff participation in drama sessions so important. We all play games together, are known by our first names and admit to difficulties in our real or simulated roles. We are all safe within the limitations of the games but, at the same time, we are all equally vulnerable within those limitations. The success of relating on equal terms with staff members to whom he has looked for help is the final step in releasing the role of patient and entering a new role with confidence.

Planning

When planning a rehabilitation group we need to ask the question, 'Rehabilitation to what?' It may be that there is little hope of the group members leaving hospital or even changing wards. Rehabilitation means learning to put the physical and mental abilities that remain after an illness to the best possible use. Therefore it is logical to start a rehabilitation programme on a long-stay ward. If the group members are likely to remain in some institutional care, then there is no point in attempting to rehabilitate them to a completely independent way of life. The role of shopper is likely to be limited to the hospital shop, the role of hostess/cook to making cakes for the ward coffee morning, the role of wage-earner to the industrial therapy unit, etc. So we need a clear idea of where we want to go with the group before we start out.

Goals

If there is time to grade the progress of short-stay patients, it is useful to have a series of group sessions towards a specific goal. In this way, a ward or group coffee morning could be the *ultimate* goal with a group of long-stay patients, but the *initial* goal of a group of short-stay patients who may then aim for a group outing for a half day, followed by a whole day, followed by a day or weekend at home. If the immediate goal is always within the bounds of possibility, then there is a feeling of optimism and achievement in a group.

Pace

The pace at which the group progresses is individual to the group and some discussion with ward staff will help the therapist to measure it. However, I find it useful to make another assessment after the second or third session when I can see how quickly the group has become cohesive. Time spent on trust exercises and co-operative games at the beginning of a course is never wasted and if there is any doubt about pace, it is always better to remain at the initial stage longer, rather than precipitate the group into activities before it is ready.

Duration

The duration of each course for a rehabilitation programme would usually be 8–10 sessions. It is better to start with easily achieved goals and reach them, rather than go on indefinitely with little evidence of achievement to the group members. The sessions could be weekly or twice-weekly, but not more frequently at first. This enables the group members to assimilate what they have experienced before meeting again and does not overwhelm them with stimuli. The length of each session will vary with the group, long-stay patients probably starting at half an hour and moving to about one-hour sessions. Short-stay patients are more likely to start with three quarters of an hour and increase to two-hour sessions. This amount of time is necessary when the group reaches the stage of practising role play.

A Typical Programme for a Rehabilitation Group

I would start all groups with basic activities to reach a point where the group is ready to work as a team. The time needed for this would vary with the group. In the first session I would break the large group down into pairs and then reassemble these to finish in a large group. There is safety in numbers when one is feeling insecure. I would aim to start each group with a general activity, then work in pairs (e.g. Figure

6.1), increasing numbers into a general group, *or* the opposite depending on the security of the group. I would *always* finish a session with a discussion of feelings.

Figure 6.1: Working in Pairs — Co-operation through Balance

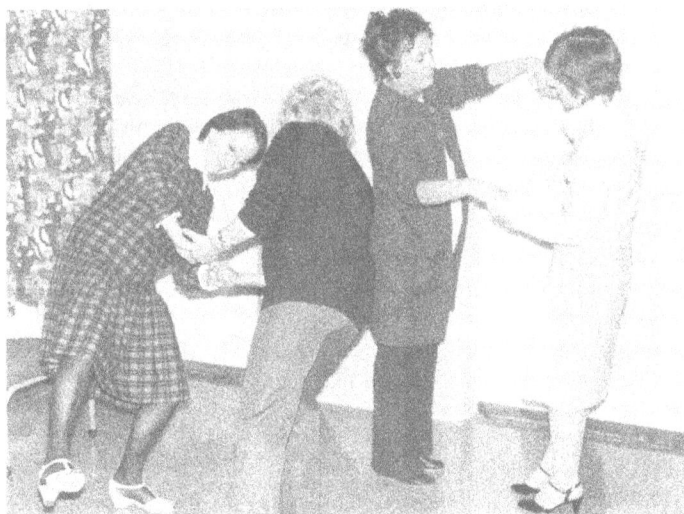

Session One:
(1) Introduce self and outline aims very briefly.
(2) Spin the platter to learn names.
(3) Divide into sub-groups and give each a hoop. See how many different ways each group can use it.
(4) Ask them to devise a game with rules and share it with the others.
(5) Discuss session so far.
(6) Blind walk to encourage trust and awareness of the need for trust.
(7) Discussion of this.
(8) Depending on the group, either
    (a) open discussion of feelings about the session, or
    (b) in pairs, tell your partner what you liked/did not like about the session.
    Share in large group.

Session Two:
(1) Name game, introduce person on your right to the group.
(2) In pairs, find three things you have in common. They can be

physical attributes, places, hobbies, etc. This starts people looking at each other to see if they both have blue eyes, etc.

(3) Discussion of this.

(4) Blind walk just holding hands.

(5) Discussion of this.

(6) Touch something red, green, purple, black etc. and go back to your place (if you choose carefully people will begin to touch each other's clothing in this game).

(7) In pairs, describe to your partner something in the room. He guesses the name of the object *or* tell partner your favourite colour and something you like that is that colour (red dress, curtains in the bedroom, etc.).

(8) Find another pair and join hands in a circle, stretching out arms full length, and then relax. This is both a trust exercise and a form of relaxation.

(9) Discuss this in large group.

Session Three:

(1) If it is an agile group, warm up by playing tag, *otherwise* take a piece of material and each group member uses it imaginatively.

(2) Blind walk, allowing your partner to feel surfaces and textures in the room.

(3) Discussion.

(4) Start a rhythmic movement individually, join with partner and co-ordinate your movements, join with another pair and co-ordinate with them.

(5) Discussion.

(6) Mime an action which your partner guesses. Now put an emotion to it, e.g. play tennis angrily.

(7) Discuss. We have now admitted to emotions — this is a useful point to discuss them either in a large group *or* tell your partner what things make you angry.

(8) Share in large group.

By this time some groups are ready to go on to more threatening eye contact and physical contact games and I would begin to introduce fantasy role-play games. Other groups would need to stay at this level for a long time, maybe the rest of the course, with new things gradually being introduced.

If we had a programme for a whole ward, then complementary activities should be organised in parallel with it. If the group members come from various wards, then contact with the ward staff is needed to ensure the reinforcement of their learning outside the group.

Short-stay patients may be able to go from this kind of group to look at roles as described in the next chapter on role play. If this seems too big a jump to make it is worth doing another course of games and approaching role play at the end of it.

7 ROLE PLAY

What are Roles?

Each of us has many roles; some are with us all the time, others at
different times in our lives. There are times when one role seems more
important than others, then it recedes and another takes over. To
clarify my discussion I will list the issues under five separate headings.

(1) Physiological Roles

These are the roles we need for physical survival. The first role a baby
takes on at birth is that of breather — this is essential for life. Failure
in this role may be treated temporarily with artificial respiration but
continued failure means death. Other roles in this category are sleeper,
eater, drinker, excreter, cougher, sneezer, etc. We do not have
complete control over these roles and they can conflict in their need
for gratification. Failure or distortion in any of these roles can result
in hospitalisation. The biological function is basic, but our expectation
of performance gives us the role. Clients who come to psychiatric
clinics sometimes have a distorted expectation of physiological roles
which results in preoccupation with that physiological function.
Anxiety over their physiological roles brings upon them the role of
patient.

(2) Activity Roles

These are the 'doing' roles of life and include cook, shopper, driver,
sempster, knitter, gardener, cleaner, etc. Some of these, such as
shopper, cook and cleaner, are essential to modern life while others
involve activities and skills by which we earn our living. Without these
we cannot survive as independent beings and failure in these roles is
frequently the precipitating factor in bringing people into psychiatric
care. The phobic person who cannot shop, the depressed mother who
cannot cope with housekeeping and cooking and the schizophrenic
person who cannot earn a living, are all likely to be admitted to day
or residential units. The above roles are very important and necessary
for independent survival. There is a tendency amongst therapists to
discount these roles as being unimportant and to assume that our
work as therapists lies with social role repair. I think that both types
of role are equally important and time spent on cooking, shopping
and craft is not wasted. Crafts can be therapeutic activities in their

own right. Who has not come home from a tense or busy working day and found relief in a hobby or in decorating the house or making something new? There is a case for teaching hobbies to our clients so that they can find their own therapy when necessary at home. Activity roles should be seen as complementary to social roles.

(3) Social Roles

The social role is a place or position in a group or social network which is dependent on a relationship with someone else. A speaker needs a listener to function in the role, a child needs a parent, etc. Familial roles can survive death and the daughter can continue in that role, behaving in a way expected of her, long after her parents are dead.

My definition of a group is a number of people whose roles are linked and who all know and are known by each other, such as a family or village or a wives' group. People in a social network do not necessarily all know each other, but there are connecting links between them, e.g. parent-teacher association, staff social club, people who live in a city street. The social network roles have wider horizons and less close contact. We all have roles in both groups and social networks, and we all perform better in some roles than in others. Some of us are happier in groups and others in our social-network roles.

If we are to grow and develop our personalities, we need to look for new roles and expand our old ones. Conflict in a marriage is sometimes created by one partner looking for role expansion or new roles. If the other partner is not prepared to facilitate this, then the one may seek new roles outside the partnership and cause a rift or break-up of marriage. Each role which we possess, brings with it an expectancy of fulfilment both for ourselves and others. Learning starts from the minute a child is born. The nurse, in her role, cleans the baby and hands him to the mother who, in her role, cuddles, comforts and feeds him. He learns to be child and patient and to have expectations of the mother and nurse roles. So begins a learning process that goes on through life. As the child develops, he needs to expand his roles and learn new ones in order to become independent and to form and sustain relationships. If, for some reason, he becomes role-bound — perhaps in the role of son to a possessive mother — then he is not able to move on to certain other roles, maybe that of friend, lover or husband and his life is the poorer for it.

A child learns by trial and error and by modelling others the behaviour appropriate to his role. If his learning process is curtailed for some reason, for example by the death of both parents at an early age, then he may not be able to fulfil that role adequately at a later stage. If he is later adopted by another family he may not have learned what is expected of him in a face-to-face situation of a family group and find difficulties with that and with the wider and looser context of a social network. Similarly, a child whose parents' role expectations of him are not in line with the social network in which he lives is presented with a dilemma — to conform to his parents' standards or that of his social network or to give up completely and not develop that particular role.

In sickness a child learns a new role, that of patient and the nurse/ mother role can become confused for him because mother sometimes is nurse to him and, in hospital, nurse is sometimes mother to him. This may, at a later stage, require him to relearn a role, that of son when he is no longer in need of nursing and mother has just one role for him. If, at any stage, a child ceases to develop a role, it can be a disadvantage to him as an adult. An example of this is when he does not develop his role of son from child-son to adult-son and this can impose on him limitations of relating to his parents only as a child. If he has based other roles on his parent-son model, he may then be unable to relate to others at an adult level too.

(4) Fantasy Roles

If we watch small children at play we find that role games occur frequently. They play endless games of 'mothers and fathers', 'doctors and nurses', 'teachers', 'policemen', 'shopkeepers', etc. This is a very important type of play and is a source of learning for them. They try the role, experiment with its boundaries and feel what it is like and how to handle different situations. As they grow and take on other roles in reality, the fantasy ones have given them some training. This is not a sudden change, but a gradual relinquishing of fantasy in favour of reality. If a child cannot make this transition for some reason, then he is termed 'schizoid', 'maladjusted' or even 'autistic'. Whatever label is placed on him he is at a social disadvantage and cannot cope with real life. Sometimes, when life is fraught, adults regress to this stage and want to live fantasy lives and become other people. To cope with real life we have to find a way of giving up most of our fantasy roles but retaining a few to which we can resort at times when we need a break from reality. We all have our fantasies of being a great pianist, dancer, artist, etc., and if we are looking for new roles we often experiment in fantasy to discover if it is appropriate and comfortable. If we have an opportunity to take that one stage further and actually try the role in role play, we get a much clearer idea of it and learn something about it before actually experiencing it. All our fantasies make a statement about us as people and are as much a part of our personality as reality is.

(5) Role Conflict

If any of our roles from any category conflict with another, either in the same or different category, it creates a problem for us. For example, a child wakes in the night and is ready for a game. Our role of parent is then in conflict with that of sleeper and we have to decide which has the priority — usually not a very difficult decision to make! Or the role of sleeper could be in conflict with that of urinator and we have to decide which physiological role has priority. Again the role of mother could conflict with that of wage-earner when the children are at home and she is at work. So a decision has to be made which role to relinquish or delegate. This is a more difficult decision to make, particularly if the mother's wage is necessary to the family's standard of living. Sometimes there are conflicts between more than one role, such as a conflict between worker and union member and wage-earner when an industrial strike is pending.

How we decide on our role priorities and deal with our role conflicts depends on our knowledge of the roles, previous experience, expectations, ability to evaluate them and our state of mind at the time. Our decisions could vary on different occasions. Sometimes people cannot deal with these conflicts or have failed in their major roles, such as wage-earner, parent or spouse. They need to allow these roles to recede and take on the major overall role of patient for a period.

The Role of Patient

Whether one subscribes to the idea of mental *illness* or not, there are times when major roles seem too overwhelming for people to cope with. The act of seeking help and desiring to hand over responsibilities to someone in the caring professions gives a new, overall role, whether we call it client or patient or anything else. The need to relinquish difficult roles is a real one and whether we approve of it is immaterial. It happens and we have to find ways of helping people to strengthen or repair their roles. As I am dealing with dramatherapy in a predominantly hospital setting in this chapter, I will refer to the role as that of patient (rather than of client).

The role of patient is a dependent one and can be a passive acceptance of treatment by one or more therapists. Even if the patient is a very active person and perhaps in conflict with the therapist, there is still the assumption that there is a difference in status — the therapist having knowledge of procedures that are unknown to the patient, which, if applied by the therapist, could be to the patient's advantage. We tend to refer to people as being 'good' or 'bad' patients by the way they accept or reject what the therapist has to offer. It is a controversial subject, but I think there is a time when the breakdown of other roles makes the patient role a therapeutic one. We only need to remember the relief with which we give up working roles and crawl into bed as a patient when we have an attack of 'flu to realise its therapeutic possibilities. Similarly, someone with an acute psychosis or depression can find relief in the patient role.

However, when the healing process has begun to work, it is time gradually to relinquish the role of patient and to work towards that of well person and the acceptance of all the other roles that go with it. Most therapists will accept this but what is sometimes more difficult to accept is an altered relationship with the patient. There has to be a narrowing in the status differentiation, so that the patient gradually becomes equal with the therapist. One important shift in this direction is to place the patient in a therapeutic group where it is not the therapist who makes all the decisions and gives out the treatment, but the group members who make their own decisions, share responsibility and help each other.

Dramatherapy groups are an excellent introduction to group therapy. The fact that there is no right or wrong way of doing drama gives confidence. A gentle interaction with others and group decisions through games help such situations to become non-threatening. The fact that staff are (hopefully) not wearing uniforms and use first names is another equaliser. It is also important for the patient sometimes to take a caring role in the group. This can be simply achieved by trust exercises. The first time a patient is led blind round a room by the therapist is a familiar situation. When the patient is asked to lead the therapist, then the responsibilities are reversed and it is a first step towards an altered perception of status.

The therapist must be prepared for a change in relationship, ready to co-operate and not to see this in terms of regressive behaviour. For example, if a hitherto quiescent patient tells the occupational therapist what to do with her knitting or refuses to comply with a nurse's request to switch off the light and go to sleep, it may be a first step in relinquishing the patient role. If the therapist is too rigid in the conception of her own role, she could in fact be preventing the patient's progress to other roles and subsequently failing in her own role as therapist.

In psychiatric illness the perception of roles can become distorted and if the illness is prolonged, the dependency role of patient can become more desirable than the role of fit person, worker, mother, etc. In schizophrenia the fantasy roles and identities may be more desirable than real ones and part of the rehabilitation programme must be geared to making real roles as attractive as fantasy roles. In other illnesses, such as depression and anxiety states, the feeling of inadequacy may be so strong as to make the role of patient more desirable than roles which hold the threat of failure. In this case, it is necessary for the patient to have the opportunity to see a possibility of fulfilling his roles successfully in order to make it an attractive goal that is worth working towards. This glimpse of another or successful role is important in rehabilitation and it may be followed by practising that role. This is a relearning process or a learning of new roles.

The kind of role problems with which we are faced in psychiatric work are:

(1) People who have ceased to develop in one or more roles because of inadequate learning in the first place, e.g. a child with an over-demanding teacher may give up and learn nothing and not develop the role of student.

(2) People whose illness has impaired their function within a role, e.g. the depressed mother who has felt inadequate and of no value to her children.

(3) People who have never had a model to imitate, e.g. a son reared without a father may find difficulty in the role of father to his own children.

(4) People to whom the role of patient is more attractive than that of well person.

(5) People whose period of illness has led them to forget how to function in a role, e.g. the long-term patient who does not remember how to be a shopper. Overlapping of roles can be confusing if a patient can cope with one role and not another, for example, cook/shopper/hostess, each role being dependent on the other.

(6) People who have learned a role in a particular social network and

find it difficult to adapt that role to another social network or even social class, e.g. the role of wife learned in a city where she is expected to be a professional person may be very different in a country setting where 'wife' could mean 'farmer's wife', centred around home and farm and acting as an ancillary to her husband and not a professional in her own right. The difficulty of coping with this role expectation could contribute to breakdown.

This is the challenge presented to therapists — how can we create situations in which patients can look at their role deficiencies and learn ways to repair them? Role play is the relevant term, but how does one approach this in the therapeutic setting? This is where therapy meets with drama, so before we can answer this question we need to look at roles in dramatic terms.

Dramatic Roles

A role in dramatic terms is the feelings and attitudes that are part of the character the actor is portraying. An actor, in rehearsal, will look at his overall role and research it. If he is to portray a real person he will need biographies of the person and the period in which the play is set. He will learn attitudes, social status, political activities, etc., of the period and from this will evolve a personalised role of the character. He will then add appropriate movements, voice, gestures, gait, which is the characterisation. This is all in the realm of make-believe and needs the personality of the actor for the character to become live and credible. Stanislavsky maintained that to do this the actor needed to draw on his own experience of roles and situations (in Bentley, 1968). The actor looks for that par of himself he recognises and uses it to inhabit the role. In this way we see that acting is not a matter of donning a mask and pretending, but of removing a mask and revealing. This makes the actor very vulnerable and he needs to learn, in his training, how to accept himself and cope with his own self-revelation. The therapist, too, has to learn this in order to survive in the role of therapist.

Therapeutic Role Play

When patients come into hospital or outpatient groups, they are preceded by medical or social reports which give us a certain amount

of information about them and their role performance. If a role is
relatively unimportant to the patient (perhaps that of golfer) and he
feels a failure in it, then he will probably admit his failure and be
able to discuss it. Another patient may value the role of golfer and
be distressed by his failing. He will be more sensitive about it and
possibly reluctant to discuss it immediately. The patient who has
been admitted to hospital because of the problems surrounding the
break-up of a marriage may feel a failure in the role of wife or husband
and possibly parent. The therapist, with foreknowledge of written
notes or staff discussion, often tries to persuade the patient to try
and talk about the event. However, our roles and how we feel we
perform in them are a very sensitive area and consequently not
something we can reveal easily. So to ask a patient to role-play (or even
discuss) real-life situations can be very threatening. The risk of exposing
one's insecurities is a real one. I recommend a gradual progression in
group activities.

It is important to form a cohesive and trusting group before
individual work begins. This ensures that no one feels alone or
unsupported, so the introduction of trust exercises and 'ice-breaking'
non-competitive games is an important preliminary. This should not
be hurried and the confidentiality of the group needs to be respected.
People are often embarrassed about their role inadequacies and find
it difficult to talk about them in a group. I find it useful to start role
play using 'play' in the sense of 'games' and work towards role
inhabiting rather than 'role play' in the sense of 'play acting'. If patients,
who are very disabled, have had adverse experiences or severe and
lengthy illnesses, are involved, one can approach roles by games such
as 'I went to market and in my basket I put . . .'. It is a simple word-
memory game that safely raises some of the basic expectations in the
role of the shopper.

Fantasy and Reality Role Play

Other groups may be ready more quickly to broach the subject of roles.
Telling lies about oneself or an impromptu scene and improvisation of
something entirely imaginary is a good beginning. We all project
something of ourselves into fantasy situations, sometimes as a direct
desire to be or to have (e.g. Figure 7.1). Sometimes it is a negative
way; fantasy is the opposite of the truth. Either way we are making
a statement about ourselves. A good introduction is an improvisation of

Figure 7.1: Fantasy — the Raising of the Ship *Mary Rose*

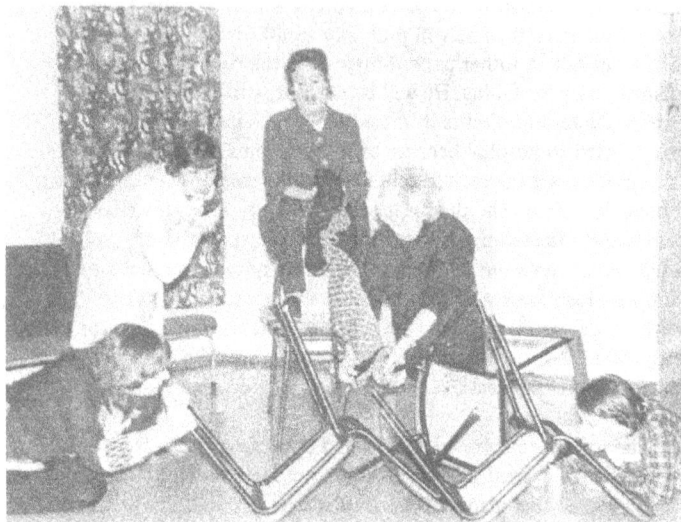

a group of travellers going on a journey. They decide who they are and
where they are going. This does not need to be within the scope of
possibility. It is still part of the 'games' approach. They could be slaves
being deported or pilgrims going to a shrine. The scene can be built up
in the same manner as an improvisation for play rehearsal and as far
from reality as the group desires. When the fun of creation is finished,
the group can look at the roles they have developed and each individual
can try to find that part of himself he has used in his creation. So the
group, working from fantasy, can become closer to reality.

The next step could be to work on family scenes. These should still
be safe, imaginary scenes, but the group could finish the session by
individuals identifying the part each used in the scene. This could be
followed by asking a group member to write a short script of a scene
that could happen in his own life. It could be treated in a similar
manner by the group, so that the gap between make-believe and reality
is narrowed to a 'play about me', but we do not yet have an open
display of 'me in my damaged role'.

By the time the group has worked to this depth, members are
probably ready to look at some of their own roles, at first just a
straightforward presentation of the individual in a role. Family roles
seem to be popular as a beginning, perhaps because the roles are familiar

and breakdowns are common, so again the group is 'playing safe'. I
would ask the group to look at their fantasy roles and situations and
find any connection with their real selves. Then we begin to see reality
through our fantasy. This is a very safe way of looking at oneself
objectively, the fantasy creating a distance between self and truth.
I think it is important for the group to be allowed to do this. Only
when we are secure in our support can we explore roles both old and
new.

When beginning reality role play with a group, I explain to them that
role play is not 'acting a part'. To portray attitudes and feelings we
need to draw on our personal knowledge of a role. For example, to
role-play a Welsh miner, I would assume the attitude of a trade union
member, his preoccupation with his rights and position in the work
force. I would assume his feelings of anxiety, claustrophobia and
physical discomfort, along with the inherited feeling of generations of
insecurity and fear of a pit disaster. To do this I would need to draw
on knowledge of my own need for a fair deal at work, my own
claustrophobic experiences, anxiety, etc., and any fears and insecurities
inherited in my own way of life. I could do all this using my own voice
and posture and sex, whereas no one would pay money to see a tall
female speaking Queen's English and playing the part of a Welsh miner
in a play. That is characterisation. There are a variety of ways of using
reality role play in a group and I list some of them under headings of
my own making:

Role Observing

A person who has lacked or needs a new model in a role could look at
some models. The other members of the group can present scenes using
that role and the same scene can be repeated with each member bringing
his own self to the role, whilst the 'damaged' member watches. This
is based on the personal construct theory described by Kelly (in
Bannister and Francella, 1971) and is particularly useful with
schizophrenics who can be confused by role reversal.

Role Practice

The same group member can then put himself into a scene and try out
the role. He can repeat it in various situations and try various ways of
coping with these situations.

Role Rehearsal

He can then go into scenes and rehearse real-life situations he may meet.

Role Support

At this point it may be valuable to look at the role he has learned. He could see where he is strong and where he is weak and perhaps find complementary roles in which he can be supported. This may come from his own roles or he may find support from another person. A weak wife helps him to be a strong husband; a strong neighbour makes him a timid neighbour, so he needs to look for support in that role from a strong brother or maybe employer.

Role Experience

We all have gaps in our role experience and regret the way we have behaved in the past at times. Many of us would have liked to be the 'teenager of today' who is outspoken and free. Role play gives us the opportunity to experience that kind of situation and behave in a manner very different from the one in which we did in reality. It gives an opportunity of filling in gaps of experience. We can have the satisfaction of experiencing in the present what might have been in the past.

Role Reversal

In order to understand the roles of other people or even discover where to look for role support, it can be very valuable to reverse roles with others who are important to the patient. He can pick his cast from the rest of the group and set up a familiar scene. He can then change identities with the other people in the scene — become his own wife, child, employer, etc. In this way he can see the situation as it appears to other people and experience himself as others do.

Role Discovery

Working within a group and playing roles, both one's own and other people's, can lead to surprises. A woman playing the role of a prostitute may discover a wantonness within herself she did not know she possessed. A man playing an engineer may discover within himself a desire for mechanical knowledge. A man who is asked to play a female role or maybe a very caring person can discover a sensitivity within himself that he did not know existed. This is a 'bonus' in role play.

Simulation

There is often confusion between role play and simulation. Where role play takes attitudes and feelings, simulation brings the whole thing nearer reality by reproducing as carefully as possible the physical conditions of the situation. Simulated pubs are set up in alcoholic units and shops on long-stay wards and simulation becomes falsely regarded as the total application of role play. I see a place for simulation in therapy but only as a climax to a carefully planned programme of games and role play.

When a group has become cohesive and trusting through the security of playing games and explored roles in the way I have described, then is the time for simulation. It can be helpful to simulate a shop to rehearse the role of shopper, an office to rehearse interviews or a family living room for a return home for a difficult family confrontation. These can be practice for reality. However, the participants are still not acting, but are being that part of themselves that is in the role. In this way a group member, who is in the role of employer to help another rehearse the role of employee, would draw upon his own experience and parallels in his own life of authority roles. Thus he may gain fresh insight into his own personality and the whole thing become a creative experience for him as well. We remove ourselves from the realms of make believe into being.

Reality

Role play is always working towards reality (e.g. Figure 7.2). The final test is to leave the group and go out and be a real parent, shopper,

Figure 7.2: Reality — a Domestic Crisis

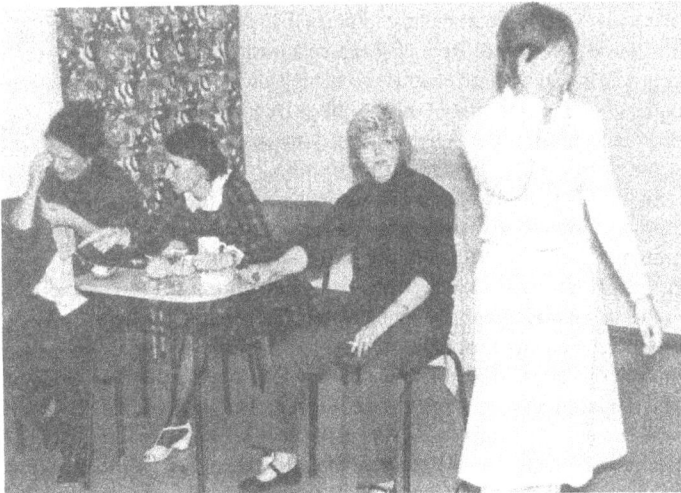

teacher, student, etc. Some group members may find their illness to be one big escape from the difficult role in reality. People who have had a psychotic episode often back away from reality and the acceptance of real roles. The aim in therapy is then to help them to accept this role. The fantasy of simulation or setting up a scene is not always necessary or a help to achieving this acceptance. I feel that a patient with schizophrenia, who can actually talk, for example, as a mother about her child as opposed to mothers in general about children in general, is just as involved in role play as another person who sets up a scene and rehearses it.

This chapter is an attempt to link social theory, drama theory and practice. I have approached therapeutic role play from the position of an actor and tried to uncover the roots of the technique. To do this, I feel we need to start with the basis of all drama which is play. My approach is from non-competitive games to role games which develop into fantasy role play and finally role activities to prepare for reality. This kind of programme can be used with long-term severely disabled people, who may find role 'repair' techniques too threatening to embark upon immediately.

Role Play in Staff Training

We have seen how sensitive people are about role performance. Our professional roles are particularly important to us because they are our means of livelihood. Role play can be a learning experience in therapy. It is also used often in staff training and can be equally valuable, but if it is misused (and I think it frequently is) then it can be damaging both to the individual concerned and to the whole concept of role play. There seems to be an assumption that staff should be able to display their role inadequacies to their tutors and fellow students and that somehow this is 'good for them' and therefore a learning experience. Vulnerability in the act of role play and the personal risk involved are discounted and students frequently come away feeling conspicuous and embarrassed. This feeling is what is remembered and any learning of the professional role is diminished or maybe forgotten. It seems to me particularly cruel to put students in this situation because they are still learning their professional skills. To ask someone to display a skill he is not sure he possesses, let alone knows how to use, is likely to leave him feeling less confident than when he started.

Simulations are frequently used in staff training and considered to be the total use of role play (see above). Sometimes physical disabilities are simulated in order to allow staff to experience disability. This may be an interesting experience but, in my opinion, role play is not so much about physical feelings but emotional ones. It involves taking the total experience that is present within the group and using it imaginatively to create a 'here and now' event. The physical make-believe and simulated disability seem to me 'play acting' in the worst possible sense. This does not mean that insight into disabilities cannot be gained by role play. The limitations one puts on oneself as granny or as a deaf child can be remarkably revealing. Trust exercises, which involve 'blind' walks, can also give some insight into blindness, but that is not the object of the exercise, just a bonus from it. Although we can simulate deafness, blindness and other physical disabilities, we can never simulate the feelings that go with it. These have to come from within ourselves. It seems to me that the value is in that inner experience and not the simulation.

When using role play in staff training I start as with patient groups to create a cohesive group. The needs of staff to trust their fellow group members are no less than patient needs and equal sensitivity from the tutor is required as from the therapist. I then go on to work in fantasy situations until the students are familiar with the technique of role play. If the group is larger than five people, then I sub-divide and have more than one role play going on at the same time. This ensures that all the students are actively involved and there is no audience. The learning comes from experiencing the role — the feeling of what it is like to be therapist, patient, relative, etc., in a particular situation It makes more demands on the tutor who has to supervise several role-play situations at the same time, but it is far more comfortable for the students and they are likely to learn more from it. If there is any embarrassment felt in an established group, it should come from within the role and not from the act of role play. Only when a group has been working together for some time and is familiar with the method do I feel that it is justified to expose individuals to personal work in a large group. Bearing all this in mind and assuming that the basic work has been accomplished, I can see the following uses in training:

(1) Modelling. If a student is not sure how to handle a situation, then it is possible to experiment in role play in the same way as the patient experiments with new roles and situations — watching other people and trying it out for himself.

(2) Feedback on Skills. Patients very rarely tell us how they feel about the way the therapist behaves. By displaying our skills to our colleagues we can receive an educated comment on our performance.

(3) Role Reversal. Experience of oneself in a patient context can be very uncomfortable and revealing.

(4) Personal Development of 'Incomplete' Roles. In order to help the patient the therapist needs to be aware of her own inadequacies and any that may have been blocked or not developed may need some work. I feel that personal development is parallel to professional growth. Even after training it is still important for the therapist to make opportunities to work on her own personality and problems. This gives her more freedom and objectivity to help the patient.

Role Play Towards that of Shopper with Long Term Institutionalised Patients

Session One:
(1) Name game.
(2) Introduction of self and explanation of group.
(3) I went shopping and in my basket I put . . .
(4) Show pictures of local shopping centre and make a list of shopping required for a tea party.
(5) Who would you like to invite for tea?
Session Two:
(1) Name game if necessary.
(2) I went shopping and in my basket I put . . .
(3) Show magazine photographs of articles. Where would you buy them? How much do you think they cost?
(4) Make a list of shopping required for a bath and hair-washing session.
(5) Where would you go to buy them?
Session Three:
(1) Bring articles — empty cartons, time, talcum powder, make-up, etc., and set up a stall. Agree on prices and take turns in being customer/ stallholder. Talk about markets. Any known to the group? What kind of stalls are there? Make a list of fruit and vegetables to buy from a market.
Session Four:
(1) Bring actual goods if possible with prices marked on them.

(2) Take turns at being shopkeeper/shopper.

(3) Talk about the hospital shop. Who goes there? What can you buy there? How do you get to the shop from here?

Session Five:

(1) In pairs, tell you partner how to get to the hospital shop and three things you could buy there.

(2) Set up shop again, this time using imitation money.

(3) Make a list of the things you want to buy which are on sale in your simulated shop. Take turns buying and selling.

Session Six:

(1) Either set up simulated shop or, if the group seems ready, take the group down to the hospital shop for a cup of tea. This is usually less threatening than having to decide what to buy. Alternatively, if the group is timid, just go and look at the shop, walk around it and go back to the ward to discuss it.

This is a good beginning, but the aim is always to go outside the hospital and shop in reality. The more rehearsal there is in dramatherapy, the less threatening the real situation becomes.

8   SOCIAL SKILLS

Social skills groups are an accepted part of hospital life, the range covered is very wide and the skills included diverse. In the mental handicap sector I have heard social skills described as involving cleaning teeth, bathing and dressing oneself. A dirty, unkempt, smelly person may not be socially acceptable, but this I would consider hygiene rather than social skills. Priestley *et al.* (1978) describe social skills as 'the ability to manage effectively the changes and problems of everyday life'. This is a broad definition which refers to behaviour and the book goes on to describe ways in which one can acquire knowledge required for specific situations. Social skills groups in hospitals often aim for the ability to speak for three minutes on a chosen subject at the end of an eight-week course. Many of the clients with whom I work would not have this kind of verbal capacity. Therefore, I will try to define what I mean by social skills.

Dealing with behaviour seems to me the tip of the iceberg and the ability to relate to others at the appropriate level is the basis of social skills. Relating to others is a matter of our own self-concept and esteem combined with regard for other people and a perception of their needs. One would not expect to address a bishop in the same way that one would approach a workmate. Some knowledge of role and expectation of behaviour is needed. Neither is knowledge of behaviour alone sufficient; it is appropriate application that makes for social skills. One can have impeccable knowledge of table manners but if one tries to apply the standards of the Dorchester in a transport café by expecting pastry forks and linen napkins, then one cannot be described as socially skilled because the application of the knowledge is inappropriate and without regard for the other people involved.

We are again talking about a concept of role and its relation to others. A group that deals with relating and interacting is basic to social skills. The client then learns different aspects of social behaviour in specialist groups, which do not necessarily require the skills of a dramatherapist but can be adequately run by a teacher, drama student, volunteer or other trained therapist depending on the level at which the group is working (psychologist, occupational therapist, etc.). It is necessary to look at the role of the dramatherapist and consider where the approach has to be specifically that of drama, therapy or a combination of both. There is continual overlap with other therapies and this is to be welcomed. We are all working towards the same end and our differing approaches ensure that there is a therapy available to suit each client. Different approaches bring fresh stimulation and interaction. However, dramatherapists need to be aware of the skills and training which they have to offer and that others do not. I think that this is specifically in the area of communicating and relating with others. It is important that the basic group is run by a dramatherapist. She may then choose to take specialist groups such as for voice or movement, but these could be delegated to other appropriately trained professionals.

Basic Group

Provided the group is carefully selected, it is possible to work at all levels of emotional or mental disability. All groups would need to cover basic activities, but some would move more quickly than others and cover different 'advanced' work. The basic essentials are:

(1) The ability to seek and maintain eye contact as long as is socially acceptable.
(2) A sense of the status of oneself and the people with whom you are relating.
(3) A knowledge of what you would like to offer the others in the group.
(4) A perception of what others may be prepared to accept from you.
(5) Some concept of the acceptability and limits of touch.
(6) An awareness of body language and some self-monitoring system.
(7) The ability to contain needs and not make premature demands on others.
(8) An awareness of personal space and acceptable proximities.

The group needs to begin gently with plenty of reassurance from the therapist and discussion of any threatening situations. Games which require looking at people precede eye contact games. Others which make people aware of their own need for body space and physical contact games are important preliminaries for discussion on these topics. Introduction games lead to evaluation of giving and receiving. Miming is a good way to start looking at body language; role play and improvisation assist in learning about roles, status and assessing how far our own needs can be met in a situation and when there is a need to compromise.

As has been stressed in Chapter 6, it is important to move slowly and to be sure the group is confident in what is being done. It is preferable, in my view, never to get beyond the basics than to move too quickly and leave anyone with a sense of failure. Achievement of some kind is essential in this group. If relating to others is difficult, an ineffective group training could be devastating, leaving the client with a sense of total worthlessness.

If the group consists of long-term clients, I would proceed in a similar way to that described in Chapter 6 on rehabilitation. However, for short-term clients with a good verbal capacity, I would proceed at a different pace.

Session One:
(1) Ball-name game.
(2) Walk round the room concentrating on walk.
(3) Follow someone, but try not to make it obvious whom you are following.
(4) Touch person you are following on shoulder. This requires some organisation and finishes with an interesting pattern.
(5) Discuss how it felt.
(6) Find a partner by similarities (both wearing jeans, the colour red, etc.).
(7) Tell your partner three things about yourself you would like the group to know.
(8) Share in the large group with each person talking to his partner.
Session Two:
(1) Remind people of your name by adding an adjective to it, e.g. artful Annie, daring Dennis, etc.
(2) Remark on anything you notice about people in the group and name them, e.g. Mabel is wearing yellow shoes, Peter is sitting with his arms folded. If this is allowed to continue for some time (or repeated on other occasions) people become quite perceptive about others and move away from the obvious.
(3) Leader of the orchestra.
(4) Clumps.
(5) This has brought people into close physical contact and discussion is probably needed.
(6) If the group is ready for it, walk in a maze.
(7) Pass squeeze around the group.

Session Three:
(1) Pin names of group members at random on people's backs. Each person has to guess the name that is on his own back.
(2) Musical islands.
(3) With a partner, A turns away while B changes something about his appearance. For example, he undoes a button, removes spectacles, etc. A then has to face B and say what has been changed.
(4) Find a partner who has the same colour eyes as you.
(5) This has brought the group consciously to seek eye contact and is a good point to open discussion on the subject.
(6) Complete the circle game. Two concentric circles standing in front of a partner. The inner circle has one person less than the outer circle. The person without a partner, A, selects someone from the inner circle, B, with eye signals alone. B then moves behind A who is now in the inner circle. B's original partner then looks for someone from the inner circle by eye contact. With practice this can be quite a speedy game.
(7) If the group is ready for it, ask each to look all group members in the eyes for three, five or ten seconds (the time can be varied as the group progresses).

Session Four:
Introduce mime as a preliminary to body language. When space, eye contact and body language have all been openly discussed and people are comfortable with them, it is time to move into an exploration of roles and personal feelings about them (see Chapter 7).

Voice

When asked to act a timid character, drama students immediately adjust posture and voice. Lowered voice is almost synonymous with self-effacement. Anxiety is expressed by a wavering voice and breathlessness. How we speak is usually an indication of how we feel about ourselves unless we make a conscious effort to conceal our feelings. Appropriate use of voice is something we learn. When it is socially acceptable to shout or speak loudly or when lowered voice or even silence is more appropriate, is more difficult for some people to learn than others.

Mentally handicapped people frequently speak too loudly, while people who are unsure of themselves sometimes whisper. Psychiatric illness can result in either more or less inhibition than the client has previously experienced. During therapy a client may want to change his self-presentation and this may need some retraining of his vocal use. Cicely Berry (1981) points out that nervous tension has a direct physical relation to voice, the taut muscles preventing air from being exhaled appropriately. For this reason I link relaxation with voice work. Berry also notes that most people who hear their recorded voice for the first time are surprised and do not recognise it. She points out that this is partly because we hear our own voice in a different way from other people (internally through the vibrations inside the ear without the effect of space on the sound), partly because tape-recorders are not necessarily accurate in reproducing sound and also because we tend not to listen to ourselves. We are frequently embarrassed by our voices and like eye contact, feel that we may be 'giving ourselves away'. Indeed, we may well be displaying our personalities by using a hushed voice rather than compete with others, for example. Equally, we may be hiding behind our voice by speaking aggressively when we are feeling timid. We use the phrase 'a voice trembling with emotion' to describe a speech and we each have a concept of that expression from past experience. For the voice is linked with our emotions and can be used to express or hide them. It may be that we are not expressing what we would really like to express. The sentence intended to be sympathetic can come across as condescending or even sarcastic if the appropriate phrasing and emphasis is not used. A client who is very self-conscious may be constantly afraid of sending the wrong messages and in his anxiety will do just that. So, use of voice is:

(1) An indication of our self-confidence.
(2) Dependent on relaxed muscles for full control.
(3) A means of showing or hiding our emotions.
(4) A matter of learning what is socially acceptable.
(5) A medium for possibly sending wrong messages.

Bearing this in mind, it is possible to produce a programme of voice training to help the client to use his voice more purposefully. As most people are initially shy about voice work, I would prepare the group first by helping them to get used to the sound of their own voices.

Session One:
   (1) Introduce yourself by name to everyone in the room.
   (2) Find a rhythm for your name and repeat the name and rhythm

to the rest of the group.

(3) Group repeats each name rhythmically, varying the sound from shout to whisper as indicated by a conductor.

(4) In pairs, at opposite sides of the room, sighted partner gives directions to 'blind' partner. Group working simultaneously so that there has to be listening and voice projection.

(5) In pairs, facing each other closely, tell a story, each giving a phrase at a time.

(6) Continue the story each giving an alternate word.

((7) Each person walk backwards taking a step with each word until the pair are at opposite ends of the room. Again each must listen and gradually increase volume to be heard above others. Continue the story moving back towards each other.

(8) Discuss what you have done so far. What has happened to the words as you distanced? (Vowels become longer, consonants more precise — Yon, 1979.)

(9) What does your own voice sound like? Each individual repeat a line and listen to it, e.g. 'Friends, Romans, countrymen — lend me your ears'. Shout it, then whisper it. Group does this together at first, then in smaller groups, then in pairs and finally, individuals are asked to say the line alone.

(10) Share with partner the feelings about your own voice.

(11) Share in the group your feelings about the whole session.

Session Two:

(1) Call name of another group member. All shout simultaneously. Try to distinguish who is calling you.

(2) How green you are. One person turns away while group hides a pen. When he starts his search, group chants in unison 'How green you are', varying the volume as he gets nearer or further from the hiding place.

(3) Group is a wide circle. One person, A, in the middle with eyes closed. A group member, B, calls him by name loudly or softly and A walks towards B until he reaches him. B is then in the middle.

(4) In pairs, A gives B directions of how to get to the nearest post office. B just listens.

(5) Repeat. This time B continually interrupts with questions, e.g. A: 'Turn left by the tree'. B: 'What kind of tree is it?'

(6) In small groups make up a story creating sound effects with voice.

(7) Take a deep breath and try to say 'Humpty Dumpty sat on a wall, Humpty Dumpty had a great fall' without renewing breath.

(8) Read some poetry together as a group, trying to keep in unison and phrasing with the leader acting as conductor.

(9) Share feelings about the session in the group.

Session Three:

(1) Chinese Whispers. Group stands in a line. The first person whispers an instruction to the second person who whispers it to the third person, etc. The last person in the line performs the task.

(2) Group takes one word each of a quotation, e.g. 'To be or not to be, that is the question' and speak it as if one person is saying the line. Say it in various ways — sadly, happily, angrily, etc. This gets the group working together, listening, timing and speaking.

(3) Tell a circle story — each person takes a deep breath, speaks until breath runs out and the next person comes in without a break.

(4) In pairs, A is a customs officer removing articles from a case; B is a passenger who has to justify the articles removed. (A has the idea and B has to think quickly and respond.)

(5) Group becomes a football crowd. Repeats alphabet with sounds expressing excitement, disappointment, etc.

(6) The scene changes to Speaker's Corner. People make speeches, others heckling using consonants or vowels only instead of words. This moves from group 'gobbledegook' speech to individual nonsense (something which can be embarrassing and so should be introduced carefully and with plenty of opportunity for discussion).

(7) Work on choral speaking. Perhaps *Murder in the Cathedral* by T. S. Eliot. The opening verses by the chorus of 'Canterbury Women'. Divide the group into smaller groups by the pitch of their voices. Allocate phrases to different groups, individuals, etc.

(8) The group has now been introduced to all the basics of voice work — breathing, volume, sounds without words, rhythm, listening, thinking quickly, working as a group and individually, and should have overcome embarrassment sufficiently to commence straight-forward elocution exercises.

I would follow with six or eight voice sessions which would include poetry and prose readings and continue with improvisations to encourage spontaneity. If it moved at a suitable pace, the group could move towards a reading programme before an invited audience as a climax to the sessions and then stop. A new group could be formed at a later date if necessary. The break gives an opportunity for the clients to assimilate their learning and the leader to make changes in personnel if required.

Effective Speech

We learn words by imitating others. If our parents' vocabulary is limited, it is likely ours will be also until we find a wider environment. Even then the models we choose have their limitations. This may not be just a lack of vocabulary but a misuse or misunderstanding of words. How we select words and string them together comes from our interpretation of them and the particular situation we may be in at the time. We change our manner of speech as we change our companions – talk in a family differs from that in the pub which is different again from office and business talk. If we have poor models, then the chances are that we have a poor command of speech and are unable to express ourselves adequately. It is not always the lack of model that holds us back. Our feelings of inferiority, insecurity and inadequacy sometimes distort our ability to project our personalities as we would like. Some clients have never been able to use speech efficiently, while others lack confidence as a result of their emotional problems and need to reassure themselves of their capabilities. If the group has the ability and the teacher is available, a course to the standards of the English Speaking Board would be ideal. The attaining of a National Certificate would be a boost to anyone's morals. However, it does require working to a standard and being assessed with the possibility of failure which may not be in the interests of all our clients. Careful selection would be necessary. It is possible to run a course on the English Speaking Board syllabus without the added stress of assessment and would be appropriate with a group with verbal ability who lack confidence. But what about those people who have lacked models? We have to consider what is necessary to answer their needs. Effective speaking requires:

(1) A versatile vocabulary.
(2) The confidence to use it.
(3) An awareness of other people.
(4) Clarity of thought and a pattern to use in different situations.
(5) Some knowledge of procedure (formal debate, committee work, toasts, speeches, interviews, etc.) according to the social needs of the group.

One of the difficulties of speech is its initiation. How do you introduce yourself and others? How do you start a conversation? How do you get the right message across without being too conspicuous and how do you know how well you are doing? This monitoring process is important. One group member, when asked about his anxieties, gave the name of a television personality. I thought he was being facetious until he explained: 'The personality (naming him) is such a twit and he obviously doesn't know it, I keep asking myself if I come across like that and don't know either, so I finish by saying nothing just in case.'

Word games can help to increase vocabulary and speed of thought. Although I would not include them as part of the dramatherapy group, I would ask the occupational therapy department to organise Scrabble, crosswords, lexicon and word card games, which group members could play at other times. Spontaneous scenes and improvisations encourage the appropriate use of words. Practice in listening, watching and sharing in drama situations gives an awareness of others and their needs. It is possible then to go on to more specific work on how to conduct interviews, deliver speeches, etc., with the needs of the group in mind.

Session One:
(1) Ball circle game. As the ball is thrown each receiver has to call a name of a country.
(2) Variation — fruit/flower/vegetable. The person in the centre throws the ball and calls either fruit or flower or vegetable. The receiver has to give a name of something in the selected group within five seconds.
(3) Adverbs — in small groups, one person is given an adverb which he has to mime to the group for them to identify.
(4) Each group is asked to write the longest possible sentence without using words of more than four letters, e.g. Jack and Jill went for a walk down the road . . . The group then mimes the sentence for the other group to guess.
(5) In pairs, create a story about a hat, a tree and a giant. Tell the story to the group, speaking simultaneously.
(6) Group improvisation of a well known myth (e.g. Midas) or fairy story (e.g. Cinderella) set in the present day.
(7) Discussion of session and how people feel about words and their uses. How do we improve our vocabulary? Suggest joining public library or give instructions about joining hospital library. Suggest each person brings a newspaper cutting or small extract from a book of an interesting dramatic event for the next session.

Session Two:
(1) Give each person a piece of paper containing a three-letter word. It must match someone else's in the group. Walk around making

conversation but using your word until you find your partner, e.g. A has 'jig', B has 'saw'. A can ask — 'Did you see those Irishmen doing a jig on TV last night?' B replies — 'No, I went to the cinema last night and saw Superman'.

(2) Charades — the old fashioned kind. Divide into two groups, each group selects a word with two syllables, e.g. classroom. The group then presents three scenes. In the first the word 'class' must be used, in the second scene the word 'room' and in the final scene the whole word 'classroom' must be spoken. The idea is to use plenty of dialogue in order to confuse the other group.

(3) In pairs, recount to your partner the events selected from a newspaper or book as if you were an eye witness to the event.

(4) Join with another pair, exchange stories and select one which the four can then act to the rest of the group.

(5) Read some descriptive poetry together.

(6) Discuss the images prompted by the poem and the feelings within it.

Session Three:

(1) In a circle one person thinks of a word with more than three letters and says the first letter only aloud, e.g. D (thinking of Dinner), the next person then gives the second letter but he may be thinking of something else (Dynamo), so he gives the letter Y. The third person maybe thinks of Dyke, so adds a K. The object is not to complete a word so the fourth person has to say something to make a nonsense. The fifth person begins a new word.

(2) One person goes into the centre of the circle and starts an action (maybe gardening). The second person enters circle and starts conversation. The third person enters and continues to extend the ideas and to bring in new ones. The first person has to find a good reason to leave the circle and is then replaced by a fourth person. Continue in this way, developing the improvisation and incorporating new ideas, but never having more than three people in the centre at a time, each having a valid excuse for leaving.

(3) In small groups, one person is asked to tell a story. The others continue to interrupt. The storyteller progresses, but is not rude nor does he ignore the interruptions. The aim is to concentrate on the narrative, having a clear idea of what he wants to say but being aware of other people.

(4) In pairs, each person tries to touch the other's shoulder, at the same time trying to defend his own from touch. He must find some logical explanation for his sudden movements and weave it into the

conversation.

(5) In pairs, A starts an improvisation with the words 'I must do it now'. B reinforces and feeds ideas, e.g.: A: 'I must do it now'. B: 'You've waited long enough to ask her'. A: 'It's been five years'. B: 'You can't go on without knowing who your real parents are'. A: 'But she brought me up from a child'. B: 'You don't owe her anything, you've worked hard to support her in her old age'. A: 'I've done my best'. B: 'It's not everyone who has been reared by a gypsy'. . . and so on, with B feeding the ideas and A responding to them. It gives practice in taking the initiative and listening ('turn-taking') in conversation.

(6) Discuss what you have been doing. What is conversation? Self-expression, exchange of ideas, give and take, action and reaction, sharing of information and interest, etc. Discuss some topics for conversation.

(7) In pairs, converse on a given topic (perhaps pop music) for two minutes.

(8) Discuss the session and ask group to bring with them some ideas for conversation at the next session.

The group should by now have some competence with words and their use. While continuing the spontaneity and word exercises, plan to cover more formal instruction: How to introduce yourself to others. What subjects are suitable for conversation? Are there any taboos? How do you apply for a job, social security, ask for a rise? When once the formal procedure is grasped the therapist should not be too directive. The client needs encouragement to be himself in a situation rather than copy another's behaviour.

Movement

As important as speech in social skills is movement. Age, fashion, personality and physical fitness all have a bearing on the way people move. A shy person will stand in a manner that he hopes will make him inconspicuous; another will try to be noticed by his manner and bearing. It is possible to make a statement by speech and contradict it by body language. These skills are learned by modelling in the same way as speech and, similarly, some people have a bad start in life simply because they have poor models. Movement can be greatly affected by emotional disturbance and psychiatric illness. As speech is inhibited by tension, so is movement. Add to that the dependency of hospitalisation and the motivation to move at all can become lost. Long-stay clients have a stiffness and sometimes compulsive patterns of movement. Acute self-consciousness can lead a client to believe that he is being conspicuous and inhibit him all the more. Post-psychotic clients may still have distorted perceptions of their bodies and move in a stereotyped fashion.

The body is also another means of self-expression and if we can overcome the conventions of movement, we can introduce people to the freedom of natural dance. Most people are conscious of movement and shy away when we talk of excessive movement and dance, so it is wise to introduce movement gently and in ways that people can understand to avoid embarrassment. In order to do this I use a simple keep-fit routine as a warm-up to each session and base the early work on walking and stretching. The more tension we put on a muscle the greater the relaxation when it is released. It seems logical then to include relaxation in a movement group. If one asks any group of clients how they are feeling, invariably several of them will answer 'tense'. Relaxation has become almost a therapy in its own right and clients are taught to relax on the floor, in bed or in chairs. They are given tapes with vocal instructions and encouraged to practise relaxation regularly. However, I do not feel that this is sufficient unless they also learn to take that relaxation with them into activity. This is where a dramatherapist's knowledge of movement and vocal relaxation can be applied to help clients move and speak in a relaxed way, thus *being* relaxed rather than practising relaxation. The control of breath in exercise is important, so this needs to be learned. Relaxation of mind completes the picture. It is possible to include, in a movement group, the complete relaxation of mind and body in motion. Controlled movement is beautiful to observe, so encourage clients to watch animals, dancers, gymnasts and sportsmen in action to increase their awareness. Groups designed specifically for movement are valuable at all levels and I would like to see them as a routine part of a ward programme. This gives a basic understanding of movement and allows specialised groups for natural dance, ballroom or country dance and body language groups to follow the needs of clients at the time.

It is a good plan to talk to the group about movement in terms of unused muscles getting slack, the need to exercise heart and lungs, relaxation and relaxed movements. Most clients are enthusiastic at this level. I usually explain that it is not a keep-fit class but a gentle movement and exercise group. The need is often to 'get fit' rather 'keep fit' and the thought of strenuous exercise is as likely to get a negative response as the word 'dance'. I take the movement slowly with plenty of time to rest and opportunity to express feelings about the content. This introduction and reassurance is just as necessary in this kind of group as it is in sophisticated role play. I have a programme of simple exercises which I use as a limbering up to each session. This also acts as a measure of progress. We start by doing each exercise once and gradually increase this during the eight weeks of sessions. The sense of physical achievement helps the group to be more confident and also aids the association of mental and physical health.

Session One:
(1) Limber up by moving limbs. Start with just a finger, then a hand, then involve an elbow and shoulder joint until the whole arm is moving.
(2) Repeat with other arm.
(3) Repeat with foot, ankle, knee and hip.
(4) Repeat with other leg.
(5) Slowly move head from side to side, drop chin to chest and up the other side.
(6) Relax and let yourself fall from waist to a bending position (not toe touching).
(7) Follow this with exercise programme (Carruthers and Murray, 1976).
(8) Stretch whole body, standing up; feel the space around.
(9) Lie on the floor and relax each muscle individually.
(10) Remaining on the floor, stretch arms above head taking up as much space as possible.
(11) Sit up, keeping arms overhead and relax forward with hand between feet.
(12) Still relaxed, stand up slowly and walk around the room.
(13) Become aware of other people in the room and touch hands as you pass.
(14) Find a partner and face him. A starts a movement and B follows, copying as if a reflection in a mirror. Reverse leadership.
(15) Form circle in group, holding hands. Stretch arms out as far as possible. Stretch arms as high as possible without breaking hands. Walk on toes to the centre of circle and stretch out again, still keeping hands clasped.

Session Two:
Repeat (1)–(7) of Session One.
(8) Lie on the floor and relax each muscle individually.

(9) Lie on the floor, stretch arms above head, using as much space as possible. Come to sitting position, arms still above head, bend forward at waist and finish with arms between legs as before in Session One. This time, however, add breath control. Breathe in as you stretch and out as you sit up and bend forward.

(10) Stand up and move about in relaxed way, exploring the space by stretching arms and legs and contracting them again. How much space can you use? How little?

(11) Stand near a partner and see how much space you can use together without actually touching.

(12) Hold hands, facing partner. A holds B steady while B experiments getting off balance. Reverse leadership.

(13) Experiment together to find a point where you balance each other.

(14) This is a good point to discuss the session so far. It brings in dependence on others, sharing and co-operation and may provoke strong emotional reactions.

(15) Mirror work in a circle, changing leadership.

(16) If group is large enough, sit in a circle clockwise with the next person between legs of person behind. Each gently massages the neck of person in front. Turn round and reciprocate. In a small group it is better to work in pairs, but if there are enough people to massage as a group, it gives a good sense of group identity and confidence and caring for each other.

Session Three:
Limber up and exercise then relax as before, (1)–(8).

(9) Same exercises as in Session Two, but this time as you breathe in think of something good you would like to bring into your life. As you breathe out think of something you would like to be rid of. Continue breathing in good things and breathing out the unwanted things.

(10) Still lying on the floor, explore the space your body is using. Use as much space as possible, then as little as possible.

(11) Stand up slowly and move gently round the room, exploring the space with eyes closed. No pressure should be put on people who cannot do this. Ask them to keep eyes closed as long as possible and then open them.

(12) Still with eyes closed, ask the group to try and form a circle. This gives a sense of personal and group space. Without sight, concentration gives the feeling and perception of space.

(13) Open eyes, but still with hands linked, move about the room as a group.

(14) Drop hands and continue to move about the room, varying the space between individuals (two paces distant, four paces distant, close together, etc.).

(15) Individually walk around the room showing different emotions: happy, sad, angry, etc.

(16) In pairs, A becomes a statue representing an emotion, B has to guess what it is. Reverse.

(17) A performs an action; B paints an enormous imaginary backcloth as if it is on a stage. Thus B adds a place to A's action.

(18) Finish session in a close circle holding hands. Hum a tune and sway rhythmically together ('Skye Boat Song', 'Sailing', 'Amazing Grace').

The group has now been introduced to: movement, balance, space, relaxation of mind and body, massage (co-operative relaxation), co-ordination, awareness of others and expression.

The way the group develops will depend on its ultimate goal. Much can be developed in body awareness, rhythms, interpretation of sounds and words in movement. Music adds a whole new realm of activity, working towards dance. However, I do not introduce music (except perhaps humming a tune) until the group is well established for two reasons: (1) it can be an inhibiting factor with people who have not developed a sense of rhythm and to whom the idea of dancing is threatening ('I can't do it, it's effeminate'); (2) more important is the fact that the group needs to learn to concentrate on movement for its own sake and become aware of the kind of movements that are possible in many combinations. Music is an added stimulus which can cause anxiety if introduced too soon (see Chapter 4).

If the group has social skills learning as its aim, then the sessions will continue by increasing the expressive movement, concentrating on feelings and how the body is placed, at the same time exploring space and the difference it makes to actions and feelings. At the end of eight sessions I would close the group and start again a few weeks later, looking specifically at body language and leading to role play. A video-recorder is invaluable in these sessions. To see oneself on the screen has far more impact than any modelling by other group members. It is possible to trace progress and note achievements. However, it is also very threatening and I prefer to use it as a climax to a programme of movement, discussion and learning rather than start at that level.

Assertiveness Training

Having looked at the use of voice, speech and movement, the final
component in a social skills programme, in my scheme, is assertiveness
training. The group should now have all the necessary abilities, but how
are they to be applied? Now is the time to look at behaviour. We have
to assert ourselves over our environment to survive physically and
we also have to assert ourselves as people to get our emotional needs
met and sometimes our rights. For some people it is a very frightening
prospect to assert themselves in any way, while others may have lost
confidence in themselves through emotional upsets or illness and need
to relearn the skills of assertion. To do this they need to:

(1) Be aware of their needs in a situation.
(2) Have some control over their emotions.
(3) Have a feeling of their status.
(4) Be able to think clearly and state their case convincingly.

If group members are looking at their emotional needs, I prefer to
do this in a separate psychodrama group. I find it the most direct and
satisfactory way of clarifying emotional situations and discovering the
true needs of the individual. Any attempt to deal primarily with
emotional needs would not come within the scope of assertiveness
training. However, the whole pattern of working I have described in
this chapter came into being because a client in a psychodrama group
became aware that one of his basic problems was his feeling about his
physical size. Although only slightly below average height, he
considered himself very small and all his life had reinforced this by
speaking quietly, moving inconspicuously and never allowing himself
to be noticed. Despite the realisation, he did not have the experience
to change his behaviour. He needed to learn to be assertive. So, again,
we have two categories of client suitable for the group — those who
have never learned to be assertive and those who need a refresher
course! Fear of emotions getting out of control is common in both
clients and staff and if we trace this to its source, the real fear is that of
emotion itself. It is important to be open and aware of all emotions
in the group. Discuss them, find out where they come from and direct
them towards the appropriate objective and they cease to be frightening.
The therapist has to be aware of her own emotions and not confuse
them with those projected onto herself or experienced by the group
members.

To ask someone to be assertive can imply dominance and that may be too remote a goal for a timid person to achieve. Keith Johnston (1981) refers to status and suggests that we can alter our status by our behaviour regardless of our social class. He describes the way in which we play either high-status or low-status roles and the effect it has on us. This appears more attainable than self-assertion and is a useful concept with which to work with clients. Johnston describes the way in which we move and speak, revealing the status with which we regard ourselves when relating to other people. He is concerned both with space, speech and body language. These will all have been discussed in the primary social skills group, so there is a good basis on which to work. However, it may still be necessary to do some simple 'getting to know you' exercises to form a cohesive group before beginning work in earnest. Assuming this has been done I would continue as follows.

Session One:
(1) (a) Group walk around the room without touching each other or objects, each being aware only of himself and his personal space.
   (b) Each becomes aware of others, greeting them if desired.
   (c) Touch everyone and everything as you pass.
   (d) Bump hard into everyone in the group. This usually causes laughter but can become aggressive. It is a useful way to release tension and reveal anxieties.
(2) Make a small circle of chairs and remove one chair to make an opening. Ask the group to enter the circle and jostle around as if in an underground train. At the shout of 'station' the two people furthest from the opening have to push their way through to get out. In fact they don't make it in time and the door closes, but two other people are now furthest away and have to jostle at the next station. A variation is to start with a large circle of chairs and gradually decrease it so that people have a small space in which to move. This exercise is about space and its use. Another variation is to imagine that you are enclosed in a glass case, wearing a crinoline or sunburned and sore all over. When working with phobic clients start with a large circle of chairs and gradually decrease so that a confined space is not too threatening.
(3) This is a good point to stop and discuss personal space.
(4) Group forms two lines at opposite sides of the room, each facing a partner, and advances towards each other. Stop at the point when

you become aware of your partner's intrusion on your space. Discuss.

(5) Group forms a large circle, volunteer stands in the centre with eyes closed. Group member walks towards him from a given direction. Volunteer tells him to stop when he feels close enough. These two exercises should show that there is some variation in the space each person requires. There can be further discussion, but it is important to emphasise that there is no right or wrong distance for comfort. We each have a space which is right for us.

(6) In pairs, the scene is a park bench. A has left the office to be alone and eat lunch in peace. B sits beside him and wants to talk. Allow the improvisation to run, then reverse roles. Discuss in pairs and also in a large group how it felt and what difference it made to the sense of space.

(7) The group forms a line, holding each other's waists, and walks in patterns around the room using varying amounts of space as a group.

(8) If any energy is left, finish with a conga.

Session Two:

(1) Group forms a circle, A goes into the middle and starts miming an action, B joins him but by his action shows that he feels of higher status than A. C now enters the circle and shows he is of a higher status than B. A leaves the circle. Either continue raising the status or lowering it alternately until the group have all had a turn.

(2) In pairs, A is master and B is servant and has to obey every command without question. Reverse roles.

(3) Repeat, but this time the servant gradually becomes higher in status until he becomes the master.

(4) Discuss what you have done so far. What status do people prefer? Discuss situations which call for altered status. How do we behave towards our bank manager and the attendant at the petrol pump?

(5) In pairs, A wants to enter a road but B tries to prevent him verbally. Look at the roles people select for themselves — policeman, gas board inspector, etc. Compare the status each has selected. Then ask the group to repeat the scene but reversing status (not roles), e.g. if A is a low-status delivery man and B is a high-status policeman, then A becomes a high-status delivery man and B a low-status policeman. This is a difficult exercise and the group may feel unable to cope with it. The point is to identify the kind of speech and body language that makes for high/low status. There should be plenty of opportunity to discuss this as it is basic to the rest of the course. If necessary let it take until the end of the session.

(6) Divide into small groups. The scene is a station waiting room. Each person decides on a role he will take and enters the improvisation when he is ready. As each new character appears the others react to the status he portrays.

Session Three:

(1) Group walks round the room and people concentrate on their own mood. Devise a walk that expresses that mood. Decide what situation you could be in and the status the mood suggests. Continue walking in the same way but alter your sense of status. Now correct body posture to new status. It may be difficult at first but is worth returning to in a later session for a sense of achievement.

(2) Ask half the group to become high-status teachers. They walk together and greet each other. The other half are low-status pupils who greet each other in the playground. When each group is used to relating to equal-status peers, ask the two groups to mingle and react with each other. Discuss, noting the changes in posture, space and speech which occurred.

(3) Ask the group to make a list of insulting words or phrases they find most hurtful, e.g. snob, moron, mental case, piss off, get lost, etc. Select four or five of these that are general terms and disliked by the majority. (If you choose things like big ears, four eyes, etc., people could take them personally. The object is for the whole group to give and receive insults, but they are not ready to work at a personal level yet.) The group members face partners on opposite sides of the room as far apart as possible with a barrier of chairs down the centre. The partners hold a conversation using only selected insults. The group gradually moves towards each other, not just shouting but using variations in tone in order to raise status over the partner. As the group gets closer it may well become louder and more aggressive. The therapist needs to be aware of what is happening and, if necessary, instruct the group to retreat gradually to avoid an uncontrolled shouting match.

(4) Allow plenty of time for discussion. Notice if anyone has been disturbed by the exercise. Giving insults can make some people as unhappy as receiving them. Discuss feelings.

(5) Ask the group to find partners using eye contact only.

(6) Hold eye contact as long as possible. Try to tell your partner something with your eyes. Change partners and repeat the process. In a small group meet everyone with eye contact only. Discuss fully.

(7) In pairs, A looks at B and says 'I see . . .' (listing what he sees

physically). Allow three or four minutes, e.g. 'I see dark hair, wearing red shoes, engagement ring, etc.', for this and then ask A to say 'I perceive . . .' and list non-physical perceptions, e.g. 'You are feeling nervous, you laugh a lot, you are a gentle person, etc.' Then ask A to state three things he thinks B would like and three things he would not like. Reverse roles and discuss.

(8) As the group has become very personal, bring them together physically to talk without eye contact (e.g. stand in a circle with arms round each other, look at a spot in the centre of the circle and each finish the sentence 'I am feeling . . ., I liked it when . . ., I did not like it when . . .'. Give every opportunity for talk so that no one goes away with unfinished business.

In these three sessions the group has looked at space, speech and movement in relation to status, and has had an opportunity to become aware of self and own feelings and also to make some assessment of other people's feelings and needs in the group. The group has become familiar with eye contact and experienced both giving and receiving insults and should be able to talk about feelings without anxiety. Some groups move faster than others, so that the material I have given may be sufficient for four or five sessions with some groups.

In subsequent sessions I would move from general activities to more personal ones. For example, the insult game could be played in pairs and not in a group. It could be later played with each pair selecting their own words so that they give and receive insults which are personal to them. Care must be taken to ensure that the group can give plenty of support at this stage and not use it if damage can be done.

The improvisations can become less general and work towards specific situations which the group face in reality — taking goods back to a shop and complaining, dealing with an aggressive person in a pub or a shopkeeper who says a bill has not been paid.

Lack of social skills can be a great handicap, but clients can be very sensitive about it, so I approach the subject with as much care as any personal therapy group, building up trust and group identity. This allows for admissions of failure and anxiety to be expressed. Clients can then go out and practise their skills, being given specific tasks to complete before the next group and, on return, have the support of the group in both successes and failures. This group can then use role play of actual situations if necessary to try alternative ways of dealing with the situation.

This way of working is a very long-term one and I am aware that it is not always possible to work at this depth. I would repeat that it is preferable to start and not complete the course than hurry the early stages. If the groundwork is done properly, the client will have something on which to build and can look for ways to help himself. It is possible to do some of the course as an inpatient and some as an outpatient. If groups can be organised, social skills can be an ongoing process from beginning to end of treatment. When once the group is enthusiastic about what it is doing, the time between each group can be lessened; it is possible to have groups perhaps daily or even in blocks of one or two days. I am aware that other professionals have social skills groups run on more behaviourist lines and I do not discount their value. The course I suggest uses predominantly drama techniques and feels right for me. It can be used at any level, can be fun and gives an opportunity for self-realisation.

In Chapter 7 on role play I referred to Stanislavski's method of drawing on experiences — creating the role from within. He also did some work on the opposite method of presenting the external façade and working inwards towards a feeling. Grotowski has extended this on his para-theatrical workshops and uses physical expression to find the true representation of an inner emotion. It seems to me that both methods — the exploring of roles by searching for the self within it and the presentation of physical and vocal expression in order to find the self (and ultimately confidence) behind it — can be used in therapy, so that a client can work in two ways. Alongside the searching and revelation of himself he can learn the outward expression of what he would like himself to be and work through that and attain his goal. It is important to keep a balance between the two and not teach the client to present a public façade behind which he cowers in fear of being found out. He must be enabled to build his knowledge of himself if he is to achieve his goal of self-esteem. I think that this way to self-discovery is something special that drama has to offer in therapy.

9 THEATRE

In this book I have attempted to show how drama can be used as a therapeutic tool. So far I have looked at the concept of drama from playing games to role play and improvisation. These spontaneous activities are performed for the enjoyment, insight or value of the experience itself. This is not the complete picture of drama and we need to consider the place of theatre in therapy.

The essence of theatre is the communication between people with complementary roles, the actors and the audience. Without the intention to communicate and the attention of the active audience, there is no theatre (Robinson, 1980). It is not necessarily a communication between two groups of people. Brook (1968) says that all that is required for an act of theatre is that one man walks across an empty space, which is called a stage, whilst another watches him. Theatre evolves from storytelling. The use of masks and movement, costume and other visual images were devised to give the impression that the event was happening 'here and now'. Reality is in a state of suspension and the audience enters into the make-believe that the actors are producing. This causes a 'dissociated condition in the minds of the audience' (Koestler, 1964) in which they know what they are seeing is not real, yet are caught up in the event to such an extent that they empathise with the emotions being portrayed. This imaginative participation of the (tragic) action purifies emotions and temporarily eliminates them from the system in an act of catharsis (Aristotle, c330 BC). How often have we claimed to have a 'good cry' or a 'good laugh' in theatre or cinema? Many of our clients would be pleased to rid themselves of their emotions, if only temporarily. Others, who are depersonalised, would be glad to feel anything at all. If a person is so afraid of his own feelings that he suppresses them, the 'once removed' feelings in theatre are safer than the real ones. Dramatic works are intended to be seen not read. There is a need for gesture and movement to assist the communication. As early as 1905 Craig stated that the art of theatre sprang from action – movement and dance (Craig, 1968) – so theatre can be a means of communication which can be understood by people who have difficulty in understanding words. Something interesting can be happening to engage the interest without the effort required in personal relationships. Unlike drama, theatre must have an end product and the final presentation is the result of a period of rehearsal. Each performance is unique in that it happens at that time, is shared by the people present (both actor and audience) and because of their varied experiences and personalities, is peculiar to that moment.

Theatre can be used in different ways to suit the therapeutic needs of the group. Most of us have experienced the change of mood that can come by watching a production. The change may not be for the better if the performance is poor but at least we have something to think about! So, let us consider the diversional side of theatre.

A play without an audience is drama, not theatre. The above reference to Peter Brook's definition of theatre includes a space which is called a stage. Grotowski (1969), however, says that you can dispense with the stage, in fact dispense with everything except the audience. He describes theatre as an encounter between creative people and says that the self-revelation of the actor gives the spectator a revelation of himself. It is this encounter that makes it theatre.

Most of our clients have difficulty in relating to others and anything that explores new ways of relating makes new channels of communicating a possibility. Esslin (1976) describes a two-way interaction as the actor communicates ideas, feelings, experiences, issues, stories, etc., and the audience listens, internalises, empathises and reacts. The actor perceives this reaction and in turn reacts himself by putting more into his performance. There is also the collective experience of the audience when a three-cornered feedback is produced — from performer to audience, audience to audience to performer. Most of this takes place in a non-verbal way which is ideal for our clients who may have difficulty in expressing themselves verbally. Here is a non-threatening, fun situation in which new ways of non-verbal communication can be experienced. The audience is relating to each other in a way unfamiliar in a hospital ward or day centre. The feeling of camaraderie, both towards other members of the audience and the performers, which is evoked by this shared experience, may encourage clients to relate to others in a more general manner at the end of the performance.

Entertainment

For some of our clients, the physical movement from the ward to the hospital hall and the opportunity to meet people from other wards may be a novelty in itself. The subsequent shared experience widens horizons and helps to develop relationships outside the clients' immediate environment. So, entertainment is something to be anticipated and remembered. Even more impressive is a visit to the local theatre and all the ritual that goes with it.

Esslin (1976) says that the audience has to make decisions about the content of the play and can only do it on the basis of their own experience and reactions in similar situations – the audience experience the action on the stage with the characters. This requires recall and assessment of past experience for comparison with what is happening on stage. This can be quite an undertaking for a long-stay client who usually has few demands made upon him. The emotional impact of the play can be as stimulating as the event itself, thus bringing feeling and cognitive experience together.

There are some clients who, because of their physical and mental disabilities, do not find their way to theatres either inside or outside the hospital grounds. For them an entertainment on the ward can be an exciting and memorable occasion. Early in my career as a dramatherapist, a local community theatre company called Medium Fair Charitable Trust offered their services. They were looking for a challenge and specifically did not want to perform on stage to a large number of people, but to a small, severely disabled group. The ward I selected was the old sanatorium which was physically isolated from the rest of the hospital. The clients living there were very physically and mentally disabled, most with organic brain disorders. The problem of transporting them, even to the hospital hall, was so great that no one ever attempted it. Added to this was the anxiety of some of the staff that the group would behave in an antisocial way and disturb others. Medium Fair came in weekly for two periods over ten weeks. Each time they brought costumes, live music, songs, dances and jokes from their current shows and a breath of fresh air. At the end of the first visit they managed to get a few people on their feet for a dance. Gradually more clients became involved and surprisingly, Medium Fair was remembered and recognised. The ward staff referred to the event during the week as a reminder and so the visits were anticipated, discussed and thoroughly enjoyed. It was a sad day when the visits ceased, but the amount of stimulation, movement, involvement and general happiness they promoted made the project very worthwhile.

Audience Involvement
A good play will reflect some aspect of life to which we can relate and

maybe learn something of ourselves. An audience can be caught up
with the emotion of a play and be engrossed by it to an extent that
they could participate in it. Sometimes the performers encourage
this by inviting the audience to sing, cheer, boo, encourage or decry
the principal characters. This is traditional in pantomine and
audiences arrive with an expectation to participate. It is becoming
more common, particularly in performances designed for the
handicapped, to involve the audience more specifically by asking
them questions and inviting them to hold props, wave flags, manipulate
puppets, etc. This is a step beyond the willing suspension of disbelief into
a sharing of the make-believe with the actors themselves. The
identification with the happenings on stage becomes intensified and
another dimension of audience enjoyment and communication is
established. It is important to give the audience roles, either
individually or collectively, to prevent embarrassment occurring.
It is also necessary to build in some kind of control to prevent
the audience taking over completely. This applies particularly if the
audience are children, mentally handicapped, or unable to define
boundaries for themselves. Audience involvement should be
presented in such a way that the audience actually *wants* to be
involved and is not bullied into it. Skills, such as those developed
by the old music hall artists, are required in order to promote the
involvement, use it and enable the audience to realise when their
participation is at an end, whether temporarily or not, in order
to allow the rehearsed action to move on.

It is important to ask why audience involvement is worthwhile
and to ensure that it is done for a valid reason and not just because
it seems a good idea. The technique can be employed at all levels
but should be appropriate to the audience for that particular
performance. Some uses of audience involvement are:

(1) To heighten the dramatic experience.
(2) To emphasise a point and facilitate learning to take place.
(3) To gain attention and stimulate an interest when working with
    severely mentally disturbed or handicapped people.
(4) To make a break in the action for those whose concentration
    span is limited.
(5) To bring the action closer to the audience. Distance is less
    threatening at first, but proximity could be a way of progressing
    with a very inhibited group.
(6) To encourage interaction between audience and players and the

building of a relationship which can be used later in therapy.

(7) If the audience is likely to be noisy or disruptive, give them a role and built-in control.

Reminiscence

Following their success in the 'sanatorium', Medium Fair returned to the hospital at a later date ready to find a new challenge. The clients they had known were scattered whilst the ward was undergoing repairs and rebuilding. At this time my husband had recently met Mick Kemp, an architect with the Department of Health and Social Security (DHSS), who was producing audio-visual aids for reminiscence therapy and we were intrigued by it. With Medium Fair prepared to tackle anything (almost) we put our heads together and came up with the idea of reminiscence theatre. This is described in detail in Chapter 10.

Theatre as a Group Experience

My first realisation of the cohesive aspect of acting came when I moved from a London suburb to a Devon village. As a family we had no contact in the village on arrival and although acknowledged as new residents, we did not feel accepted as part of the community until I took a small part in a village play. There was an immediate feeling of inclusion as we went into rehearsals and the sense of group identity remained long after the play had been performed. We met on a level previously unattainable, but now the shared experience of the group activity brought us all very close.

It is this kind of closeness that can bring another dimension to a therapy group. The performing of a play is the climax of a long ritual of casting, rehearsing, creating, discarding and recreating. During that time the cast has many experiences together:

(1) Decisions have to be made.
(2) Authority has to be delegated (and with it responsibility).
(3) Discipline has to be maintained as a group and on a personal level.
(4) Ideas are discussed, tried and maybe discarded.
(5) Co-operation and compromise are necessary, even with people we don't like very much.
(6) Roles have to be explored, internalised and come to terms with.

(7) Memory, movement, ability, voice, adaptability and self-confidence
(or lack of it) are all revealed to the rest of the cast and are later on
display to the audience.

All the tensions, anxieties and self-doubt are brought together in
'nerves' and it is this flow of adrenalin that gives us the impetus
(hopefully) to put on a good performance. The relaxation that follows
this tension brings about a sense of euphoria and comradeship that is
peculiar to the shared experience of performance.

Theatre brings with it an expectation of standards and sometimes
competition, so that selection and the needs of the group should be
carefully considered. If the audience is to be confined to people with
a particular interest in the group, such as the other occupants of the
ward or clients attending a day centre, then they are not likely to be
critical and will enjoy the entertainment because they know the actors
involved. Even so, the standard should be as high as possible, and if
necessary one should ask for assistance from professionals. A group
of drama students, actors or a community theatre could be involved
to bring their professional expertise. Perhaps they could direct the
play or bring technical assistance or even act roles that are beyond the
ability of the rest of the group. This is particularly necessary when
there are a lot of words to be learnt and the group has difficulties with
memory.

One way round the memory problem is to improvise a play. The
group is made familiar with a story and the roles are allocated. Each
person then develops his character and the story by impromptu scenes.
These can be revised as often as necessary until arriving at a suitable
script. The learning of the script is facilitated by the fact that the actor
has written it himself and people are more likely to 'ad lib' during the
performance if they forget their lines. This kind of playwriting goes
through three distinct phases:

(1) The period of enthusiasm and excitement when everyone is
keen to start.
(2) The period of complete chaos and anxiety when it appears that
nothing presentable will ever emerge.
(3) The period of final hard rehearsals to get it to performance standard.

The second period is the most difficult to handle and the director needs
to remain confident that all will be well. If he allows himself to be
overwhelmed by his own or his cast's anxiety, he will not be able to

help them achieve their final goal, an improvised play. There are always people on the periphery of production — technical assistants, other members of staff, etc. — who will project their own anxieties into the situation with gloomy comments that it will never pull together, or even into hostility towards the director. The dynamics of producing a play embrace those of any other group and the director needs to be aware of them to survive personally and bring the whole thing to fruition.

Careful selection of the play is necessary in order to ensure that no one is overtaxed. If no member of the group is capable of learning a large part, then select a play with several small parts. Casting should be undertaken with this in mind. There is little point in casting someone with impaired memory in a leading role no matter what his acting ability. It is better to present a rehearsed play-reading than cause embarrassment to both actors and audience by asking the group to work beyond their limitations. I have, however, seen a client with impaired memory gain a sense of achievement by remembering his one line and coming in on cue. Entering into stage roles requires self-discipline and imagination and can be the means of extending one's personal role repetoire. For a client who is role-bound, a theatrical role can be the first step towards trying new roles (Langley, D.M., 1982).

Theatre does not necessarily need verbal communication and problems in this area can be overcome by dance drama. One project of this nature in a hospital for mentally handicapped people was of such high standard that it was produced in the local theatre (Edmunds, 1983). It took the form of a masked ritualistic performance by staff and residents, masks providing anonymity for both. It involved a large number of people each performing a small part well, rather than undertaking a lengthy role which could not be sustained. The director attributed its success to the fact that they were not trying to make an important statement about mental handicap or confront the public with a moral issue, but the aim was to share something beautiful and creative with the community. Some advantages to be gained by such group performance are:

(1) Clients relinquish the 'patient' role and take on other roles.
(2) They enter into a unique shared experience with the other members of the group.
(3) There is a sense of group identity and achievement.
(4) For a short time the actors become 'public figures', valued and applauded by their peers.
(5) It is an opportunity to involve other departments in the hospital or

from the community outside.

Theatre demands standards — the highest we can achieve — and should not be undertaken lightly. Consideration needs to be given to the time involved. Does it mean that less time will be spent on other client groups? Does it justify the temporary curtailment of 'insight' dramatherapy? How can the therapist help the group to cope with the 'flat' feeling that follows the period of rehearsal and performance? What are the objectives to be achieved? Where does it fit into the pattern of therapy? Can it involve members of the community in the activities of the institution? One group I know sought the assistance of the beauty therapist and hairdresser to help with the make-up, the vicar was asked to give the blessing at a nativity play and brought with him the choir from a nearby village — truly community theatre. Poor theatre is not only boring but leaves the audience feeling embarrassed and possibly sorry for the entertainers. This is not an attitude conducive to therapy. Appearing on stage makes the actor very vulnerable and is likely to reveal physical and psychological weaknesses rather than conceal them. We should not allow disabilities to be an excuse for poor theatre. The last thing we want for our clients is a patronising pat on the head! So, if we involve our clients in theatre, the material should be carefully selected to enhance ability, with an emphasis on the things that people do well rather than a display of lack of skills.

Theatre as a Warm-up to Personal Work

The group whose work is centred round roles and role play can find endless material in the theatre. There are so many roles available for study and because they are characters in a play, there is a security about them. The fantasy removes it a little from reality. A group of actors, maybe students or maybe an amateur dramatic society, can act short scenes that make a statement about a role which can be watched and discussed. *A Taste of Honey*, *When We Are Married*, *Look Back in Anger*, Pinter sketches and plays by Ibsen and Chekov are just a few ideas. There are various ways in which theatre can be used:

(1) The group can watch a production and discuss it.
(2) The group can watch a scene and speculate on its ending.

(3) One group member could take on a role in the scene, read it with the actors, performing with them, and see what it feels like.
(4) Several people can take on roles and improvise the end of the scene.
(5) If the group has the concentration, they can look at characters in plays and try to establish the goals of the characters. They can then see if the behaviour as shown in the play achieves any of these goals and personalise it.

Costume and theatrical role play can present a good warm-up to a group. I arrived at one session wearing a 1920s 'flapper' dress and entered in the role of dancing teacher at a finishing school, who on the last day of term was daring enough to teach her pupils the Charleston. After an energetic warm-up in which we had a lot of fun, I came out of role to explain that the Charleston movements were derived from the fact that the dress is so tight that movement was restricted above the knee. We then looked at our own personalities to find anything that restricted our development and made us behave in a particular fashion. It was an amusing yet meaningful session in which the whole group participated.

I have given a few ideas of ways in which theatre can be used in therapy. The important issue seems to be not so much how we use theatre but why. Our aims and objectives should be carefully considered in relation to the needs and abilities of the group. If we are clear about our motives, then theatre can add a new dimension to our group therapy.

10 REMINISCENCE

Gordon E. Langley

Why reminisce? Is it to indulge a well-remembered past that competes favourably with less flattering and ill-retained recent memories? Is it an attempt by a person nearing the end of his life to leave a verbal or written memorial? Is it an updating of values and lifestyle, a levelling process, in which the present is met by drawing from a lifetime of experiences? If the latter, then is it not a practical and immediate problem-solving tool? Is it a social event in which ideas and images are shared and valued, identities established and communication initiated? Is it the process of recording history, distinguished or humble, written or oral and therefore of perpetuating the culture of the storyteller?

Reminiscence may be any of these and at its best is probably all of them. It is defined as the art or habit of thinking about or relating past experiences, especially those considered most personally significant. It is characteristic of late life but not confined to it (McMahon and Rhudick, 1964).

Once upon a time the old men and women were the storytellers. Now, regrettably, it is the media who tell the tales and another role, together with the status and esteem that go with it, is lost to the elderly. Reminiscence is very much an affair for the family, close friends or workmates. Older persons who have lost or moved away from such a nurturing environment, particularly if it is replaced by an impersonal institution, are deprived not only by their physical circumstances but also by their diminished opportunity to share the past. If, by reason of mental illness, memory for remote as well as recent events is impaired, then the barriers to reminiscence are even higher. The loss of motivation and increased narcissism that accompanies advanced age has an effect similar to depressed mood and the apathy that stems from isolation. In the face of these stresses the older person can actively disengage to protect himself from further distress and a cycle of deprivation is initiated.

What is the Effect of Reminiscence?

The evidence that reminiscence is helpful in bridging past and present, in promoting adaptation and self-esteem and as a social catalyst is presented in a series of papers and reviews: Cumming and Henry (1961), Butler (1963), Kastenbaum (1974), McMahon and Rhudick (1964), Lewis (1971), Coffman (1979) and Erickson (1950). This is supported by descriptive accounts of reminiscence projects: Kemp (1978), Langley and Corder (1978), Langley and Kershaw (1982), Recall (1982), Johnstone (1982) and Norris (1982).

The claims for reminiscence are summarised in Table 10.1 and the barriers to its successful practice in Table 10.2. It should be emphasised that such barriers are not absolute.

Table 10.1: Claimed Effects of Reminiscence

Source	Item
Lewis (1971) and McMahon & Rhudick (1964)	(1) Identifying more closely with one's past and strengthening present identity.
	(2) Achieving past/present continuity of self-concept.
	(3) Achieving greater personal identity and coping ability.
	(4) Resistance to stress and disturbances in homeostasis.
	(5) Increased self-esteem in the face of declining powers.
	(6) Increased ability to reach out and enthuse others in a way that negates disengagement.
	(7) Dissonance reduction.
	(8) Protection against depression.
	(9) The promotion of serenity, wisdom and social awareness.
	(10) Encouraging the anticipation of future milestones, e.g. birthdays, anniversaries.
	(11) Enjoyment from the exercise of mental function for its own sake.
	(12) Life justification and coming to terms with guilt and unrealised aspirations.
	(13) Handing on the culture of the race and the preservation of views and experience, both distinguished and humble.
	NB: Ability to reminisce is unrelated to intellectual ability and is not a feature of failing intellect.
Butler (1963)	(1) Life review involves a gradual return to consciousness of past experience and the resurgence of unresolved conflicts.

Table 10.1: Claimed Effects of Reminiscence (continued)

	(2) Life review promotes candour, serenity and wisdom.
Kastenbaum (1974)	(1) *Validation* — 'I was worthwhile then . . .'
	(2) *Boundary setting* — 'That is over, this I can still do.'
	(3) *Perpetuation* of the past as if in the present — 'I am still me . . .'
	(4) *Replaying* of past experience — 'Wasn't it nice when . . .?'
Cumming & Henry (1961)	(1) Passive mastery — pride in what has been rather than what is.
Witkin (in Langley & Kershaw, 1982	(1) Contact with the feeling side of life — a problem-solving tool.
Langley & Kershaw (1982)	(1) Entertainment/enjoyment.
Johnstone (1982)	(1) Reassurance of personal development.
	(2) A vehicle for collaboration.

Table 10.2: Barriers to Reminiscence

Advanced age	Sensory deprivation
Physical immobility	Severe depression
Social disengagement	Memory and intellectual impairment
Separation from family and occupational ties	Institutionalisation
Negative emotionally charged memories	Impatience and lack of understanding by others

A number of themes run through the literature. Reminiscence is sometimes referred to as a defence; for example, the retired recall past occupational status in order to ward off anxiety from failing self-esteem. This can be seen as a rather negative, regressive approach, particularly if it involves the mechanisms of denial and projection (McMahon and Rhudick, 1964), e.g. elderly footballers decrying the abilities of present players and attributing to them the lack of zip that they themselves feel but deny. Nevertheless, we all need defences and, within limits, these approaches may be better than raw anxiety.

At other times reminiscence is described more positively as a coping strategy (Lewis, 1971). In the latter sense, past memories are used to solve present-day problems and via communication establish social relationships, a very real achievement. Even passive mastery (Cumming and Henry, 1961), i.e. being able to feel pride in what has been rather than what is, is constructive. Reminiscence is said to produce contentment, serenity and wisdom and this is valued by patients who themselves want a quiet life and, by others, who wish for compliance in those for whom they care. However, discontent leading to political activism on behalf of their peer group, noted by Lewis in *non*-reminiscers, can also be valued. One should not slip into the assumption that all elderly persons need passive care.

McMahon and Rhudick suggest that some of the more obsessive, mildly depressed elderly review their life out of a sense of guilt and the need for self-justification. It may be that this helps to prevent the development of more severe disorders, but it should also be noted that the severely depressed are so preoccupied with their present distress as to be incapable of reminiscing. In clinical practice these distinctive attitudes will need to be recognised and handled appropriately. Both McMahon and Rhudick and Coffman (1977) note similarities between the repetitive aspects of reminiscence and the processes of mourning. Coffman also notes, like Butler (1963), that life review prepares for the terminal disengagement of death.

Techniques and Variants

Reminiscence can be promoted in different ways as set out in Table 10.3. In my discussion, the techniques involving drama will be emphasised, but further study of the wider field will repay serious students.

Table 10.3: Forms of Reminiscence

Reminiscence theatre	Reminiscence creative drama/workshops
Reminiscence audio-visual aids	Scrapbooks
Photography	Storytelling
Pilgrimages	Genealogy
Interviews	Oral history
Family memoirs	Hospital and local radio
Biography and autobiography	Informal dialogue
School/museum/volunteer projects	Architecture
Music and dance	

Reminiscence Theatre

Reminiscence can be formally stimulated in performance or less formally through workshop activities. Reminiscence theatre provides an event in what may otherwise be a monotonous institutional life. The skills and the presence of the actors and the deliberate involvement of the audience all add to the impact.

The practice and problems of staging a reminiscence theatre show are described in *Reminiscence Theatre* (Langley and Kershaw, 1982) from which a summary of the stages of the process is here reproduced by kind permission of the authors and publishers.

Stages in the development of a typical reminiscence show

(1) Company discussed the general area, topic or historical period to define loosely the lines of research.

(2) Visits were made to libraries and museums to research the area, topic and period.

(3) Visits were made with tape-recorder to selected old people's homes to get to know residents and to collect material for the show.

(4) Company reviewed all material collected and made decisions about a more specific focus for the show itself, followed by further and more detailed research to find suitable songs, photographs, objects and further background information.

(5) Improvisations tried out different ways of presenting the material. Characters, situations and structure of the show were explored and developed, always using the collected material as a starting point and focus. Songs were tried out and selected.

(6) Improvisations gradually shaped into rehearsals as different ways of performing the material effectively were finalised and the show took shape. Songs were rehearsed intensively. Props and costumes were selected.

(7) Previews for invited audiences of specialists — doctors, psychiatrists, matrons, etc. — were given, especially if there were powerful emotional scenes in the show, or material which may have produced trauma.

(8) Performances of the show were given in old people's homes, especially those in which material had been collected.

(9) Follow-up visits were made to discuss the show with residents and staff to entertain and sing songs informally, during which more material could be collected for further shows.

Further details and background to reminiscence theatre are also given in Langley and Corder (1978).

Reminiscence in the form of theatre is best suited to less disabled elderly residents and has been produced successfully in residential homes, dining clubs and wards. The most successful format was tripartite, consisting of:

(1) *Research* – especially where the elderly themselves were involved.
(2) *Performance* – including audience participation.
(3) *Follow-up workshops* – of a more intimate nature, in which the staff of homes and any interested volunteers could be involved in order to maintain the impetus after the highlight of the company event. In the follow-up workshop activities reminiscence theatre merges with, and involves, all other variants.

Creative Drama

An American variant on the theme (Coffman, 1979) is the use of reminiscence as a component of a creative drama programme with the elderly. In an interesting, informative and practical review, Coffman presents the theoretical background to both creative drama and reminiscence and describes ways in which both concepts are applied in practice. She found that while well-preserved, retired elderly persons enjoyed reading and performing plays, the less able residents of nursing homes preferred reminiscence and personal themes in a workshop setting. Non-personal themes, even within the creative drama format, were not so attractive to them as personal reminiscence. Coffman, claims that creative drama is effective because it allows temporary re-engagement with lost roles and experimentation with new ones. It also promotes sharing amongst aloof and isolated nursing home residents, and as such is a viable tool for enriching the quality of life of the institutionalised elderly. In a balanced review she wisely states that to offer rejuvenation would be unethical but to offer creative expression of the past is therapeutically and philosophically correct. The use, at one point, of the term 'remembrance' rather than 'remembering' aptly summarises the point of view.

It would seem that, in its most sophisticated form, Coffman's work amounts to personalised therapy, whether individual or in a group, but she rightly points out that there are various levels of emotional involvement and risk-taking and that with wise leadership the participant will find his own level.

Audio-visual Aids

The initial impetus to use reminiscence in the UK came in the form of
an audio-visual aid developed by Kemp and his co-workers in the Architects'
Department of the Department of Health and Social Security (Kemp, 1978).
With the support of Help the Aged the material is now available as a
tape/slide presentation in either an audibly pulsed or synchronised form.
The latter, because of the absence of audible bleeps, is more aesthetic
but requires specialised apparatus. Each of the three tape/slide packs
consists of 2 x 20 slides, appropriate music and commentary on the
tape, supported by a handbook with background information, and cue
questions by which the operator may initiate discussions. The periods
concerned are appropriate to elderly residents of the United Kingdom
in the 1980s and cover 'Childhood, The Great War, Youth, Living
Through the Thirties, The Second World War and A Different World'.
By participating in the discussion the operator forms an integral part
of the system.

It was not intended to combine this material with performance, but
if appropriate skills are available, there seems no reason why this should
not happen. As the published material is of general and national interest
in the United Kingdom, much opportunity exists for producing local
versions.

The Application of Photography

Local scenes from past years were shown by back projection as an
integral part of many of the Medium Fair Reminiscence Theatre
shows. Views of the interior of Dellers, a well known local café
meeting place in the 1920s and 1930s, always produced much discussion
and in one case a courtship tale that was later dramatised and used as
part of a show. If photographs are used as a prop they should be of a
size and mount that can be easily and safely handled. Some may later
hang, but pictures that can be seen only in this way are less useful
than those that can be handled. If local photographic clubs, museums
and historians can be involved in collecting and presenting the
material, the work becomes a useful catalyst involving a wider section
of the local community in the service of their aged members.

An interesting account of a community photographic venture with
strong, though perhaps unwitting, reminiscence connections is given
by a photographer, Paul Carter, in *British Images I* published by The
Arts Council of Great Britain (1975). As part of a community service
venture in a deprived South London Inner City Borough, he made
slides from favourite snapshots submitted by members of a pensioners

club. Those illustrated have strong personal and reminiscence value. He then made current slide portraits of each of the persons concerned and used the past/present contrasts in order to promote group discussion and identity.

Other Reminiscence Techniques

Formalised presentations should not detract from the value of simple reminiscence dialogue in the course of other duties. While it may be difficult for nurses to encourage reminiscence while taking a temperature, there is no reason why conversation during a bath or the changing of a dressing should not be about the past, perhaps using related themes such as, 'What sort of soap did you use when you were a child?', 'How clothes have changed since we were girls.'

Discussion may lead to scrapbooks, pilgrimages or research into history or genealogy and the recounting of researched material to others. Hospital radio is mostly confined to acute hospitals where, increasingly, the elderly form a large proportion of the total clientele, and could be used with effect. For those confined to their own or residential homes, the increasing presence of local radio has shown that it can be a powerful companion to those who are isolated, especially when linked to phone-ins.

The use of props, preferably, like photographs, those that can be handed around, is stimulating. Costume for the ladies, particularly if authentic, and tools for the men, go down well. In one reminiscence theatre show a genuine, though safe, Mills bomb from World War I was the centre of attraction. In participation the props need not even be elderly for, in another show, an aluminium-framed walking aid was used with vigour to demonstrate the way to handle an old-time wash dolly.

Music is related to drama and for the elderly a sense of rhythm is preserved long after many other senses are dulled. Appreciation of pitch may be affected by high tone deafness but music hall songs (suitable updates for my generation would be Glen Miller!) are potent reminders of the past. Memories are most firmly laid down when reinforced by emotion or action, so it is not surprising that music and dance can evoke vivid images at a later date. Dance has its limitations in practice because of the relative immobility of some elderly but dance workshops have been practiced by SHAPE (Reid, 1982) and others in geriatric hospitals and in one reminiscence show a patient joined in to demonstrate to the actors (the situation was deliberately contrived) how to dance the Valeta.

Matthews and Kemp (1979) have also experimented with period

architecture as a reminiscence aid and, although this particular experiment is difficult to evaluate, the idea presents an interesting challenge to others.

Table 10.4: Allied Techniques

Reality orientation	Attitude therapy
Behaviourist techniques	Psychiatric rehabilitation
Non-reminiscence drama/games/music	

Reminiscence is not the only technique for helping the elderly and other related, and complementary, techniques are listed in Table 10.4 and will now be briefly described.

Reality Orientation

This is an active, participative technique for keeping those who are confused, forgetful or isolated as far as possible in touch with the world around them. While it may not stem certain inevitable deteriorations, it can at least make the best use of those faculties that are preserved. An early variant on this technique is described by Kennedy (1959), while later a systematised approach was initiated by Folsom (1968) in the USA and developed in the UK by Holden and Sinebruchow (1978), Brook *et al.* (1975), Saxby and Merchant (1981) and Holden and Woods (1982). In essence it starts from the simple here and now of day, date, time, weather, place, etc., and proceeds, in the later stages, to something very akin to reminiscence. It may be practised formally in a daily session or informally throughout the 24 hours. Repetition is of the essence. Reality orientation is based on a behaviourist approach, of which it is one specific form. Woods (1979) showed that reality orientation improved residents' memories, information and orientation to a greater degree than enhanced social attention. He could not, however, confirm Brooks' findings of improved general behaviour.

Behaviourist Techniques

The attitude of behaviourist psychologists has been reviewed by Miller (1977), Woods and Britten (1977), Mueller and Atlas (1972) and Simpson *et al.* (1976). The behaviourist approach, if it is to be effective, emphasises the crucial importance of the way in which attention or other reward must immediately follow appropriate behaviour. Sometimes the reward can be in the form of tokens given immediately and exchanged later for money or goods; alternatively, the reward can be social in the form of attention and praise. The value of each specific form of behaviour has to be well-defined, well-understood by all staff concerned and applied consistently. In the residential setting it is essentially a group exercise for the patients and staff. An important element before even the treatment begins is the thinking through of desirable behaviour and the mode of giving rewards.

In a comprehensive review, Miller (1977) makes an important point that is applicable to most work with the elderly. He notes that with the cessation of 'treatment' subjects rapidly recede to previous levels of functioning. What is required is a philosophy of environmental adjustment, sometimes, although perhaps too passively, called a prosthetic environment, in which the therapeutic changes are continued and are not, like many other treatments, applied for a limited period and then withdrawn. Architectural changes (Matthews and Kemp, 1979) will of course well meet this criterion.

Attitude Therapy

Attitude therapy, described by Ginzberg (1953, 1954), stresses the importance of milieu, attitude and non-verbal cues. When cognitive processes are impaired, contact through the emotions is still possible. As verbal communication is impaired the psychiatrist and nurse must interpret needs from behaviour. Neglect of these principles will lead to disturbed behaviour and for the most disturbed, choice must be limited to that which can be apprehended and tolerated. An important derivative of this work is the use of touch in therapy. The importance of handling objects when other senses are impaired has been stressed already. Touch is one of the few senses that are not projected. We can see and hear across a room but when we touch we know that pleasure or pain is near at hand and imminent.

The Role of Education

In its broadest sense, education can cover many of the activities already mentioned but Jones (1977, 1982, 1983) makes a strong case for the place of the professional educator in working with the elderly over a wide range of topics, including poetry (speaking and writing), drama, current affairs, collage, music and movement, local history, art and craft, languages. Those engaged in such activities, if they are from outside the caring professions (e.g. from local education authorities, workers' education services or volunteers), provide a useful supplement to professional nurses and remedial staff. For the patient they provide personal satisfaction and greater group cohesion.

Psychiatric Rehabilitative Approach

Much useful and perceptive work has been done in psychiatry with younger patients by Wing (1973, 1977a, b), Bennett (1977) and Clark (1981a, b), but for the elderly, because of the different role structure of their lives, the work needs to be translated in order to become appropriate (Mian, 1982; Quiltich, 1974). In the later years of life many work and family roles are lost and survival roles may predominate but, as Coffman points out, reduction in specific roles and responsibilities allows more time for creative pastimes or, in Maslow's (1943) terms, self-actualisation. The point made by Bennett (1977) about role performance is, however, still valid. To be performed efficiently, roles must be defined and understood, the appropriate skills must be available and motivation assured. In achieving the role adjustments necessary between middle and late life there would seem to be a place for reminiscence and therapeutic drama. As Coffman (1979) points out, there is no terminal age to creativity. Furthermore: 'The therapeutic milieu defines the patient as the actor, innovator, co-operator and manager of his own affairs and everyone else as assistants in this process' (Cumming and Cumming, 1962).

Some Specific Issues

The Role and Training of the Presenters

Most, and certainly the more potent, forms of reminiscence therapy depend upon the skills and attitudes of the presenters. In a deliberate attempt to modify attitudes it can be used in varying degrees of sophistication and with varying degrees of emotional risk for both the presenter and the participant.

The most personal, and therefore risky, form is when reminiscence is used to explore personal problems and adjustment in a creative dramatic, almost psychodramatic, session. At this level the presenter/ therapist will need a minimum of performance skills but good personal contact and empathy with the client, together with competency as a therapist to deal with emotional crises if they occur.

In contrast, reminiscence theatre needs good performance skills, good and spontaneous empathic contact with the audience and minimal overtly therapeutic training. The first two attributes can, however, in combination, be quite demanding. The actor, and indeed the ensemble, need to be able to deviate from an agreed script at precisely the right time in order to pick up audience responses and develop them there and then until such a time as it is prudent to return to the script. The 'freeze frame' technique developed in performance by the Medium Fair 'Fair Old Time' Company was a good example but is taxing on the actors and is not for the prima donna who wants to impress within a role.

The audio-visual format requires neither performance nor therapy skills but does require good contact and empathy and, in this respect, is similar to most of the less formal variants.

It is one of the assets of reminiscence therapy that it can be used in one format or another by people of most divergent skills, providing they all have a common ability to make contact with their clients. While knowledge of the historical background is helpful, even that may not be necessary in the first instance. Research and practice with clients will soon cast clients in the role of teacher, with the presenter as his student. As Norris (1982) has pointed out, this is one of the increasingly rare opportunities for the elderly to give rather than to take. While it is certain that distress can sometimes occur in a client, in all but the most personal forms it is rarely overwhelming. It has been made clear by both Butler (1963:1964) and McMahon and Rhudick (1964) that the recalled memories can sometimes be painful. Catharsis, however, can be helpful. The sharing of a troubled past has been recognised as beneficial by those who have been through the experience. The listener must be prepared to understand and modify (although not necessarily conceal) his own reactions to the patient's distress in a way that is objective and free from anxiety and resentment. Presenters, in this respect, would be wise to share their reactions to the work with those skilled in interpersonal techniques so that their own personalities can be used wisely but with conviction.

Is it Treatment? Is it Scientific?

The effect of reminiscence in the treatment of disease (in the sense of dis-ease) is difficult to prove by strict scientific criteria. Nevertheless the importance of description and the illuminative incident are increasingly recognised even by arch-scientists (Reid, 1982; Parlett and Hamilton, 1977). Voting with your feet (and practice) is not necessarily valid, as many episodes in the history of psychiatry have shown, but an enjoyable and creative experience that people wish to perpetuate in a good start.

Evaluation

For those interested in evaluation the reviews by Ward (1980) and Kuh (1982) are recommended.

Reminiscence certainly does not cure senile dementia and may not even retard the progress and pathology but, nevertheless, the preservation, by exercise, of undamaged skills is a realistic aim of treatment. For those whose mental function is recovering after temporary impairment by a toxic delirium, reminiscence and reality orientation will run with the stream of improving physiology and mental function. In the present state of knowledge reminiscence is contrà-indicated during a severe psychotic episode, depressive or otherwise, but may be helpful when depression of mood follows a situational or neurotic crisis.

Treatment for the more disabled sufferers from dementia centres around basic nursing care and a proper concern for their quality of life. This is challenging work but, for all that, rewarding, even though progress may be small and disengagement, close to the ultimate disengagement of death, great. The clinical art is to find the level at which the patient is still responsive. Music, touch, games and audio-visual work even on a one-to-one basis, may be best and there is great scope for the creative approach at this level. Sessions will need to be shorter because of a reduced attention span and the ready appearance of fatigue. In these circumstances, frequent mini-pauses, even within sessions, can be advantageous. Distractions and interruptions will have a deleterious effect and are best avoided. Regularly timed events, such as meals, may be imprinted even on a failing memory and are delayed only at the risk of non-compliance with the substitute.

Other Uses of Reminiscence

Reminiscence has been studied mainly as a therapeutic tool with the elderly. It has been noted, however, that reminiscence can occur spontaneously at times of stress and crisis at all ages. There is a similarity between the repetition of reminiscence and that of mourning, and bereavement is no prerogative of the old. Mourning is also more distressing in the younger age groups and in those whom the process has been precipitated by losses other than death, e.g. the break-up of a relationship. Such ideas may point to further uses for reminiscence in the future.

In Conclusion

It is suggested that there is a sound, theoretical basis for the use of reminiscence with the elderly and possibly in other age groups. Certain practical applications, based principally on the use of drama, have been outlined with brief reference to related techniques. Together they provide a broad strategy for the use of interactive and creative processes both in treatment and in preserving the quality of life of older persons in and out of residential care. The art of clinical practice is to convert this strategy for social nutrition into a balanced diet, devise the recipes and then prepare regular and varied individual meals.

11 AUDIO-VISUAL AIDS

Dramatherapy overlaps with other creative arts. It is but a short step from beating rhythm to playing music, movement gradually becomes dance and painting and sculpture are other forms of non-verbal communication. Although the boundaries are not clearly defined, it is important that a dramatherapist has knowledge of her own limitations. Creative arts are broad subjects, and none of us can hope to embrace them all. An awareness of our own skills and how they differ from those of our colleagues can enable us to work together to form a comprehensive therapy of creativity. This does not prevent us from using other art forms, for they can heighten the dramatic experience, making it more meaningful to the client. We should, however, bear in mind that art and music therapists have their own professional training which extends beyond the overlapping area. Their knowledge of the application of their particular art in therapy is beyond our own experience of it unless we undertake more than one training. So any use of other art forms should be designed to extend or enhance the drama, not to replace it. We need to be clear in our own minds the reason for its use and not include other art forms because it seems a good idea. This applies equally to the use of technical equipment. It can be a valuable addition to a session if used for a purpose, but needs to be expertly handled to keep the interest of the group.

There are two ways in which I use art or technical aids. One use is in creating group cohesion, in which a sharing of responsibilities, decision-making and doing of the activity itself is the means by which the group comes together as a whole. The other is to use the art/ technical aid for a specific purpose.

Art

Dramatherapists who work in occupational therapy departments or alongside other creative therapists have the opportunity to produce a combined programme. The therapist who is not in this position can include art in the drama sessions (or drama in the art sessions). It may require a change of room and the effect of a different environment

156

should be taken into account in the planning. It may be disruptive at first and time used to assimilate the new surroundings may be well spent. I find the most successful sessions have been ones in which I have initiated an activity and then used the spontaneous ideas the group presented.

Group Cohesion

Creating pictures together is fun and encourages co-operation, group decisions and compromise. The shared creation brings people closer and can be used as a stimulus for other activities. Here are a few ideas:

(1) The group lies in a heap on the floor, bodies overlapping on a large sheet of paper. Each person in turn draws round the outline of his neighbour until the picture is complete. This can then be coloured, filling in the outlines of the bodies or the segments presented by their overlap.

(2) The group makes a picture or collage together, each person contributing to it. This can be the result of a group story or an improvisation or used as a basis to commence one.

(3) A large sheet of paper and a variety of art materials are placed in front of the group. One person draws something, e.g. house, person, bed. Others add to it in turn. A variation is to try and think of a song for each picture represented. This is usually popular with elderly people who have a good repertoire of songs.

(4) Some of the group form a tableau and others paint a suitable background. This can be used to start a new improvisation.

(5) The group draws a picture (usually abstract), each person representing his feelings of the moment. This can be used at the termination of a series of sessions when each person can share something he has felt during the life of the group. It is also useful as an introduction to looking at the dynamics of the group.

(6) Each person draws a single stroke which relates to others on a board.

Communication

A group that has problems with communication can benefit by combined non-verbal art activities with drama sessions. Some of these, done in pairs, can help individuals who have difficulty relating to the rest of the group. If the therapist pairs initially with the most withdrawn clients, she can gradually encourage them to enter into group activities.

(1) In pairs, each person has a crayon and, alternating strokes, has a 'line' conversation with partner.

(2) A large sheet of paper on the floor. In pairs, draw round partner's feet as he moves across it.

(3) Take a journey across the paper, each making a mark alternately. If you cross the path of another pair make a special mark to note it.

(4) Plot a journey for your partner across the floor, drawing pictures of the places he passes.

(5) In two groups, using separate sheets of paper, each person draws a trail for his partner from the other group to follow.

(6) Paint a picture of a place you think your partner would like to visit.

Heightened Experience

We can use art to add another dimension to the dramatic experience. Here are some ideas:

(1) Create masks and use them in improvisations.

(2) Try to get into each other's feelings by wearing other people's masks.

(3) Look at other people's paintings and try to express their mood in movement or drama.

(4) Paint pictures of scenes we have created in drama.

(5) Make models to express our feelings. Comments from the rest of the group (not of the artistic merit but of emotional content) can be a valuable learning and sharing experience.

(6) We can use a group or individual's picture as a stimulus for improvisation.

Music

The combination of music and drama is a familiar one. Backgrounds for plays and films are an accepted part of theatre. If we use it in drama we need to be sure that it does add to the session and not cause more confusion (see Chapter 4). It can certainly create atmosphere for an improvisation or dance drama, is useful in relaxation and sense training, and can be used as a means of communication. Singing, moving to music and dancing are obvious extensions of drama and frequently arise spontaneously. Live music always attracts attention but the musician has to be a competent one. Nothing is more distracting than to work with someone who has to keep hesitating or apologising for mistakes. The rhythm of the session is destroyed by the lack of rhythm from the musician! If using record players or tape-recorders, be sure you have the right track or place on the tape. It is worth arriving early and spending time on the technical details before commencing the session.

Group Cohesion

Working together to make music brings the group together with a common aim. Percussion instruments are good for giving an opportunity to participate, but unless the therapist has musical ability, there is usually a need for background music to keep the players together. Small groups with ability could learn to play a recorder or whistle. Chime bars, drums, clapping and improvising instruments from articles in the room all help the group to work together creatively.

Communication

(1) Have a conversation with a partner, each using a percussion instrument in turn to say something non-verbally.
(2) Create a story using percussion instruments to make sound effects.
(3) One member leaves the room; hide an object. On return, the rest of the group play, getting louder as he nears the object and softer as he gets further away.
(4) In two groups, one group plays a song with the name of a person or place in it and the other group has to guess the name. A variation is to play expressing an emotion, e.g. anger, happiness, sadness, etc.
(5) In pairs, A starts a movement and B plays a rhythmical accompaniment. Each can vary and produce either a conversation or a co-ordinated pattern of movement/sound.
(6) In two groups or pairs, each produces a meaningful sound pattern for the other to interpret or reply to.

Heighten Experience

Music can help to produce rhythmical and flowing movement and stimulate creative movement. Selection of music can set the mood and theme for a session. If it is used as a background to improvisation, make sure it is not too obtrusive. Some other ideas for its use are:

(1) The group listens to an expressive piece of music. Each person shares the images or memories it conjures up. Improvisation on

one of these themes can follow.

(2) The group listens to selected music, perhaps of two minutes duration. Divide into sub-groups and prepare a story in movement to the music.

(3) Individuals bring their own records to play to the group. Group suggests uses for music or uses it for improvisation. This can be used in social skills sessions for clients to speak for a few minutes about their reasons for bringing the record. Others can speak for a few minutes on their personal reaction to it.

(4) Play a song that tells a story, e.g. 'The Lonely Man' (Garfunkel), 'Lady with a Braid' (Dory Previn). The group takes on the role of people who know that person and improvisations around that person or the area in which they live can take place.

(5) Play a song that tells a story. Ask people to identify with any part of it. Use as a warm-up to role play of personal problems.

(6) Play music with one instrument only (flute, violin, etc). Create movements that are suggested by the sound. This can be extended by orchestrating sound/movement as a group, or making up a story or improvisation around the movement.

Art/Music/Drama

It is possible to use all three art forms together in therapy. To avoid using too many stimuli at once, it may be advisable to have separate sessions which are linked. There is so much to offer that we do not want to undermine the value of each creative experience by overwhelming the clients. Here are a few ideas which can provide continuity from one medium to another:

(1) Listen to music and paint a picture stimulated by it (or express feeling or images of it); use picture as basis for improvisation.

(2) Listen to music, paint picture to represent the sound, create movement simulated by the movement in the picture.

(3) Listen to music, tell a story, paint it.

(4) Paint a self-portrait in a particular situation. This should be expressive rather than artistic, so pin men or caricatures can be used. Exchange pictures with someone else and improvise around the roles you now hold. Select instrument and hold non-verbal conversation about the experience with a partner.

(5) Self-portrait in a particular mood or situation. Role play using

instruments instead of words.

(6) This is especially useful for small groups. Select music you think your partner would enjoy. Play it if possible (have selection of records available). Partner then paints his experience of the music. Both can improvise movement or a scene from this painting. This is useful for clients who want to give to others and don't know how to start; they can give an experience.

Tape-recorders

Most departments possess a tape-recorder and if you are buying equipment it is worth investing in a good one with stereo speakers. It is important that the recorder is suited to the size of the room. When working in a large space more volume is required than in a small one. It may seem elementary, but I have seen good sessions undermined by the use of inadequate equipment. Take the time to learn how to use it properly before relying on it in a session. You can lose the interest of the group or the poignancy of the moment by wasting time with technical mistakes. It is possible to be accurate with a tape and have it ready for use at the right moment. For this reason I tape any music I am going to use rather than use a record player. Cassettes are easier to manage and less likely to go wrong during a session, but spool tapes can be edited more easily. There is a large spool recorder in the hospital where I make and edit tapes. I then record them on to cassettes for use in group sessions. Some years ago I was fortunate enough to be consulted when new audio-visual aids were being bought for use in the hospital. A good stereo recorder was purchased for my personal use and another for each unit dealing with elderly clients. The latter is available for each ward on application to the unit officer. I recorded a set of four tapes suitable for use with the elderly that ward staff can use outside drama sessions. I have also recorded tapes for special needs.

Group Cohesion

Using a tape-recorder with a group can be rewarding. Many people are surprised to hear their own voices for the first time and simply recording and listening can take up a whole session. It is important that people are happy with the medium before trying to use it creatively. Some ideas might include:

(1) Record a play reading.

(2) Record a group story with sound effects.
(3) Make a tape of various sounds around which you create a story.
(4) Each bring a record and make a tape of group favourites.
(5) Record a music session.
(6) Record each client's description of an event, e.g. ward holiday, outing, party, etc., and replay later in the year when the event has been forgotten.

Communication

(1) Play a tape of sounds which the group identify.
(2) Play sounds relating to a particular theme.
(3) Play recording made in the grounds (these could have been made as a group experience). Have each person tell a partner what the sounds mean to him.
(4) Record and play an event which the group has been unable to attend (hospital harvest festival, etc.).
(5) Play recordings of group members speaking and try to identify them.
(6) Record individuals recounting reminiscences and build up a group 'memories' tape.

Heighten Experience

(1) Play a short extract from a play to be completed by the group as a story or improvisation.
(2) Use sound effects to create an atmosphere (trains, water, ships, etc.) on which to improvise.
(3) Play recordings of group members making a prepared speech in social skills training.
(4) Record a description of a person, place or event from which the group can enter into role play.
(5) Play sounds of events and places to the group in rehabilitation programmes, e.g. noises in a busy supermarket, on the bus, etc. Members can identify sounds and become familiar with them. Also compare with past experience.
(6) Record and play group members interviewing or conversing in social skills group.

Pictures/Photographs/Slides

Visual aids have been part of teaching for a long time and they can be equally valuable in learning social skills and in creative or projective activities. If you have a photographer available you can build up an interesting record of groups and ward events. Photography as a group activity is an interesting thought and a possibility if facilities and expertise are available. It is not something that I have experienced myself, but, the uses of slides, photographs and pictures in drama are numerous. A few suggestions are:

(1) Create a role using a picture as a starting point. Who is this person? What does he do? What is his history? It is possible to build a character in this way.

(2) Each person has a picture of a place — house, park, street, etc. Tell a partner what it reminds you of — events or places you have known in your own life.

(3) Show a slide on a screen as a simulation and a background for improvisation.

(4) Show a slide or picture of a crowd of people. Each person takes up the physical position of someone in the crowd. The group decides on the situation and commences improvisation, starting from the still position. Another entry into role play.

(5) Show pictures of group members as babies. The group guesses which picture belongs to whom. This can be used as an introduction to sharing of childhood experiences, reminiscence and personal role play.

(6) The group physically represents a picture, each person becoming part of it, e.g. one person becomes a wall, another a window, another a door, etc., in a picture of a house. This is useful as a general warm-up, as a means of promoting physical contact and introducing representation of inanimate objects by human beings (a psychodrama technique) to be used either in personal work or fantasy role play.

Video

Most hospitals have video equipment. This varies from sophisticated sets in a special room to mobile apparatus that can be used anywhere. It does not require a lot of technical expertise to use simple video, but it is important to have sufficient knowledge to feel at ease with it. Useful advice on buying equipment is given in Powley (1980). Again time needs to be spent learning to use it and preparing for a session. My experience is that things frequently need adjusting during playback so I prefer not to use it with groups who are easily distracted. Sometimes technicians are available to help the therapist and I now confine my use of video to groups where this can happen. I found that the anxiety of coping with the machinery and the precision required distracted me from the group activities and I did not do justice to either without plenty of assistance.

I am still ambivalent about the use of video in drama. I feel that the value of drama is in the moment of creation, so unless the group is engaged in theatre, presentation of the session loses its meaning as soon as it has happened. It is the engagement and experience that is important and therapeutic. To view it at a later stage or to show it to others who were not present at the time is to represent only half of the event — that which can be seen — and that can easily be distorted or misinterpreted. In order to prevent that happening, I insist on erasing tapes when they are no longer of value to the group (usually when it disperses). This means that useful teaching material is destroyed, but I feel that the confidentiality of the group is paramount. What we have created together is personal to us and I would not like to risk it being misused or misinterpreted by others. I also feel that one-way screens are in total conflict with the essence of dramatherapy and I cannot think of an occasion when I would use one. Anything done in the group should be open and anyone who wants to see dramatherapy is welcome to come to group sessions but must be prepared to participate. I am always available for question or comment on my work and indeed welcome it. It is only by experience in drama that you begin to feel its power and understand it as a therapeutic tool. This is my opinion, but others may disagree.

Group Cohesion

Working together to understand and use video equipment can be a valuable way of obtaining co-operation and a sense of group identity. The equipment is really quite robust and not likely to be damaged by unskilled handling. I was so impressed by the effect it had on a staff training group that I used it as a method of introduction with a new client group. The group contained three people with personality disorders, who all found a role for themselves through their expertise: technical, artistic and directive. The co-leader was a doctor and the change in client-doctor relationship in this situation was marked. Both were grappling with a technical problem and learning something new together. It was a good step towards rehabilitation (see Chapter 6).

I also used this method of group involvement in a ward of long-stay elderly clients. To be trusted with the equipment and technical handling of cameras and to have the power to select whom you would put on the TV screen was a novel experience. It was difficult to judge whether it was more confusing to those who could not communicate. The second time we worked with this group we also had a visiting music therapist and the multiple stimuli were too confusing – it was not such a successful session.

Specific Uses

Video is not something to use without a purpose. If it does not heighten the dramatic experience then don't use it. I think that video has limitations in staff training because of the experiential nature of drama. In my view it is unethical to film a client session for training purposes only. It must have a value to the participating group to justify its use.

I do not attempt to use video for a specific purpose until a cohesive group has been formed. We are about to see ourselves without any disguise and we need trust in those with whom we share the experience. It is practical to spend the first session getting used to the equipment. Film the group playing games, then a close-up of each individual in order to accustom them to the medium and get over the embarrassment of seeing themselves on the screen. It is as well to warn them that everyone looks about half a stone larger than in reality. There will be so much laughter and comment that no extensive work will be done, so do not expect it.

Social Skills

People whose intellectual or emotional reactions are slow have difficulty in recognising themselves when group members model their behaviour. This was particularly noticeable with a group of clients with both personality problems and low intelligence. However, as soon as they saw themselves on video, they could see how misleading their own body language and behaviour could be. This facing up to reality is an important part of social skills training. Other professionals have built up their own pattern of social skills training using video recording. Rather than repeat a pattern which they are already doing successfully, I prefer to work at a client level where drama skills have their most value. At this point the clients are not usually ready for video.

Staff Training

Video is used widely to help staff see themselves at work and improve

their techniques. While this is often done formally, one can gain
considerable knowledge by playback in client groups. Not only can
the therapist see herself, but she also gains by the comments of the group
members. Making a video film can be a valuable experience in itself.
One staff training group set out to make a film on the management of
violence. It was unanimously felt it was more important to portray the
prevention of the potentially violent situation. A group of twelve
sub-divided into three smaller groups and each produced two rehearsed
improvisations. One showed how the conduct of the staff contributed
to an aggressive scene and the other showed the same scene handled
differently to prevent aggression. The whole was finally filmed. I do not
think the film has ever been shown outside the group but the insight
and knowledge which the group gained by the experience was
considerable.

Group Dynamics

If a video-recorder is allowed to run during a group session, it is
surprising how much comes to light. Filming a staff training group
playing warm-up games showed how little interaction there was between
sub-groups — who initiated activities, who was on the periphery of the
group. Group dynamics have been highlighted in a similar manner in
client groups. It is interesting to record a whole session and play it
back, stopping the film to look at grouping, body language, etc.
Group members can take up the physical postures shown and maybe
improvise from it or make a statement of the feelings created.

Warm-Up

Open-ended improvisations can be filmed and the group decide on its
ending. This, too, could be recorded for detailed discussion. Rehearsed
scenes from plays can be recorded to start discussion or improvisation.
Video recordings of events, parties, concerts, etc., can be used for
long-stay clients who cannot attend or to reinforce the memory of
those who were present. As I do not use video often myself, it has not
stimulated creative ideas, but I am sure the enthusiast will find ways
of heightening the dramatic experience with a client group. This is the
joy of drama. If the therapist develops a new interest, new uses arise
spontaneously and enthusiasm gives birth to further creativity.

APPENDIX II: SOME USEFUL MUSIC

Compiled in collaboration with Leon Winston. This represents a personal selection and we are conscious that readers' taste may differ!

Records used for Dance/Drama and Music and Movement

Fantasy and Atmosphere

Berlioz	:	Symphonie Fantastique
Bizet	:	L'Arlésienne — Adagietto
Bliss	:	Miracle in the Gorbals (parts)
		Things to Come
Debussy	:	L'Après Midi d'un Faun
Holst	:	Planets Suite — Venus, Neptune
Kodaly	:	Harry James Suite — The Fairy Tale Begins, Song
Mussorgsky	:	Pictures at an Exhibition (parts)
Respighi	:	Fountains of Rome — The Triton
Rimsky-Korsakov	:	Scheherazade — Story of the Kalender Prince
Rota	:	Legend of the Glass Mountain
Saint-Saëns	:	Carnival of Animals — Aquarium
		Danse Macabre
Sibelius	:	Swan of Tuonela
Stravinsky	:	Firebird Suite — Dance of the Princesses with Golden Apples, Dance of the Firebird, Dance of King Kastchel

Conflict and Violence

Copland	:	Billy the Kid (parts)
Holst	:	Planets Suite — Mars, Uranus
Liadov	:	Baba Yaga
Liszt	:	Mephisto — Apparition Ballet
Ravel	:	Bolero
Sibelius	:	Finlandia
Turina	:	Danzas Fantasticas — Orgia

Action and Excitement

Bizet	:	Le Cid and Carmen — Prelude
Khatchaturian	:	Sabre Dance
Liszt	:	Hungarian Rhapsody No. 2
Tchaikovsky	:	1812 Overture and Marche Slav
Wagner	:	Rienzi Overture

Comedy

Beatles Records		
Kodaly	:	Harry James Suite — Battle and Defeat of Napoleon,

167

Kodaly (cont.)		Entrances of the Emperor and his Court, Viennese Clock
Mussolov	:	Steel Foundry
Rossini	:	Thieving Magpie Overture
Saint-Saëns	:	Carnival of the Animals — Personages with Long Ears, Hens and Cocks
Schubert	:	Divertissement
Shostakovitch	:	Aged of Gold — Polka
Stravinsky	:	Petrouchka — 3rd Tableau — In the Moor's Room
Vaughan Williams	:	The Wasps — March Past of the Kitchen Utensils
Walton	:	Façade — Plaka, Popular Song, Yodelling Song
Wolf-Ferrari	:	Susanna's Secret — Overture

Quiet Themes Also Suitable for Relaxation

Bach	:	Jesu, Joy of Man's Desiring, Air on a G String
Dvorak	:	New World Symphony (parts)
Elgar	:	Chanson de Nuit, Chanson au Matin
Folk Songs	:	Simon & Garfunkel etc.
Grieg	:	Peer Gynt — Morning
Kodaly	:	Harry Janos Suite — Song
Mussorgsky	:	Khovanshtina — Preludes
Saint-Saëns	:	Carnival of the Animals — The Swan
Samuel Barber	:	Adagio for Strings
Tchaikovsky	:	Andante Cantabile
Wolf-Ferrari	:	Jewels of the Madonna — Intermezzo

Records Used for Dance Drama

Bizet	:	Carmen — Prelude
Bliss	:	Miracle in the Gorbals
Copland	:	Billy the Kid
De Falla	:	El Amor Brujo
Dukas	:	Sorcerer's Apprentice
Gershwin	:	Rhapsody in Blue (parts)
Grieg	:	Peer Gynt
Hart and Rodgers	:	Slaughter on 10th Avenue
Holst	:	Mars
Kodaly	:	Harry Janos Suite
Jarnefelt	:	Praeludium
Khatchaturian	:	Gayeneh Suite
Mussorgsky	:	Night on a Bare Mountain — Conclusion, Pictures at an Exhibition (parts)
Offenbach	:	Orpheus in the Underworld
Picarelli	:	La Montanara
Prokofiev	:	Cinderella Ballet Music, Peter and the Wolf
Ravel	:	Mother Goose Suite
Respighi	:	Fountains of Rome — The Great Gate of Kiev
Rimsky-Korsakov	:	Scheherazade
Rossini	:	Thieving Magpie Overture
Rota	:	Legend of the Glass Mountain
Schubert	:	Unfinished Symphony (parts)
Shishov	:	A Jumping Game

Sibelius	:	En Saga and Valse Triste (parts), Finlandia
Strauss	:	Til Eulenspiegel
Tchaikovsky	:	Swan Lake, Hungarian Dance
Wagner	:	Rienzi Overture
Walton	:	Façade — Polka, Yodelling Song, Popular Song

Records for Walking, Moving and Miming

Delius	;	La Kalinda
Herb Alpert	:	Tijuana Sounds
Mike Oldfield	:	Tubular Bells
Purcell	:	Trumpet Voluntary
Red Army Choir	:	Songs for Marching
Rossini	:	Thieving Magpie — Overture (opening)
Schubert	:	Marche Militaire, Polonaise
Scott Joplin	:	The Entertainer and other Rags
Shand	:	Policeman's Holiday, Baby Sweetheart, Whistling Rufus, Whistler and his Dog
Sibelius	:	Karelia Suite — Alla Marcia
Tchaikovsky	:	Hungarian March, Nutcracker Suite — Dance of the Sugar Plum Fairy, Miniature Overture

Special Interest for the Elderly

Mrs Mills Party Records
Glenn Miller Big Band Sounds
Salvation Army Hymns
Brass Band Music (selected)
Oh! What a Lovely War
Songs from World Wars I and II
Charlie Kunz Piano Solos
George Mitchell's Black and White Minstrels
Peter Dawson Songs of the Open Road
Russ Conway Piano Music
100 Best Hymns

Jazz Bands

Acker Bilk
Chris Barber
Kenny Ball

Pop Music (selected)

Elvis Presley	ABBA
Bill Haley	Shakin' Stevens
Beatles	Cliff Richard
Showaddywady	Hot Chocolate
Boney M	Odyssey
Kids from Fame	

Songs for Role Play (selected)

Simon and Garfunkel   Gilbert O'Sullivan

John Lennon   Alan Price
Paul McCartney   Johnny Cash
Dory Previn

Film Music

Lisztomania   The Year 2001
Psycho   The Lion in Winter
Star Wars   The Big Country

(A useful record series – The World of Your Hundred Best Tunes, The Great
Classics)

12 LOOKING BOTH WAYS – A PSYCHIATRIST'S GUIDE TO DRAMATHERAPY

Gordon E. Langley

What should doctors, or for that matter, members of the other caring
professions, know about dramatherapy? What should dramatherapists
know about doctors and the services within which they work?
Paradoxically, dramatherapy is not always applied to the sick (the word
'patient' is getting unpopular anyway); nevertheless in many countries
most of the mentally ill and handicapped are treated as patients.
At present, within both health and social services, dramatherapists,
as such, are few and far between, but there is increasing recognition
of their skills and the need for mutual understanding. Even in other
settings an account of the interface between two professions will
find common ground.

Those who are not dramatherapists will need some understanding of
subsidiary questions such as: What is drama? What is dramatherapy?
Who are the dramatherapists? How are they trained? Where do they fit
in?

Dramatherapists themselves will need to ask: Where do I fit in?
What disabilities will I encounter in patients? Which of my skills are
relevant? How do they interact with other forms of treatment that the
patient will be undergoing? And within the structure and dynamics of
residential care?

In an attempt to answer these questions a brief personal overview
is presented in the hope that it will be of value to clinicians as prescribers
and to the therapists themselves as participants. Detail will need to be
added by dramatherapists in their own way.

Drama and Dramatherapy

Most general psychiatrists, if they recognise them at all, will see
dramatherapists as creative therapists similar to those already working
with the visual arts and music and will classify them as members of the
remedial professions. Not all dramatherapists would agree with this
viewpoint and many would regard their profession either as independent
or as related to the practice of psychotherapy. However classified,

dramatherapists will be seen by most doctors as providing a range of skills within the much broader spectrum of the multiprofessional team. Access to their skills will be through a mixture of prescription and negotiation with individual therapists. In so far as motivation is essential, the client will also play a part in this process. Some practitioners of dramatherapy will belong to other professions such as occupational therapy, clinical psychology or medicine, and of these some will be more dramatically orientated while others will work towards the psychodramatic and psychotherapeutic ends of the spectrum. A similar range of activities will be seen amongst those practising entirely as dramatherapists.

For the sake of the already confused psychiatrist, let me go back to first principles and start with pure drama. Dramatherapists must, and do, speak of their art in their own terms but a psychiatrist will see the matter in his own way and, for me, certain key issues are significant.

The statement 'drama is doing' is basic. The Greeks included the word 'struggling' in their definition (James, 1979). Drama may, but does not necessarily, involve performance. Drama in the form of theatre, for those to whom it appeals, is at least a physically passive and predominantly middle class way of increasing sensitivity to the human situations in which we live. Drama in education takes the form of participation in creative activity. Community theatre involves an element of both theatre, with a relatively passive audience, and more active participation, and is applied in shorter focus to a wider audience. Drama workshops use techniques originally developed in the training of actors in a way that develops social skills and personalities. So, without leaving the field of pure drama, we are already getting close to the idea of 'therapy'.

Looked at in more medico-social terms, drama is a creative group activity between two or more people involving self-awareness, verbal and non-verbal communication, trust, movement, risk and body awareness. It also permits the review of established strategies of living and experimentation with new ones. It expands the individual's repertoire of interpersonal skills and, where necessary, allows him to examine more closely the grammar of his interactions with other people, making, in the end, for a more flexible performance, whether the change be towards behaviour that is more controlled or more expressive.

To apply these normal and creative processes to the treatment of disease, in its literal sense of dis-ease, implies some differentiation between health and illness. What makes a person into a patient is a big issue that cannot be examined here in great depth, but let us assume that it implies a disability or internal conflict that makes the sufferer maladapted within either himself or in his social environment.

In some ways it is easier to define health. Moreno (1953) states: 'The most effective people are those who can readily adjust to new situations. Such adjustments require flexible, spontaneous reactions. The man incapable of reviewing his outlook when confronted with a new situation is the likeliest to develop mental illness.'

To paraphrase C.G. Jung (1979), maturity is the ability to find satisfaction in what is realistically available. Sutherland (1971) has a definition of mental health that is similar:

> The healthy individual feels he is leading his own life, taking responsibility for action and inaction, and taking credit for success and blame for failure. He must be able to love and work effectively and come to terms with social demands not by simply conforming but by making his own distinctive contribution to society, however small. In this respect he has some autonomy.

Later, Sutherland says the aim of treatment is to nourish stability and promote achievement and self-respect.

Thus health, like drama, is about doing, feeling and communicating. Drama has the added advantage that it allows rehearsal and experimentation during a temporary suspension of reality. In that respect it is allied to play as an agent of development and, like play, is not confined to children. Its appeal and effectiveness may lie in its ability to contact and exercise the normal and unaffected aspects of personality rather than those that are imparied by illness.

While the proof of the pudding lies in the eating (i.e. in its acceptability and effectiveness), there would seem to be at least a theoretical case for regarding drama as a therapeutic world parallel to that of real life. The language of the dramatherapist, in addition to its roots in drama, has been extended by ideas from sociology, dynamic and behavioural psychology and anthropology. It is the stronger for this knowledge which may give it an important advantage over theories derived essentially from the study of disease. Starting from pathology and working outwards towards normality, as do most of the medical sciences, does not necessarily give an unbiased view of what is normal. Working from a concept of drama as portraying normal life may provide an important counterbalancing and complementary function.

It we have to think about how a person becomes a patient, we must also think about how an actor, or director or, for that matter, a nurse, becomes a dramatherapist. There are, after all, a number of people from the dramatic arts who already work in institutions without styling themselves as therapists. 'SHAPE', 9 Fitzroy Square, London, W1P 6AE, Director: Seona Reid and HAI (Hospital Audiences, Inc.) 1540 Broadway, New York, NY 10036, and similar organisations facilitate the work of artists with the disabled and disadvantaged. If their work is of benefit to patients, how do they differ from those artists who style themselves formally as therapists? The answer to that question, in my mind, lies in that the creative *therapist* must have, at his command, a greater knowledge of the disabilities that he will encounter and of the specific and appropriate techniques in his own discipline that can be used in their remedy. In addition, he may benefit by learning other techniques culled from related therapies such as psychotherapy. This is not to say that the pure artist cannot contribute to the quality of life in hospitals, for he can, but the therapist must go further.

Techniques

The techniques of dramatherapy, detailed elsewhere in this book, have their parallels in conventional psychiatric practice. The warm-up, in this case it may be a game, is the initial encounter in which patient and therapist can size each other up and decide how to relate. Communication games, eye contact, trust exercises and creative exercises can be seen as the specific therapies exercised in a group or social setting. Thereafter there may be relaxation, de-roling and informal discussion comparable to the termination of an interview or treatment epoch, with all that that implies for resolving unfinished business and tensions. Like chess, there is an opening, a middle game and an ending. Many of the dramatherapeutic techniques are simple and non-threatening; they form the basic grammar of interaction. They are enjoyable, promote confidence and teach skills that are useful in other settings. If greater depths of feeling and intimacy are required, then more specific role play techniques, simulations, sociodrama and, in the greatest depth, classical Moreno psychodrama, can be used. The latter is a sophisticated and potent form of psychotherapy. The participants go through a similar three-stage period of warm-up, work and wind down. One of the group, the protagonist, emerges in the early stages as the central figure for that session and is encouraged to relive a personal experience or experiment with fantasy. Under the overall control of the therapist (director), he is aided by other members of the group who may perform auxiliary roles as doubles or play other persons in the drama. Although the emphasis is on the problems of the protagonist, the rest of the group, by identifying with him, have the opportunity to share their own experiences and reassure him that his feelings and problems are not unique (Blatner, 1973; Davies, 1978).

Who Are the Dramatherapists?

In order to answer this question some knowledge of the development of dramatherapy and psychodrama is required.

In the United Kingdom the work of Jennings, Sherbourne, Wiseman, Shuttleworth and others in the 1960s began particularly as an interest in remedial drama with children and moved outwards into wider fields. Other organisations, such as Sesame who originally worked in mime, developed in parallel. Art and music therapy were already established with their own criteria for competence and the progression to dramatherapy seemed in place.

Already in existence in the United States of America was a strong school of psychodrama originating from the work of Jacob Levy Moreno. Born in Bucharest (1892) and moving to Vienna at the age of five and to the USA at the age of 33 years, Moreno was a man of wide experience and learning. His formal studies included philosophy and medicine and his diverse interests included social action with the underprivileged, self-help groups, group psychotherapy, children's play, social psychiatry, theology and literature, including drama. From the Theatre of Spontaneity (1921–3) and its application to the treatment of individuals and small groups, psychodrama was born. In 1936 he established the Beacon Center in New York as a treatment clinic and theatre of psychodrama. (For further information see Blatner, 1973.) Although Moreno visited the UK in the immediate post-war years, little interest was shown there until the work of Davies, a British psychiatrist, and Marcia Karp, a Beacon-trained therapist now resident in the UK, brought it into greater prominence in the 1970s and a training centre was established by Karp at Holwell in North Devon.

The establishment of the British Association of Dramatherapy (now British Association for Dramatherapists) in 1977 and training courses in dramatherapy in St Albans in 1977, York in 1980 and Torquay in 1981, firmly established the dramatherapy movement while, at the same time, links were being established with the classical psychodramatists.

Dramatherapy is, in part, a skill and, in part, a professional activity in its own right. As a profession there is a growing need in the UK for a formal identity and a place formally within the policies of the two departments of health and social security (DHSS) and education and science (DES). No less is the need to develop an appropriate salary structure which is flexible enough to acknowledge that it is a skill for some and profession for others. Some will have entered professional dramatherapy with a previous training as nurses, occupational therapists or social workers. On transfer, their earlier professional skills will stand them in good stead, but they will need to acquire the additional skills and knowledge of drama. Others, who already possess a thorough training in drama, will have to acquire the basic knowledge of the caring professions. This is, in part, accomplished by theory, practice and placements during dramatherapy training courses, but may need to be further developed. On qualification a number of dramatherapists seek additional training in individual and group psychotherapies or in psychodrama. In the end, although all dramatherapists will have much in common, there will be differences depending upon skills acquired before or after their specific professional training.

Further developments being discussed include degree courses, probationary periods of practice before full qualification and the training and employment of aides.

Courses at present run on a one day per week day-release basis and supportive employment must be found for the two years of the course. The possibility of bursaries as occupational therapy or nursing aides for those coming directly from the arts, so that they may thereby increase their experience of practical caring, is worth exploring.

What Should Dramatherapists Know about Psychiatric Services?

Whatever the method by which services are managed and delivered, the therapist, if he or she is to work competently within them, will be well advised to study their organisation. In the United Kingdom, although many dramatherapists work outside the psychiatric and mental handicap components of the National Health Service, there is growth potential for dramatherapy in the service, even though current financial constraints will first have to be loosened. In any country increasing emphasis on treatment at home rather than in hospital will inevitably lead to more attention to family and social processes in support of the still essential biological and medical techniques.

It is this breadth of orientation that has led, certainly in the UK, to the development of a multiprofessional team as the unit of treatment. The consultant psychiatrist is still important in orchestrating and conducting the score, but there will be leaders in other sections of the orchestra as well as soloists. The creative therapist will have to play, and sometimes write, his own score (script) as part of the concerted effort of the orchestra (cast). If the team is to work together properly, certain basic skills and assumptions will need to be shared. Some will be derived from training and others from working together within the team. There must be some empathy with the rest of the orchestra as well as with the music. Full integration is not easy for new and junior professionals coming into a traditional, strange and rather frightening hospital, particularly when the music (patients) can be obscure and difficult. The traditional venue for such communication is the ward round or case conference which is, in most cases, not conducted by the bedside and not always in the presence of the patient. The process of bringing together the ideas of numerous discipline in such a setting is, itself, a creative art even if techniques and technology are used in practice. Without necessarily being an expert with all instruments, the artist will need to know something of the theory and techniques of other disciplines in the team. With some, such as psychotherapy and occupational therapy, there may be a degree of overlap; with others, for example a traditional medical or biological approach, these may be less distant. Where there is overlap there will need to be sufficient personal security not to feel threatened into a sense of rivalry with a profession with which there is, essentially, an affinity. The therapist must realise that within a team many roles will be blurred. Here the musical analogy of an orchestra may break down, but dramatherapists could perhaps translate the model into their own terms of 'company' and 'production', with their own symbolism.

Where, physically, does the team work? Mostly it is still in hospitals but, increasingly, some activities are moving nearer to the patients' homes although still remaining in secondary (specialist) care. Other rehabilitation processes are now undertaken by social services. Finally, there is no theoretical reason why some of the activities traditionally provided by the hospital-based service should not move entirely into primary care and be co-ordinated by general practitioners within the health centres rather than by consultants from the hospitals.

Management Structures

The structure of clinical operations must, however, be differentiated from that of management, often represented as a hard financial reality. The relationship of a dramatherapist to management is clouded by the issues of skill versus profession that have already been discussed. The politics of the debate are beyond the scope of the present work, but it is important for the dramatherapist that the issue is resolved. Many pure dramatherapists work comfortably in association with occupational therapy departments. Some in the UK practise within established National Health Service professions (e.g. occupational therapy), and yet others work in relative isolation. All will need professional support from their team colleagues, from like-minded professionals and from management if they are to function happily and effectively. There are few hospitals where more than one dramatherapist works and in such professional isolation it is important for management to realise that time will need to be devoted to travelling and keeping in touch with professional colleagues in the appropriate workshops and courses.

The therapists needs to know to whom she is clinically and managerially responsible and to understand something of the management structure of the organisation within which he works, be it either hospital or community orientated. Additionally, she should know something of the culture and community which she serves and how the public and the consumer make their voices heard. These social and organisational aspects of her life are no less important than skilled clinical considerations.

13 THE PATIENT, THE THERAPIST AND THE GOAL

Gordon E. Langley

It is clear that patients are not a homogeneous group. Even though they are individuals they need to be sub-classified in some way. Some, the mentally handicapped, have never been well-endowed mentally and in some cases physically also. Others, namely those suffering from the dementias of middle and late life, will have experienced riches in their personality but will have subsequently lost them. Yet others, while intellectually able, will be emotionally crippled or suffer from distortions in their emotions or thought processes, as in schizophrenia. In some, the very structure of the personality itself seems deranged. Any classification, like that of library shelves, is not absolute; it is the product of someone's mind. Just as the shelves guide us in our choice of history, biography or novels, so clinical classifications guide us within the mass of specific disabilities seen, serving at the same time as a guide to outcome and response to treatment. The dramatherapist will need to know something of this ordering of material but, nevertheless, should not lose the freshness of approach that comes from seeing a patient primarily as a whole person and responding to that part of his personality which is not disabled.

Some patients will get better, some will remain static and others will deteriorate. The therapist has to be prepared for the vicissitudes as well as the pleasures of his task and deal within himself with his reactions to success, failure and pressure. This can be no easy task and is one of the prime reasons for the professional and managerial support already noted as necessary.

At this point it is worth looking more closely at our attitudes to the conventional care-versus-cure dichotomy, in which value judgements are usually made in favour of cure. In these circumstances, if the care end of the spectrum is publicly and professionally devalued, it can also be neglected. It is one thing to respond positively to healing. It is another thing to maintain interest and morale in the face of continual exposure to incurable disabilities. That such problems can be resolved is, however, shown with great effect in the hospice movement for the care of the terminally ill. Psychiatry should respond no less.

There is, fortunately, another way of looking at the matter that avoids this uncomfortable and prejudicial dichotomy. For those patients with whom cure cannot be achieved, the question of the quality of their life becomes all important. Quality of life may be difficult to define in purely medical terms and one way of looking at it is to judge it in relation to Maslow's 'Hierarchy of Human Needs' (Maslow, 1943), as mentioned in Chapter 1 and shown in Table 13.1.

Table 13.1: Maslow's Theory of Human Motivation: Basic Needs and Goals

1	Physiological homeostasis	Food, rest, shelter, sex
2	Safety: physical and psychological	Protection from: threat, danger, deprivation
3	Love and social recognition	Belonging, association, giving and receiving friendship
4 (a)	Self-esteem	Coping
(b)	Esteem of others	Prestige
5	Self-actualisation	Being oneself, creative and inventive needs

In essence, the higher (numerical and valued) needs are the most vulnerable. When threatened, the individual's lower needs will be afforded priority. Satisfaction has to be worked for at all levels. We are rarely fully content and are usually reaching out for more. Some needs may be imperative; wants may have to wait for another day. Conventional medical hospital practice deals reasonably with levels 1 and 2, although even a hospital is not an entirely safe place to be in. In the higher realms, hospitals contribute less to the need for love, esteem, prestige and creative activity and can even be damaging in these areas. Some would say that hospitals are outmoded and should be dismantled, but as long as they are with us we have a responsibility for counteracting the worst of their effects. By all means let us rejoice in biological cures but let us also feel that helping our patients to satisfy their higher emotional needs is also satisfying professionally to ourselves. Once clinical stability has been achieved it may even be that, at these higher levels, patients can *give* us something rather than be continually receiving 'care'. In poetry, art and reminiscence they are already contributing to the social life in a number of hospital communities.

With this notion in mind we can now look at the care-versus-cure dichotomy in a different way (Table 13.2).

Table 13.2: A Hierarchy of Activities and Responses

1	Activity	Response	
1	Conventional medical treatment	'Cure' of symptoms	
2	Other treatments	'Cure' of symptoms	
3	Social interaction		*
4	Education	Personal growth	*
5	Enjoyment	Growth: pleasure	*

*also primary prevention? (see below)

Cure in the sense of conventional medical treatment is still necessarily at one end of the spectrum but at the other, instead of care, there is the idea of personal growth and creative activity. For some patients gains in these directions may be very humble, but they can still be appreciated and they are still more positive than the outmoded notion of 'care'. From what has already been said about the purpose and function of drama it should have much to contribute in these matters.

Prevention

Prevention is further aspect of medicine that may appeal to dramatherapists. It may occur at different levels. In its purest form it may prevent an illness ever occurring, as when inoculation may prevent diphtheria, flexibility in roles may prevent neurosis, etc. But avoiding a recurrence after an initial illness is also an aspect of prevention, e.g. avoiding re-infection or relief from family tensions after a crisis in which one family member became ill. Reducing the length of an illness or the disability caused by it is a third aspect of prevention; it is a way of preventing excess or protracted disability. It would seem possible in psychiatry that creative therapies have potential at all three levels by improving self-awareness and the individual's repertoire of interpersonal skills. Ideally, if these skills can be maintained, social breakdown as evidenced by admission to hospital can be prevented or delayed. If it occurs, however, then the rapid return of role function,

once the acute phase of an illness is past, is of the essence. At this point
the ideas of prevention merge with those of rehabilitation.

Rehabilitation

In social terms, rehabilitation can be seen as the restoration of role
function (see Chapter 6). Living in a normal community involves
playing many roles, for example those of worker, friend, family man,
worker for the community, hobbyist, etc. Each role commands a
degree of status and each involves us in a social network of
interactions that may be supportive, rejecting, ambivalent (or even
non-existent). Initially, the concept of rehabilitation in psychiatric
hospitals revolved principally around the work ethic but there is now
more to it than that. The effect of institutional attitudes in the ward can
be damaging, but equally, properly handled, the 'family' dynamics of the
ward community may be used therapeutically. There is then still the
question of how to manage one's personal leisure time and, in a
hospital setting, how to translate it all into the world outside with
its shops, clubs, churches and the wider community. Adequate role
performance requires that the role be defined and understood by the
persons expected to play it. Relevant skills will need to be acquired
and motivation secured. Role flexibility is held to be central to
dramatherapy (Jennings, 1982) and is the goal of many of the techniques
already described. Therefore it comes as no surprise to see that
dramatherapy is already used in the rehabilitation process in a number
of centres (Clark, 1981a, b; Scoble, 1978).

Before leaving rehabilitation, some words of caution are needed
for the over-enthusiastic. Rehabilitation is not necessarily related to
discharge from hospital. Let us call that resettlement, to distinguish
it from the rehabilitation of those patients who may never leave, but
who may still be helped to perform at their best, however grave their
disability. Looked at this way, all patients are capable of rehabilitation,
including those with protracted terminal illnesses. The concept of
rehabilitation in these circumstances becomes very similar to that of
'quality of life' that has already been discussed. Therapists should be
prepared to recognise that what to them may seem simple work and
limited progress is nevertheless significant for the patient and
worthwhile for themselves. There is much work to be done at this
rather humble end of the spectrum.

Even if a patient is discharged he may not be rehabilitated in the full sense of being integrated with local communities. Resettlement without integration is no more than moving him to a smaller institution. Less than full community integration is still all that some patients can achieve and for them discharge may still be worthwhile if an appropriate range of supportive day centres and work opportunities can be provided. The enjoyment, motivation and skills that come from dramatherapy would be well placed in day centres working in this way.

Dramatherapy in Clinical Practice

In clinical practice dramatherapists currently work in three main areas in the psychiatric and mental handicap services (Mitchell, 1982).

(1) With acute patients in admission wards.
(2) In the rehabilitation of the long-stay and not so long-stay psychotic patients.
(3) In special areas: e.g. with the elderly, with children, adolescents, drug abusers, etc.
I would also add a fourth category, namely:
(4) Staff development and training.

Each area presents its own problems.

(1) Acute Admission Wards

Acute admission wards take a wide variety of patients with divergent disabilities. Some will be disruptive to groups by reason of psychotic or antisocial conduct. Others will come and go rapidly and all will be subject to many other influences. Continuous and developing work in such a setting is well nigh impossible yet dramatherapy groups are active on a number of admission wards so, surprisingly, there must be some benefits. These would seem to be:

(1) As the open and short-stay nature of the group restricts the level of involvement to basic drama, the groups are enjoyable and non-threatening. There is not a lot of deep personal work and subsequent acting out does not occur. The groups are seen as 'the nice side of treatment' (see below).
(2) The groups are shared by other caring staff, such as nurses and occupational therapists, who see their patients in a more positive light than on the ward and who can gain an impression of function.

The group is therefore valued by these staff for assessment
purposes.

(3) It may act as a shop window for dramatherapy and give those
patients who take to the technique an insight into its nature
and potential for further development in a separate setting if
they so wish. Similarly, staff may learn something of the
techniques and seek further experience or training.

As to its disadvantages, working for ever at the simple end of the
spectrum prevents the progression to more personal work that would
occur in a closed group. This disadvantage can be offset by providing
closed groups to which the patient can go both during the admission
period and, if necessary, after discharge. The merging of in-patients
and day patients can be helpful in its own right.

Difficulties can also arise over acutely disturbed psychotic or
acutely depressed patients. While their management in a dramatherapy
setting may not be impossible, they are not for the noviciate and
good staff support and continuity with those caring for the patient
after the group are essential.

(2) The Long-stay Patient

The general theory of rehabilitation has already been considered but,
in the main, there are two groups of long-stay psychotic patients in
mental hospitals: those who have been resident for very many years
and those who, even with modern and active treatment, remain in
hospital because of residual disabilities. These patients are sometimes
referred to, unelegantly, as 'new chronics'. Although the disabilities
are similar, socially they pose rather different problems. In both groups
many will have disturbances of their body image, will be shy socially
and unsure of their sexuality. Some cannot contain their ambivalence
to life and paranoid (hostile or grandiose) mechanisms will be seen.
For the use of voice, awareness of body image, social skills,
management of difficult situations and the promotion of coping, esteem
and natural self-expression are all areas where the dramatherapist can
make a contribution. With the mentally handicapped movement, rhythm
and bodily awareness seem particularly important.

(3) Specialist Groups

I can only speak personally of work with the elderly and other authors
must deal in detail with other sub-groups. Some illustrative accounts in
the literature of work with other groups are provided by Fairclough

(1977), Wright (1978), Bracegirdle (1979), Langley, D.M. (1979b) and Edmunds (1982a).

With the elderly, the place of drama in reminiscence, reality orientation and life review has been dealt with in Chapter 10. The importance of being satisfied with limited goals has also been stressed. Multiple disability is the rule rather than the exception in the over 75s in whom the movement aspects of dramatherapy can provide important and pleasurable, physical as well as emotional, treatment. Both physical and intellectual activity are said to improve intellectual performance, so that dramatherapy will be helpful in a general and non-specific way. Body image disorders may occur after strokes and provide a more directly useful place for movement techniques.

Concern is sometimes expressed at asking the elderly to play games for fear that it is patronising. Dramatherapists do not need to be told of the importance of play in human development, but they will need to make their point to both their patients and their colleagues. As in reminiscence, wherever possible, provide the opportunity for patients to make contributions. They probably receive enough essential help for their dependencies anyway and a chance to give is refreshing. Choice is another element that may be limited and providing a decision is within the patient's level of ability, opportunities should be created in which choice can be exercised. There is, however, a great deal of emotional pain involved in coming to terms with ageing and disability so that denial and hostile projections onto institutions and therapists alike will need to be recognised and acknowledged. The expression of these emotions in a non-judgemental atmosphere may go a long way to securing the resolution of the conflicts posed.

The Neuroses. These are hardly a separate group in the sense used above but perhaps do justify some individual comment. Dramatherapy is not entirely psychotherapy (Jennings, 1978), but that part which is will mostly be directed towards the psychoneuroses and will include drama therapeutic and psychodramatic techniques. Styles of psychotherapy are changing and the therapist is now less of a passive screen and is moving towards a more conscious and acknowledged interaction with his patient. Dramatherapy and psychodrama extend this trend from emotional involvement into physical action, including doubling, role reversal and sculpting. At the same time the emphasis on intrapsychic events is being replaced by interest in the individual and his roles in life, particularly within the family. In this respect, classical psychodrama is related to sociology and to personal construct and systems theory

(Davies, 1979). Just how far the dramatherapist can move from pure drama into these newer psychotherapies will depend on his training, but his general orientation certainly seems in keeping with the move towards the more active participation of the therapist.

(4) Staff Development

Just as dramatherapeutic techniques may help patients to understand their own place in social systems, so they may also help staff to work through the problems posed by patients and by the organisational structure in which they work. In both these areas group dynamics and counter-transference phenomena may be prominent and an opportunity to vent and share feelings away from normal line management hierarchies could well help to prevent the periodic breakdowns in institutional organisation that surface as public enquiries. It can be looked on and has been practised as training (Shuttleworth, 1977; Langley, D.M., 1981) but it can also be seen as an operational necessity when pressures are particularly acute and negative feelings prominent (Cantle, 1980).

Selection of Patients

Within the complexity of skills and problems described above, some selection by therapists of patients is necessary, but as yet the criteria for selection are more intuitive than defined. Dramatherapists, in their own gatherings, frequently partake of their own medicine in order to share new skills and keep old ones alive. Less commonly do they define the type of patients with whom they work, or communicate their results.

The commonest selection process at the moment is,that within a very broad and general remit from doctors, dramatherapists will get together with their nursing and remedial colleagues and suggest certain patients for the dramatherapy session. In admission wards one suspects that this is more by a process of excluding those who are too sick. The patient's consent is of the essence so, in so far as he may choose whether to participate, there is an element of self-selection. Choice by therapists may be exercised more on the basis of personality than of symptoms but the picture is still confusing. Some therapists feel that patients who consciously use body language and non-verbal communication are appropriate, others think that introverted people may find release. An artistic mind or background may help but is not

essential. Once involved at the shallow end, those patients who take to
the medium may self-select themselves for further 'in depth' work.
Whatever the starting level, the therapist will need to be perceptive
about those patients who are too sick really to be able to participate and,
for others, will need to gauge the rate at which they can progress. All
therapy is a creative art and is largely a matter of judging, as the old
shaving cream advertisements used to say, whether the lather is 'not
too much, not too little but just right'.

The Nice End of Treatment

It has been suggested that the creative therapies made contact with and
indeed overlap with the verbal psychotherapies and perhaps even with
the more medically orientated psychiatric treatments. For the artist the
additional urge to be a therapist may pose dangers that are not at first
apparent. Art, in the finished product if not the act of creation, is
about wholeness, beauty, balance and emotional enrichment. The
observer becomes involved with the mind of the artist. Though
pleasurable, the message is essentially serious. For example, who could
not enjoy and be entertained by the recent play *Children of a Lesser
God* even though it made a sensitive and serious statement about the
need to come to terms with disability, in this case deafness. Although
pure theatre and good box office it is also potentially therapeutic and
not just for the deaf. Life, like drama, is about conflict and its resolution
into harmony; discord is resolved; uncertainty is replaced by security;
homeostasis is restored. There is, on the one hand, the work, discomfort
and risk of the creative process and, on the other, the relaxation and
pleasure derived from the final product.

Conventional treatment is not normally regarded as pleasurable.
The medicine has to have a nasty taste, the operation makes us sore,
psychoanalytic uncovering may be challenging and reveal primitive,
negative emotions that we would rather disown. This is not the stuff
for a night out or the conventional audience's response to art. It may
be more akin to the pains of creation within the artist as he struggles
to express himself. Sickness in itself can be awful, be it from fragmented
limbs or egos. Perhaps it is the parallel between the difficulties of
treatment and the pressures of creation that makes the artist want to
become a therapist; he feels that he has been there before. He senses
that he can help the patient, but until evaluative studies are undertaken
this is largely an intuitive reaction. He is sure of his art, music, drama

and pictorial but, in addition, feels that he must justify himself as a therapist by getting involved in the more conventional, messy end of treatment that is usually left to doctors, nurses, psychologists and social workers. It is right for him so to be involved but he must not belittle the effect of his pure art in its own right. To stay with the previous analogy, certainly there are times when the immediate active intervention of surgery is required and the patient remains passive. There is also the recovery process when the object of rehabilitation is to lead the patient, increasingly from his own efforts, back to normal life. In this process a representation of normality and of the ability to resolve conflict, as presented by the artist, may act as a useful model of the goal and a focus around which fragmented personalities can reform. The artist is reaching inward towards the recovering patient and truly assisting him to pull through and back into a social world from which he had temporarily departed.

14 THE ROLE OF THE DRAMATHERAPIST

Recent Changes

Dramatherapy has come a long way since the days of the remedial drama centre (see Chapter 12). There is a demand for dramatherapy posts to be created and more students are training in order to become full-time dramatherapists rather than use drama skills in their own discipline. Until now, appointments and salaries in the UK have been negotiated on an *ad hoc* basis but the growth of its use and wider understanding by other disciplines has created a need to negotiate salaries and terms of employment on a national scale. In order to do this there have inevitably been changes. Perhaps the most important is the entry into full membership of the British Association for Dramatherapists. (formerly 'of Dramatherapy'). Originally, people who had completed a certain number of hours of drama training and personal group training could apply to the BAODth and on approval by the executive committee, become full members. Associate membership was for people who did not want to call themselves dramatherapists but had an interest in the association. The latter has not changed. However, as the training courses became established, more people applied for full membership after completing a course than by the less formal entry of hours completed. In order to negotiate terms, a method of training will have to be established which shows evidence of clinical expertise to a standard acceptable to the Whitley Council.

With this in view informal membership has had to cease and full membership becomes available only to those who have completed an approved course. Each of these courses has an external assessor, who monitors the standard of training and is available for consultation by the tutors via the training committee and sets out guidelines for training. Consequently, the association and its function is changing from that of informal contact to a supportive professional body. This may be regretted by some but it is necessary in order to meet the demands of an emergent profession.

The Practice of Dramatherapy

During the last decade, dramatherapy appointments have been created.

Some of these are in schools, have evolved from remedial drama and are still regarded as part of the educational system. Yet there is a difference between the role of the drama teacher and that of the dramatherapist, although there is common ground. A teacher is by definition employed to teach and even if she is using the medium of drama to encourage personal development she is ultimately responsible for teaching skills which may involve examinations. One could argue that both teacher and therapist are teaching the skills of living. That may be so and I am sure such discussion will go on for a long time yet. However, being a teacher implies the teaching of skills towards a certain standard and self-knowledge is secondary to the learning of those skills. Therapy employs the skills primarily for insight and the resolution of conflicts and has secondary benefits in personal growth. There is no accumulating of skills in order to produce written work or achieve a standard. Effective therapy is giving the experience in which a client can learn to understand and come to terms with his individual needs. Standards of education and the acquiring of knowledge are irrelevant. Brightwell (1979) says that it is impossible to be both teacher and therapist to the same pupil. There is a need to define roles.

Appointments of dramatherapists in hospitals and day centres have been equally haphazard. Most have started to work as part of occupational therapy departments and there are certain advantages in this. There is the support of an established professional role, the availability of its resources and the opportunity to work in close co-operation with other trained professionals. Some hospitals also employ art and music therapists to form creative art departments and a co-ordinated framework for therapy. The main disadvantage of this seems to be the limitations that may be imposed by the parent department. If, as trained therapists, we are capable of planning and carrying out a course of treatment for an individual or group, should we not also have the responsibility of running and developing our own department? I am in this position and there may be others whom I have not met. Whilst I value the autonomy and professional freedom it gives me, I have had no one within the department with whom I could discuss matters on equal terms. There has been no strength of members to support my request for accommodation and equipment and no budget which I could allocate personally. Every need has been presented to a committee for a decision and all salary negotiations have been my own responsibility. If I had not embarked on this with a recognised qualification, which gave me some status in the hospital, had considerable experience of work in hospitals and knowledge of their hierarchies, I do not think I could have survived. Despite the difficulties, it was right for me and I have always had a reasonable hearing even if the response was sometimes a refusal!

It was not easy to be taken seriously at first, especially as originally my skills were limited and I had only a vague idea of how to apply them. Movement sessions with the elderly were acceptable and I spent a few years developing these before venturing into other branches of the hospital. Sometimes I have been asked to work in specific areas; other times I have seen a need and asked to try and meet it. There is always more work than one part-time person can possibly do alone. I was told on appointment that my time could be spent in client practice or staff training at my discretion and my role has been changing constantly. At the moment it is that of innovator and supervisor except for psychodrama groups. This was a choice governed by the need to 'spread myself thin'. I find staff training and client groups equally enjoyable and challenging, but time does not allow long-term work with any particular group at the moment. Treatment of clients and training of others are both components of the role of dramatherapist as I see it.

Group Facilitator

The dramatherapist's major responsibility is to the group with which she is involved at the moment. The therapy is rooted in what is happening 'here and now' to a group of people. Within that setting, individuals are experiencing their own particular drama. If one person is disturbed by the experience and requires individual attention, then a conflict arises for the therapist. Does one tend the needs of the individual or those of the group? Usually it is possible to deal with the situation in the context of the group, who will be supportive and maybe contribute towards a solution. This is the ideal, but people do not always conform to ideals! The most difficult situation is if someone leaves the room in a disturbed state. Does the therapist follow or stay and help the group deal with the feelings of loss, rejection, anger, etc., that the action has provoked in them? One person's impulsive behaviour can have a disturbing effect on the others.

I feel my responsibility is to the group and to avoid such a conflict, I always work with another member of staff present. If an individual client needs special attention, then the co-therapist can deal with it whilst I attend to the group needs. This applies regardless of the status of the co-therapist. There have been times when, by virtue of my training in counselling, I was better equipped than the helper to deal with the individual problem, but I was present as a group therapist and not counsellor. A good relationship with charge nurse or head occupational therapist ensures that further help is available for both client and co-therapist if necessary. Students frequently act as co-therapists and it is important that they can have the support of trained staff who may not be present in the group. It is my responsibility to ensure that every group member has an opportunity to express and deal with feelings arising from the session, so adequate time for closing is necessary (see section on starting a group). However, the role of group facilitator means that I am not available to clients for personal counselling. Anything that cannot be discussed in the group must be referred to a nurse, social worker, doctor, etc., whose role includes that of counsellor. The fact that a co-therapist is present makes an immediate link, especially is she is someone to whom the client can go direct. There are two reasons for my insistence on this:

(1) Some clients manipulate the group leader into a situation of being 'special' to them. In doing so the client manages to evade personal work through the group process, which is the purpose of group therapy and may also destroy the relationship existing between other members.
(2) My time is limited by the number of sessions for which I am employed. If I spend too long with one individual, then the balance is disturbed and other groups may be affected.

This does not mean that I am unsympathetic to individual needs and the difficulty some clients have in talking about their problems. There have been occasions when I have accompanied a client to a charge nurse or doctor to give support in the initial stages of a difficult interview. My role then was that of team member, becoming a bridge between group and individual therapy. One these occasions I was not present in order to speak for the client but to be a silent support, at most clarifying difficult issues.

Team Member

I do not make any claims for dramatherapy as a total therapy. It has a wide scope and I believe can be of value to everyone. It should always be viewed in the context of treatment as a whole. It can be part of a rehabilitation programme and alongside occupational therapy, home management and industrial rehabilitation can play its part in total rehabilitation. If used in social skills training, dramatherapy can help in the treatment and rehabilitation of both neurotic and psychotic clients. It can be the major group therapy in which a client is involved, yet we must consider other factors too. The client may see doctors, social workers or psychologists in regular therapy sessions. The shift from a difficult situation into a hospital ward or the attention and interest shown as a day or out-patient will all have an effect on the client. So we have an added responsibility to the team of professionals who undertake the total care of the client.

Team Meetings

Wherever we work, it is unlikely that we are isolated from a team, however small that may be. If working in a hospital, then it is likely that the team will meet either in a general team meeting to discuss clients and administration, or in ward rounds and case conferences to consider the care of individual clients. The importance of these meetings should not be underestimated. It is in our clients' interest, as well as our own, that we should not only attend but participate in the meetings. We have an opportunity to see clients in a situation that is unique to dramatherapy in which creativity, imagination and past experience are all brought together in an experience which is happening 'here and now'. Their behaviour may be very different than in other settings and there may be surprises for us. Only once have I asked for a client to be excluded from a continuation group. I felt I had no working relationship with him, he saw no need to change and no point in the dramatherapy group, his behaviour was disruptive and held the rest of the group 'frozen' in the 'What's this all about?' stage. I was astounded to hear the referring doctor say 'The nurses have reported a marked improvement in his attitude and behaviour on the ward since attending your group'. This was an aspect of his behaviour I had not seen!

I have referred to the diverse opinions of psychiatry, which can cause problems if the team is not in agreement. If we are working with colleagues, whose views are not the same as ours, we have to tolerate them. The medical practice of interviewing clients in front of all team members is an added stress for them which some professionals feel unnecessary. Others see it as the most direct way of deciding a course of treatment and of teaching students in the team. They are not necessarily uncaring and insensitive to the client's needs. Boycotting meetings of which we disapprove or using them as a platform to express our controversial views does not help our clients. Physical treatments and team hierarchies can be another source of disagreement. Dramatherapists are a new and developing profession and have to earn the respect of colleagues. Our attitude to our established professional colleagues must be as tolerant as to our clients — accepting the person or role, if not the opinions that go with them. Dramatherapists may be regarded with curiosity and may be ridiculed by some people and it is only by behaving in a professional and competent manner ourselves that our special form of therapy will be accepted. If our feelings are so strong that we cannot contain them, then we should look for a place of work in which we can agree with the views and methods of our colleagues.

My personal experience has been in a hospital setting. The training I received as a psychiatric social worker gave me an understanding of the medical viewpoint and the environment in which I practise. We each need a model for working and find the one that is most suited to us individually. A strictly medical viewpoint may not be sufficient to meet all our clients' needs but provides a broader frame of reference than is sometimes attributed to it. I view the diagnostic categories not as a rigid classification of people with medical labels but as a kind of shorthand. Without labels there would be no discussion (Jones, 1982). The hierarchies are a structure for the sharing of responsibilities and allocation of roles. It would be chaos if every member of staff was expected to perform every task. Specialisation is an economic use of resources. Teamwork provides a broad selection of therapies for the client and support for the staff. Whilst I am happy to plan a course of dramatherapy for a group or an individual, I do not desire or feel qualified to take the final responsibility for the total treatment, which may be a life or death one if the client is suicidal or homicidal. Working under medical hierarchies relieves me of this burden yet allows freedom for me to make decisions at a level at which I feel capable.

Informal Contact

Whilst the team meetings are important, informal contact should not be ignored. Time spent 'dropping in' to the ward office or occupational therapy department can develop relationships, clarify issues and facilitate the smooth running of client groups. It can sometimes give a new perspective for therapy. I called in at the day centre office one Monday lunchtime to find the staff concerned by the number of people who needed counselling after difficult weekends. They felt there was not enough time to give adequate attention to each. 'Why not form a group?' I suggested jokingly. When we discussed the matter seriously, we found a group of women, all experiencing difficulties in their feminine role, who coped by attendance at the day hospital during the week but found their weekends difficult to manage. So began a Monday morning role-play group which solved the staffing problem and laid a foundation for a series of graded group experiences. This was in the days before 'women's groups' became popular and developed from an internal need rather than external political pressure!

Dramatherapy is new to many people and because it is not understood can be threatening. Informal contact can help to allay these fears and win the support and confidence of colleagues.

Information

All clients treated in hospital settings have written records of treatment. These are available to qualified staff and contain a variety of information. Personally, all I ask initially is:

(1) Is the client likely to have a psychotic episode?
(2) Is he liable to impulsive or aggressive behaviour?
(3) Is he potentially suicidal?

In this way I approach individuals with an open mind, uninfluenced by others' comments or by the client's own history. Later, if I need specific information I usually ask for it rather than read through a file with much that is irrelevant to me. If I feel the need for information, I ask myself 'Why? What purpose will this information serve?' If it is to satisfy my own curiosity, then I have no right to ask. It is not within my role to pry into other people's lives, behaviour, emotions or fantasies for voyeuristic reasons. I prefer to gain an understanding of the client as he unfolds it to me. In this way I know I am moving at his pace and allowing him to participate at the level he chooses. To probe unnecessarily may precipitate him into a situation in which he is out of his depth. This does not mean that I never seek information. If it is relevant I usually ask 'Would you like to tell us more about this?' or 'Would it help to enlarge on what you said about . . .?' It could be argued that opportunities could be lost by my ignorance of events but I think the client will disclose important issues when he is ready. I can only facilitate work on what he is prepared to give.

Although hospital notes are highly confidential, I do not write in them myself, usually preferring less formal verbal exchange. Any information I pass on to colleagues is usually general in nature. 'He worked on his conflict with his mother' or 'He worked well in the group and I have not seen the disruptive behaviour you mentioned'. If it is a matter of personal information, such as previously unexpressed suicidal thoughts or some aspect of a relationship that seems relevant to his treatment, I try to persuade the client himself to report the information to the appropriate member of staff (charge nurse, doctor), if necessary giving him moral support. If a client is unwilling to do this, I ask permission to give the information myself. There has been no occasion when the client has refused either of these options, but in that event there would still be the co-therapist who is aware of the information and could counsel the client privately after a group session. The nature of the dramatic experience is such a private one that I feel complete trust in the confidentiality of both group members and leaders to be absolutely essential and binding.

Staff Training

At present dramatherapy is young and those who practise it have difficulty in meeting all the client needs that are presented. There is scope for professionals to use dramatherapy within their own discipline, but unless they have experienced it elsewhere, they will need both dramatherapy experience and supervision and support to practise extensively. I have tried various ways to cover training needs and have found a pattern that seems to work that is adaptable enough to include new openings as they arrive. I have organised on-going evening training groups, weekend workshops and day release courses which have been directed by drama teachers and specialists not employed by the hospital. I have taught basic drama as an in-service course weekly over six weeks as well as advanced on-going groups. My present scheme is to organise one-day in-service workshops in introductory, intermediate and advanced dramatherapy. These are

complete in themselves and solve the problem of disruption of the group
by duty rosters. They provide a continuity for individuals but not a
stable group progression. The introductory day covers basic drama,
games and examples of their use. The intermediate day is about roles,
role play and its uses. The advanced days are on specialised subjects.
A local branch of the BAODth provides additional one-day specialist
workshops which extend the group membership beyond the immediate
hospital personnel and bring in workshop leaders from other sources.

In addition, I work regularly with student nurses in their bloc
training. All nurses will have an opportunity of experiencing
dramatherapy and may develop a special interest during their normal
course of training. In future this should eliminate the need frequently
to explain dramatherapy and its uses to my nursing colleagues. Staff
training groups present a dilemma. Do we teach techniques and supply
ideas or do we aim to give a meaningful experience to the group? I
have tried both approaches and have come to the conclusion that the
experience is of more value than techniques. The expectations of the
group are important and so is the overall period of training available.
It is useful to see each particular session in the context of a whole. If
I am not likely to meet the group again, emphasis on techniques,
ideas and suggestions is necessary to give a comprehensive picture or
if there is much resistance from the group and it is a short-term one,
I hope that people who are interested in the practice will look for
further experience. I move at a slower pace, entering into the
experience in more depth with those groups whom I will meet over
a series of training sessions. The depth of experience is determined
by the group. If trust and a cohesive group are established quickly,
then we move into the realms of experience. Staff who are using drama
for the first time are often unsure of themselves. I offer to join the
first six sessions as a group member to support and supervise the
leader. I do not take the group myself as I feel it is important to
develop an individual way of handling the group. Each therapist must
lead in the way she feels most comfortable and I do not want
to model a 'right' way. What is right for me may not be appropriate
for others. We plan sessions together and discuss them afterwards
but the presentation and leadership of the group is with the
trainee.

Some hospitals are able to offer staff support groups and this is ideal.
I have done this in the past but at present my work schedule does not
allow it. I am always available for individual consultation and the
BAODth branch workshops offer an opportunity to share ideas and

problems with others. Unlike the client groups, I feel my role includes
that of counsellor in staff training. Any group matters must be dealt
with in the group but personal matters involving conflicts outside the
group context are another matter. Many people do not want colleagues
to know their private problems and this I respect. Training sessions in
the hospital vary. Some are part of a nurse or occupational therapy
training programme and I do not think staff should be expected to
explore personal problems in a compulsory training situation. Other
training days do not have continuous group membership and one cannot
always achieve a deep level of involvement and group trust in a short
session. I feel my responsibilities are to deal with any feelings that
may have arisen during the session. If it is necessary to do this privately,
I make time immediately the session has finished. Then I can suggest
people or groups to whom staff can go for personal work — a
counsellor within the hospital, a staff psychodrama group or
professional contacts I have outside work. Unlike clients, staff do
not always have a clear structure for seeking help and often feel they
should be able to deal with all their own conflicts themselves! I
believe one of the responsibilities of training in psychiatric work is to
acknowledge that we all have difficulties, both personal and professional,
and make available any information on where the therapist goes for
therapy!

Education

The difference between training and education is one of theory and
practice. The reaction when a child comes home from school and tells
you that he has received sex education is likely to be different than if
he tells you he has received sex training at school! Broadly speaking,
education is the learning of theory and skills and training is the practical
application of those skills. There are many colleagues — doctors, nursing
officers, senior staff as well as junior members — who will not want
to practise dramatherapy or be involved as co-therapists, and who ask
'What is dramatherapy?' There are many opportunities for informal
explanations. Talks to groups of people not only save time but allow
for some experiential learning. If asked to talk to a group, I usually
explain that I prefer to involve people if possible. I then present a
mixture of talk and games to demonstrate a point. There are
generally some people who are happy to volunteer for games, etc., and

the whole group is usually involved by the end of the session. The danger is that some people may feel embarrassed or conspicuous, so adequate discussion time is essential. Writing is another teaching tool and papers published in journals, the hospital newsletter or even notes for specific groups of people can help others to understand the methods.

Liaison

The dramatherapist is a link between artist, therapist and the medium of drama. The increased use of volunteers in hospitals and the creation of organisations like SHAPE has brought artists into regular contact with clients. If they are to work effectively, the artists need to be able to turn to a therapist for guidance and support. Sometimes ward staff are able to give time to volunteers but in understaffed wards with nurses working in shifts, regular contact may not be possible. The dramatherapist should be in touch with clients needs throughout the hospital and be available for consultation in the placing and support of actors and drama teachers who come into the hospital. Contact with amateur dramatic societies, Women's Institutes, students from local drama courses and professional teachers and actors can be an important part of the dramatherapist's work. I contacted sources of possible voluntary help when appointed ten years ago and am still approached by artists (usually students) who want to work on a project involving the disabled.

There is one college of further education that regularly sends students to me during their second term. I meet the students and talk about the clients they are to work with and then accompany them during their project. A weekly visit by a group of young people is a novelty and a stimulation in itself for the clients. The limited period of the project ensures that neither clients nor students tire of each other's company, ward staff on long-stay wards appreciate the interest and it is a stimulating and learning experience for all concerned. Other students come as groups or individuals for a varied number of sessions. They gain material and experience for their studies and the clients enjoy the sessions. It is a reciprocal arrangement which brings contact with youth and the world outside. It also helps break down the barriers of fear and ignorance that often surround psychiatric illness. The dramatherapist understands the medium which the volunteer is using as well as the client's need, and so acts as a liaison between the two.

Drama/Therapist

Although volunteers are accepted in hospitals, their methods are
sometimes foreign to ward staff. Dramatherapists should be in a
position to interpret what the volunteer is doing and the value to the
client. The therapist herself may have experienced the anxiety and
hostility that can be aroused by ignorance of the applications of the
arts in therapy. Most volunteers find both client and environment
unfamiliar and the added stress of staff who do not appreciate the
potential of their art form can be destructive. The dramatherapist
should be available to act as a liaison between the art form itself
and therapists from other disciplines.

Where Next?

Already dramatherapists are moving away from strictly therapeutic
roles into other areas. Some are working with young people in youth
clubs, with the unemployed, with ethnic groups, children with school
problems, the elderly in residential homes and day centres,
'Wellwoman Clinics', etc. The term therapy implies the healing of
sickness, so do clients in these new fields of work have to be termed
sick in order to have the attention of the dramatherapist?
Courtney (1979) refers to two dimensions of language which are
grounded in experience at earlier levels. Any gaps in this experience
puts people at a disadvantage. At this point we are beginning to move
into the world of personal development and hopefully prophylaxis.
The same skills that are used to restore equilibrium and gain help can
be used to prevent gross imbalance in times of crisis. The field is
wide open, but just as we need to learn the impact of drama on those
who are not disabled before we can apply it as treatment, so also
we need knowledge of disability in order to apply our skills
preventively.

Who Can Benefit from Dramatherapy?

In my experience everyone can enjoy drama provided it is presented
at the appropriate level. If the therapeutic application is at the same
level and the rate of progress adjusted accordingly, then I believe that
all our clients can benefit from it. When working with brain damaged,

severely demented or mentally handicapped people, I sometimes ask the question 'Where is the drama in this?' Wagner (1979) says that all but very damaged or psychotic people have the ability to identify and through this can gain new insight by the dramatic process. How are we to know when identification has not or cannot be reached? Does there have to be some comprehension and at what point does drama begin?

Courtney (1979) says that drama exists in the act of spontaneous performance. So, can we call the movements a client makes when copying the therapist spontaneous performance? Imagination is an essential part of drama and we cannot say whether a client is using his imagination creatively; however, something is certainly required to 'mirror' the action. If the action is not part of everyday life, then it can be viewed as spontaneous. Bowskill (1973) points out that whilst spontaneity does not always result in meaning, creativity cannot happen without it. In dealing with clients who are so disabled that they are maybe unaware of even basic needs, we can only use primitive forms of drama such as rhythm, movement, ritual and play at their particular level. If there is a spark of imagination or spontaneity, then creativity is possible and with it drama. Whether this is used in the strict therapeutic sense of treatment or in the broader one of enrichment is unimportant. Anything that can be done to improve the quality of life is worth while (Langley, G.E., 1982) and for the very disabled drama, as the basis of all art forms (Courtney, 1979), is the only medium which can reach them. The more profoundly disabled the client the fewer means are available for communication and enrichment. Although there may be little evidence of achievement, the time which a dramatherapist spends at this level of work is of equal importance as time spent with clients who are capable of more obvious responses. She learns to set limited goals, the achievement of which is as valid and rewarding as for any other group.

15 SOME OTHER CONSIDERATIONS

Who Can Do Dramatherapy?

Any trained therapist can take a drama course and begin to apply the new skills in therapy. Some hospitals have inservice training schemes. The British Association for Dramatherapists organises courses at both national and regional levels and will supply the names of people approved to direct workshops. The British Association of Occupational Therapy includes drama in some of their national and regional conferences. If the therapist has no administrative support to go to dramatherapy courses, most local authorities offer drama classes in their evening further education programmes. It is possible to apply the techniques almost immediately and confidence to experiment comes as skills increase.

People with drama training are welcome in the therapy setting. Actors, drama teachers, students, directors and technicians can all apply the skills in which they have been trained. There is a need for this, particularly in institutions where clients have been deprived of creative development. I would like to encourage any artists who are interested to take their place alongside the therapist. It is important for all concerned to be aware that these helpers are bringing skills in ways which may not be seen as therapeutic. Clients can experience the satisfaction of acquiring skills and self-expression in the broad sense of 'therapy' in the same way that any member of a further education class or drama group does. This is a valuable experience and should not be underestimated. The application of drama as used in treatment should be left to the trained therapist and not undertaken by untrained people.

Confusion can arise when a drama teacher or actor, working in a clinical setting, or a therapist with some drama skills, is termed a dramatherapist. Only someone who has taken an approved course or who is fully trained in both drama and therapy is qualified to practise unsupervised. People who are inadequately trained in either speciality can find themselves unable to meet the expectations demanded of the role of the dramatherapist. An example would be an excellent teacher who is termed 'therapist' after working in a hospital situation for some years. Her written and verbal exchanges indicate that she does not really understand the therapeutic process. This devalues her in the eyes of her colleagues, yet as a teacher she had earned their respect. Similarly, a therapist who displays a lack of drama skills or knowledge can debase the professional expertise of dramatherapy.

Training

How Do I Become a Dramatherapist?

This is a question I am frequently asked. There have been informal ways in the past but the pattern is changing and the trend in the future will be through an approved course. Drama and therapy are such vast subjects that intensive training is required for each. It is unrealistic to expect every dramatherapist to be exhaustively trained as both therapist and dramatist, but the training must be sufficiently broad to provide basic competence in both. In the United Kingdom there are, at present, three courses approved by the British Association for Dramatherapists. These are two-year part-time day release courses. The students are expected to be working in a situation which allows for the practical application of their subject during training, the theory and practice being developed in parallel. Applicants are selected from trained therapists (nurses, occupational therapists, social workers, etc.), who have some knowledge of drama and people with a theatre or drama training, who have some experience of work in therapy. So we are faced with the dual problem of teaching drama to the therapist and therapy to the dramatist to a level at which they can work with confidence and expertise. As drama is a group activity, the therapist should also have training in group therapy. It cannot be assumed that a therapist will have had specific training in group dynamics. Although she may have worked in groups, relatively few therapists have experience of psychodynamic exploration of group processes within their basic training. Our task, as tutors, is to offer an adequate training in all three — which is no small undertaking!

Drama

An understanding of the process of drama, its power and uses, experience of all aspects of drama, theatre in practice and knowledge of the theory behind it are fundamental. We can only hope to give a wide basic training which develops interest and stimulates people to go on to other specialised courses. The subject is so wide that there is every opportunity for people to follow their own interests and apply them in therapy. Dramatherapy is as individual as each person practising it. Drama is an experience and it is difficult to impart the nature of that verbally, so much of the student's time is spent in practical sessions. The development from games to improvisation and role play is basic to the drama training and students learn the potential for change through personal experience. Theatre must not be neglected. Visits to the theatre and critical discussion are necessary to recognise the value of being a member of an audience. Some students will not have taken part in a theatre production; therefore a dramatic presentation is included in the course. This gives an opportunity to learn technical skills, develop interests such as costume and make-up and gain first-hand knowledge of the problems, tensions, thrills and enjoyment of stage craft. It is not designed to train people for the stage or produce skilled actors but give sufficient experience to be able to use theatre intelligently when the opportunity arises (see Chapter 9). Reading books and plays, writing essays and critical reviews are included to give a broad overall view and an understanding of the therapeutic tool we are handling.

Therapy

Most professional training (nurses, occupational therapists, etc.) in therapy consists of a three-year full-time course. During this time the student studies physical and mental development, psychology, psychiatry, the social implications of mental health as well as the theory and practice of the selected discipline. The time allocated to each subject will vary with the training and schools put their own emphasis on different aspects. Each discipline has its own national criteria for selection and standards of basic training. Thus a group of trained therapists on a dramatherapy course will arrive with some common basic knowledge and a variety of specialist applications. The task in training is to supplement this knowledge so that each student has an opportunity to widen her approach. For example, a nurse in the mental handicap sector would be given theoretical and practical experience in working with mental illness. The student who comes with a drama background will have some experience of therapy but maybe no systematised training or reading of the subject. Lectures are designed to cover the specialist areas, but students have to make a detailed study of subjects according to their individual needs. We work on the tutorial system in order to achieve this, catering for individual needs in small groups.

There are diverse schools of thought about psychiatry. Is it a mental illness or a social one? Is it an illness at all? (Szasz, 1974). Whatever the dramatherapist's personal views may be, she has to work with colleagues who may have different ideas. It is necessary for her to be conversant with diagnostic procedures, medical theories and treatments in order to communicate with others. If she works in a hospital setting, she must know about physical and drug therapies as well as psychotherapy. Colleagues and clients will expect her to understand when they discuss treatment with her.

Training courses cover basic theory and treatment of mental handicap, forensic psychiatry, mental illness, psychology, social anthropology and relevant social studies. This is the background of training but individuals will, of course, develop their own special interest.

Group Experience

Dramatherapy is usually a group therapy. Occasionally clients can be helped more effectively in individual sessions but these are rare and frequently aimed towards inclusion in a group at a later time. Apart from work with clients who are severely brain damaged or demented, I can see no point in prolonged individual work. Drama is essentially a group medium. Stimulation and interaction with other people enrich the experience. The dramatherapist needs to know about groups. Each course provides an opportunity for the student to experience herself in a variety of group situations:

(1) *The drama group*, in which she learns drama skills. She will be a member, with the tutor as leader. Later she will take her turn in leading this group in order to gain some appreciation of skills in handling groups. Clients rarely tell us how we appear to them — our peers are less inhibited!

(2) *The large tutorial group*, in which she is encouraged to express her own views and training needs and evaluate the course as it progresses.

(3) *The small tutorial group*, to discuss written work, present book reviews and look at specialist needs.

(4) *The production group*, in which she may be allocated any role from director to actor or technician.

(5) *The placement group*, in which she may be asked to take a group of fellow students to her place of work to widen their experience and she will be asked to visit others at work.

(6) *The personal group experience.* Time is set aside each week for students to study their own behaviour in a group. As group leaders

we need to know our own strengths and weaknesses, be aware of the manner in which we act, react and interact and the repercussions that these can have on other group members. Unless we recognise our own feelings as coming from ourselves and do not project them on to others, we will be unable to help our clients towards self-discovery.

(7) *Group dynamics.* As part of the above experience, time is given to the understanding of the way in which groups work, the patterns of behaviour comes to all groups and the manner in which they achieve or avoid their goals.

(8) *The psychodrama group.* As psychodrama is linked with dramatherapy and overlaps with role play, it is important that the student has an experience of the psychodramatic process. Some students arrive for training with only a vague idea of the scope and boundaries of each. It is important that the student is aware that she is doing drama-therapy and not psychodrama, where the two overlap and where the peripheries lie in order to be explicit in her discussion with colleagues from other disciplines. The psychodrama group works on the emotional conflicts and is predominantly client-centred (Langley, D.M., 1979a). It gives the student an opportunity to experience herself in yet another group setting.

Application

Alongside the learning of skills goes the practice of them. Students are expected to be in a working situation in which they can use drama skills as soon as possible. The theory makes more sense when it is applied practically. The manner in which they work is determined by place of employment and the students themselves. Some may have been using drama techniques for some time and be confident in their group work. Others will be fresh to the field and may have anxieties at starting something new. From the commencement of training, students are encouraged to widen the scope of practice and develop fresh skills and interest in their own place of work. In their second year, there are visits to other institutions and supervised placements in different environments. The aim is to produce therapists who are competent to apply their skills in a broad range of situations. Inevitably people will specialise but a dramatherapist should have a sufficiently flexible training to allow her to adapt to working anywhere.

This discussion on training is based on my own experience as a tutor at the South Devon Technical College, Torquay. The other courses in the UK may vary slightly as each has its individual identity, but we cover the same general schedule.

Personal Training

When setting up the course at Torquay, I took a close look at my own eclectic training which had developed according to my practical needs. I realised that my clinical judgment and experience were rooted in the basic professional training I received as a psychiatric social worker. My need was to learn about groups and how to use the dynamics creatively. A course in group dynamics taken early in my dramatherapy career was most valuable. The drama skills I practised as I learned them in a variety of short drama courses and production experiences. After five years I felt the need to learn about psychodrama, and my first introduction was sufficient to convince me of its relevance in therapy. The training was extensive and long but very necessary to enable me to practise psychotherapy competently. I was proud to be the first graduate with the Holwell Diploma in Psychodrama and equally delighted to become a Certified Practitioner of the American Board of Psychodrama, Sociometry and Group Psychotherapy. It seemed that psychodrama was the only way in which I could develop new skills. Then came an opportunity to take a two-year part-time course in theatre skills. It was a comprehensive course covering all aspects of theatre, involving written and practical examinations and an original project. I took the theme of 'The theatre skills used in dramatherapy' and I found myself getting more excited as I worked on the project. It revealed whole areas of dramatic resource which I had not yet applied in therapy and prompted me to review my work with added enthusiasm. I recount this personal experience in order to emphasise the fact that a dramatherapist does not necessarily need training in psychodrama and I hope this book has shown that there is plenty of scope for the application of drama skills.

Specialist Training

Most dramatherapists want to extend their training at some time and as both psychodrama and dramatherapy have their roots in the two areas of drama and therapy, it is a logical specialised training to undertake and can supplement the basic training. I did not realise the power and versatility of role play until I had considerable training and understanding of psychodrama. It was then that I developed the pattern described in Chapter 7. I must add a word of warning, that psychodrama should not be undertaken lightly or by inadequately trained therapists. The training is long and expensive, but so is any reputable training in psychotherapy. Go to psychodrama groups and use them for your own personal development; the experience is invaluable but if you want to practise, then a full training is essential. Indiscriminate use and misunderstanding of the term psychodrama by under-trained practitioners can cause both psychodrama and dramatherapy to fall into disrepute.

Movement

Another area of special value is that of movement. There are comprehensive courses available in the Alexander technique and training in the martial arts, particularly T'ai Chi, gives a good basic training. Veronica Sherbourne has developed movement as a means of communication and incorporates it in her training for teachers. Natural dance is a popular extension of movement training and short courses are available, but I do not know of any comprehensive training established in the UK to date.

Theatre Skills

Further training is available at further education establishments and some include adult production groups. These will vary in detail and content and with the individual colleges and drama teachers concerned; I have always found drama teachers interested and helpful in meeting the needs of the disabled.

Technical Specialisation

Training in audio-visual aids is available in some colleges, but it is worthwhile looking around your own place of work. Many hospitals provide in-service training in technical skills and are more likely to supply the instruction suited to the therapeutic needs.

Counselling

These courses are useful for any therapist whose basic training did not include counselling skills. Although dramatherapy is a group therapy, there are sometimes encounters within the group that require careful handling and an understanding of individual counselling techniques can help the dramatherapist to deal with these problems.

Music

Short courses are available for anyone with musical ability who can already play an instrument. Again it is worth enquiring at local colleges of further and higher education. If there is no existing course, you may find the tutors sympathetic to your need.

Massage

As much of our work involves physical contact, some knowledge of massage can be useful. I find it can be a non-verbal way of mutual giving and receiving and often include gentle neck, hand and foot massage when working in pairs. Most people respond to its relaxing sensation and enjoy the reciprocal nature of their communication. It is given greater significance by the importance of non-verbal communication in both drama and therapy. If the group is large enough to sit in a circle with each person massaging the neck of the person in front, it can be a meaningful group experience. I believe that the therapist should have more than a vague knowledge of the tools she is using and would recommend a short course of instruction in body massage. Most natural therapy and alternative medicine centres offer massage and are usually helpful when approached about training needs.

Other Group Therapies

It is important to realise that our chosen form of group therapy is one of many. There is much to be learned by experiencing other ways of working, in particular a widening of knowledge and awareness of what others have to offer. Basic training is only the beginning and not something to be learned once and for all. We need to be open to new ideas and ways of personal development. If the therapist ceases to develop her own personality her work will stagnate. It is for each individual to decide how she extends her basic training. Experience of Gestalt therapy, transactional analysis, bioenergetics, family therapy training, women's groups, in-service support groups, etc., all have their place. Personal development does not only take place in groups. We can grow within relationships and if we appreciate this, we make time to develop them both personally and professionally. It would be a contradiction if we, who aim to facilitate personal growth and confident relationships in our clients, fail to take such opportunities ourselves.

What about Other Creative Therapy?

Art therapy has been accepted in hospitals for a long time. Music, dance, poetry and creative writing are more recent newcomers, each finding a place in therapy. So where does drama fit in? The dramatic experience is not only in the happening but in coming to terms with events: life *is* theatre (Lyman and Scott, 1975). If we subscribe to this theory of social reality, then we accept drama as inherent in everything we see, do, feel and experience. Southern (1962) describes the work of art as communication by one individual to others. There are two ways of achieving this, by making or by doing. All that is desired to be said is embodied in the action. The writing, picture or musical notation is the thing done, but theatre is doing. It is distinguished from the communication of casual conversation by the fact that it contains two meanings; the apparent and the symbolic, the latter being the more important. This view of drama as a metaphor is demonstrated by Heathcote (Wagner, 1979). Working with a group of young, pregnant, unmarried girls she took the theme of Cinderella, emphasising the social discrepancies and unfair treatment of Cinderella by her sisters. Within this improvisation the girls were able to express their anger about their own situations. The 'doing' in the dramatic sense brought the feelings about reality to a point where discussion and resolution could commence.

Other visual, oral and verbal art forms may be contained within this action, making drama a 'truly composite art' Stylan (1971). Courtney (1979) extends this idea when he talks of overt and covert drama. An action does not have to be overtly dramatic but as it contains the seeds of dramatic activity it is part of the wider concept of drama. He draws from this the conclusion that dramatherapy, as well as being a methodology in its own right, can include any other artistic medium according to the client's need. I do not take this to imply that the dramatherapist is capable of working in depth with all art forms. She must be aware of her limitations and work as part of a team.

Drama is a social activity (Stylan, 1971) and therefore best suited to clients whose needs are to be met in a group. Most of our clients have problems relating to others and this is most obvious in group situations. It is logical to start remedial work in a group setting. Drama offers alternatives to verbal communication and so is appropriate for people who are withdrawn, inhibited or have a limited verbal capacity. Acting (drama) is not simply self-expression, but communication with an audience (Swift, 1976). Maybe a client needs to learn self-expression as well as communication. A client who is very handicapped in this way (which does not necessarily bear any relation to the severity of his psychiatric disability) may need to work individually at self-expression before he can allow himself expression in a group. The material used in drama springs both from the individual and from what is happening in the group itself. We take the life that exists at a certain time with a gathering of individuals in a particular place and use it to create an experience that is of and for each member and yet personal to him as well as the group. In this way it is different from other art forms which, whilst they can be experienced in a group, the group is not essential to its existence. Art, music, dance, poetry and writing applied as therapies can be both 'making' and 'doing' in Stylan's sense but are not necessarily 'being'. Stylan points out that 'making' can be completed at any time and possibly in isolation, whilst 'doing' concentrates the effort into one particular occasion for an audience limited by those present at the time. It is the 'being' that attracts me to drama both as an art form and as a therapy. It is the shared experience that is both creative and therapeutic in one spontaneous happening. What happened to group members in the past, might have been and could be in the future, meet in the present to allow us insight into our individual personalities and behaviour.

Some institutions do not employ a variety of creative therapies or do not encourage them to work as a team. Shortage of personnel, sessional employment and rigid hierarchical systems are partly to blame for this. The therapists themselves do not always see the advantage of co-ordination and the limitations formed by a narrow outlook. Ideally, creative therapists should work as a team, working together, merging and emerging similar to the blending of an artist's paint. If separation is necessary, here are some reasons I would give for sending certain clients to creative therapies other than drama:

(1) To learn self-expression before joining a group.
(2) To extend interest or skills already learned and use them as a means of therapy, e.g. an artist or musician experiences another dimension of his art.
(3) As a sensual experience in order to encourage sensual awareness (sculpture, pottery, etc.).
(4) Beginning an individual creative therapy relating to more than one person at a time is too threatening.
(5) If the individual prefers another medium, providing his motivation is not to evade the dynamics of group therapy. Some people have a natural preference for one particular art form.
(6) If the individual is disruptive in a group but would benefit from a creative therapy.

The therapy should be flexible enough to allow one art form to arise naturally from another, each being utilised appropriate to the needs of the individual client or group. I would repeat my views stated in the chapter on audio-visual aids. The dramatherapist should know her own limitations and be aware of the overlap with other creative therapies, but not try to apply any other art form psychotherapeutically unless she has taken the appropriate training.

How to Start a Group

I asked a group of students what they found most difficult about dramatherapy. The reply was almost unanimous — 'getting started'. This is not peculiar to therapy groups and I know I am not alone in finding ambivalence an intrinsic part of creativity. It is not the writing of this book that has been difficult but the discipline of starting to write on each new theme! When once pen has touched paper the creative act has begun. Until that point I have done all manner of things in an attempt to put off the moment of creation. It has to do with time; the embryo needs to develop and it is more comfortable to acknowledge its growth than experience the pangs of its birth! When considering a dramatherapy session, the therapist is planning a group creation which she will facilitate. It is this responsibility plus the ambivalence of creativity itself and the natural nervousness arising from addressing a group which creates anxiety.

Southern (1962) points out that the actor realises that the group has the ability to destroy the individual or at least his reputation, both physically and psychologically. It is this knowledge that results in nervousness or stage fright which many experienced actors suffer. This same knowledge is apparent to the group leader. Although not enjoying the sensation, I welcome these 'nerves'. There is a flow of adrenalin that energises and gives the extra stimulus to action and a heightened awareness of other people in the group. The intensity of 'nerves' varies but is usually determined by the degree of unfamiliarity in the situation. I can offer no antidote except to say — 'Don't allow yourself to be overwhelmed by them but use them as part of the creative process'. Like an actor who has learnt his lines and is well rehearsed, adequate preparation allows the dramatherapist to meet the group with confidence if not without nervousness. So here are some practical steps which can generate a confident approach to dramatherapy:

(1) Ask yourself, 'What have these group members in common?'
    It may be a group you have purposely selected or you may have been given a preselected or random group and asked to work with it. Have group members sufficient in common to enter into a joint venture?

(2) Look for support for group and therapist. If you are to work on the ward, do the staff understand and approve? Look for a co-therapist.

(3) Talk to the charge nurse or senior occupational therapist and explain your aims and objectives. If necessary talk to the next upper line of management of the appropriate departments. Always pay attention to hierarchies and work with them, not against them. It takes time and energy but when people at the top of the hierarchy are familiar with your work, new ventures become less fraught with difficulties. Lack of co-operation is sometimes caused by ignorance and time taken to supply information and create good relationships is well spent. It is important that the nursing officer or head occupational therapist is aware of what is happening in their areas. They are responsible for the organisation of the ward or department and have a right to know. If you do not consult them you cannot expect their co-operation.

(4) If he has not made the referral personally, check that the consultant psychiatrist agrees to the client's membership of the group. He has an overall picture of the client's treatment and is ultimately responsible for it. It is possible that dramatherapy is not appropriate at this time and may upset the long-term plan of treatment. Failure to consult puts you in a difficult position if a paranoid client becomes litigious. You are giving him a treatment which has not been prescribed. You cannot expect the consultant to accept responsibility for something of which he has no knowledge.

(5) Look for an adequate space in which to work. This will depend on the nature of the group. A closed role play or personal development group needs strict privacy. A more socially orientated group may take place on the ward, allowing the more reticent to join in as they wish. Disturbed clients may need freedom to come and go during the session and this has to be taken into consideration when choosing the site of the work space. If the area is too small it may be cramped and inhibited but too large a space can be equally inhibiting or threatening.

(6) Decide the aims and objectives of the group and length and number of sessions. Plan the first three sessions. These can be reviewed after the first group meeting as they may need to be modified or changed. If you have been asked to work with a group you have not selected and are unsure of its aims, then make the first few sessions introductory and exploratory. When working with clients who are all new to dramatherapy, a few sessions just introducing the method are valuable. A session has three phases. (i) The *warm-up* in which

you prepare body and mind — this phase gives an opportunity to put aside thoughts and feelings belonging to other activities and to concentrate on the present. No one should embark on any physical activity without allowing his muscles to get into action gradually. (ii) The *main activity* embodies the objectives for the session. (iii) The *closing*, which allows the group to (a) express feelings arising from the session, (b) 'wind down' from activity, both physical and mental, and (c) share experiences, feelings and needs with the rest of the group. It allows support and warmth (physical and mental) and encourages group cohesion.

Adequate time should be allowed for each phase which should not be rigidly applied but be flexible.

(7) Have a planning meeting with the co-therapist and any other staff who will be attending the group. Explain their roles and make sure they understand the reasons for use of first names, non-uniform and the fact that there is no standard of performance.

When you start working with a group remember to:

(1) Let the charge nurse (or senior occupational therapist) know you have arrived on the ward and when you leave. She is responsible for all the clients in her care and needs to know where they are and who else is on the ward in case of crisis, e.g. fire. It is also common courtesy!

(2) Arrive early for each session, prepare the room and make sure any technical equipment (tape recorder, etc.) is working.

(3) At the end of each session wait until all clients have left the room (or delegate to co-therapist). Put away any equipment and leave the room tidy. You cannot expect ward staff to be responsible for your equipment or blame clients for damage to things left unattended.

(4) Review the session with the co-therapist and possibly charge nurse, noting anyone who may have been disturbed by the group. Make sure that the ward staff know if anyone has left in a distressed state.

(5) Find time to think about the session again the next day. You may have a different perspective and be aware of things that were not apparent earlier.

(6) Plan the next session.

Some Final Comments

Maybe this book appears to say nothing new — 'I've been doing that for years' is your reaction. Drama is as old as humanity but we do not always recognise it. When we are aware of this, practising drama becomes a new way of looking at the familiar. This fresh perspective applied to therapy can generate interest in new areas. There are so many possibilities and so many needs to be met that the enthusiast can apply skills in almost any area of therapy. If the ideas presented here are new to you, then I hope you will be encouraged to look for places to experience drama for yourself. When you have enjoyed the first training course (you should if it is sensitively presented), then start to apply your skills in small ways. It is such a wide field that you cannot start in all places at once. So begin by using your own interests and do only the things with which you feel comfortable. If movement embarrasses you or music does not come naturally, don't force yourself to use them. If you are ill at ease with any 'tool', then your clients will be also. Let the things that feel 'right' for you be done and your confidence will grow. Be on the lookout for material you can use or adapt. Drama is for everyone and ideas should be shared and not kept to oneself. If you see someone using a good idea, store it in your memory, personalise it and use it in as many ways as you can!

Go to the theatre and see how actors and playwrights apply their skills. You may come away with ideas, inspirations or enthusiasm or perhaps thinking you could have done better. In that case put your thoughts into action and find a fresh outlook for creativity. (That's how Shelagh Delaney came to write *A Taste of Honey!*) Contact local professionals. All local authorities employ drama advisers and most teachers and actors are interested in finding new fields in which to apply their skills. Drama is intrinsic to life and is there for us all to find. When we make the discovery we enter into a whole new world which brings us closer to other people and gives us an opportunity to look at ourselves through the medium of a shared creative experience. What more powerful therapy could we offer our clients?

APPENDIX III: SOME USEFUL ADDRESSES

For training courses approved by the British Association for Dramatherapists contact:

Sue Jennings,
Hertfordshire College of Art & Design,
Hatfield Road,
St Albans, Herts.

Leon Winston,
Combined Arts Department,
South Devon Technical College,
Newton Road,
Torquay, Devon

David Powley,
Drama Department,
College of Ripon York St John,
Lord Mayor's Walk,
York

British Association for Dramatherapists
   (formerly 'of Dramatherapy'),
c/o Hertfordshire College of Art & Design,
Hatfield Road,
St Albans, Herts

British Association of Art Therapists,
c/o Hertfordshire College of Art & Design,
Hatfield Road,
St Albans, Herts.

British Society for Music Therapists,
48 Lancaster Road,
London N6

Association of Dance Therapists,
7 Ashlake Road,
Streatham,
London SW16

Radius Sesame,
27 Blackfriars Road,
London SE1 8NY

SHAPE (Director: Seona Reid),
7 Fitzroy Square,
London W1P 6AE

British Library of Tape Recordings
   for Hospital Patients,
12 Lant Street,
London SE1 1QR

Council for Music in Hospitals,
240 Lower Road,
Little Bookham,
Surrey KT23 4RE

Drama with the Blind Advisory Group,
c/o Royal National Institute for the Blind,
224/8 Great Portland Street,
London W1N 6AA

The Drama Board and Central Council
   for Amateur Theatre,
PO Box 44,
Banbury,
Oxon. OX15 4EQ

Inter-Action Trust,
Talacre Open Space,
15 Wilkin Street,
Kentish Town, London NW5

National Operatic and Dramatic
   Association,
1 Crestfield Street,
London WC1H 8AU

Natural Dance Workshop,
Play Space,
Peto Place,
London NW1 4DT

Royal National Institute for the Deaf
105 Gower Street,
London WC1E 6AH

Scottish Association for the Deaf,
Moray House,
Edinburgh EH8 8AQ

PHAB (Physically Handicapped and
   Able Bodied),
42 Devonshire Street,
London W1N 1LN

Help the Aged (Recall Project),
Education Department,
218 Upper Street,
London N1

MIND (National Association for
   Mental Health),
117–23 Golden Lane,
London W1N 2ED

Scottish Association for Mental Health,
Ainslie House,
11 St Colm Street,
Edinburgh EH3 6AG

Scottish Society for the Mentally
   Handicapped,
13 Elmbank Street,
Glasgow G2 4QA

American Association of Dramatherapist
c/o Dr Barbara Sandberg,
William Pattison College,
New Jersey
New York, USA

Marcia Karp,
Holwell Centre for Psychodrama,
East Down,
Barnstaple,
North Devon.

BIBLIOGRAPHY

Aristotle (circa 330 BC) *Poetics*

Bannister, D. and Francella, F. (1971) *Inquiring Man* (Penguin, Harmondsworth)

Batchelor, I.R.C. (1969) in Henderson and Gillespie's *Text Book of Psychiatry* 10th edn. (Oxford University Press)

Bateson, G., Jackson, D., Haley, J. and Weakland, J. (1956) 'Towards a theory of schizophrenia', *Behav. Sci., 1*, 251-64

Bedaines, J. (1977) 'Psychodrama concepts, principles and issues', *J. Brit. Assoc. Drmthpy, 1, 2*, 4-9

Bennett, D.H. (1977) 'Psychiatric rehabilitation' in *Rehabilitation Today* (ed. S. Mattingly) (Update Books, London)

———— (1978) The Camberwell District Psychiatric Service 1964-67: 'The Provision of Alternatives to Mental Hospital Care in *Alternatives to Mental Hospital Treatment* eds. Stein, L. and Test, M. (Plenum Press, New York)

Bentley, E. (ed.) (1968) *The Theory of Modern Stage* (Penguin, Harmondsworth)

Berne, E. (1964) *Games People Play* (Grove Press, New York)

Berry, C. (1981) *Your Voice and How to Use it Successfully* (Harrap, London)

Bion, W.R. (1961) *Experiences in Groups* (Tavistock, London)

Blair, D. (1975) 'Medico-legal implications of the terms psychopath, psychopathic personality and psychopathic disorders', *Med. Sci. Law, 15*, 1.

Blatner, H.A. (1973) 'Acting' in *Practical Applications of Psychodramatic Methods* (Springfield, New York)

Bowskill, D. (1973) *Acting and Stagecraft Made Simple* (W.H. Allen, London)

Bracegirdle, H. (1979) 'A dramatherapy group for anorexia nervosa sufferers', *J. Brit. Assoc. Drmthpy, 3, 2*, 1-5

Brightwell, M. (1979) 'Therapist and teacher?', *J. Brit. Assoc. Drmthpy, 2, 3*, 10-13

Brook, P. (1968) *The Empty Space* (Pelican Books, Harmondsworth)

Brook, P., Degun, G. and Mather, M. (1975) 'Reality orientation: a controlled study', *Brit. J. Psychiat., 127*, 42-5

Brown, G.W., Birley, J.L.T. and Wing, J.K. (1972) 'Influence of family life on the course of schizophrenic disorders', *Brit. J. Psychiat., 121*, 241-58

Butler, R.N. (1963) 'The life review: an interpretation of reminiscence in the aged', *Psychiatry, 26*, 65-75

Cantle, A. (1980) 'Hate in the helping relationship: the therapeutic use of an occupational hazard', *J. Brit. Assoc. Drmthpy, 4, 1 & 2*, 11-31

Carruthers, M. and Murray, A. (1976) *'F/40. Fitness on Forty Minutes a Week* (Futura, London)

Carter, P. (1975) *British Images I* (ed. Campbell, R. and Lane, B.) (Arts Council of Gt Britain, London)

Chapman, J. and McGhie, A. (1963) 'An approach to the psychotherapy of cognitive dysfunction in schizophrenia', *Brit. J. Med. Psychol., 36*, 253-60.

Clare, A. (1980) *Psychiatry in Dissent*, 2nd edn. (Tavistock, London)

Clark, D.H. (1981a) *Social Therapy in Psychiatry*, 2nd edn (Churchill Livingstone, Edinburgh)

———— (1981b) *The Cambridge Psychiatric Rehabilitation Service* (Fulbourn Hospital, Cambridge)

Coffman, V.T. (1979) 'Creative drama in the elderly: the use of reminiscence and role playing with nursing home residents', University Microfilms (Ann Arbor, London)

Courtney, R. (1979) 'Dramatherapy: some theoretical questions', *J. Brit. Assoc.*
Drmthpy, *2*, 3, 1-9.
Craig, E.G. (1968) 'The art of the theatre: the first dialogue' in *The Theory of*
Modern Stage (ed. E. Bentley) (Penguin, Harmondsworth)
Cumming, E. and Henry, W.E. (1961) *Growing Old: The Process of Disengagement*
(Basic Books, New York)
Cumming, J.H. and Cumming, E. (1962) *Ego and Milieu Theory* (Atherton Press,
New York)
Davies, M.H. (1976) 'The origins and practice of psychodrama', *Brit. J. Psychiat.*,
129, 201-6
——— (1978) 'The origins and practice of psychodrama', *J. Brit. Assoc. Drmthpy*,
2, 1, 1-7
——— (1979) 'Moreno's|social theory now', *J. Brit. Assoc. Drmthpy*, *3, 1*, 16-20.
DHSS (1971) 'Better services for the mentally handicapped', Command 4683
(HMSO, London)
——— (1975) 'Better services for the mentally ill', Command 6233 (HMSO,
London)
——— (1981) 'Growing older', Command 8173 (HMSO, London)
Edmunds, B. (1983) *Apex*, January
Elefthery, D. (1975) in *Basic Approaches to Group Psychotherapy and Group*
Counselling (ed. Gazda) (Charles C. Thomas, Springfield Illinois)
Erickson, E.H. (1950) *Childhood and Society* (Hogarth Press, New York)
Esslin, M. (1976) *Anatomy of Drama* (Abacus, London)
Fairclough, J. (1977) 'Drama for the blind', *J. Brit. Assoc. Drmthpy*, *1, 2*, 14-16
Flew, A. (1973) *Crime or Disease?* (Macmillan, London)
Folsom, J.C. (1968) 'Reality orientation for the elderly mental patient',
J. Ger. Psychiat., *1*, 291-337
Ginzberg, R. (1953) 'Geriatric ward psychiatry: techniques in the psychological
management of elderly psychotics', *Amer. J. Psychiat.*, *110*, 296-300
——— (1954) 'Attitude therapy in psychogeriatrics', Conference Report, *Old Age*
in the Modern World (E. & S. Livingston, Edinburgh), pp.457-63
Gottesman, T.T. and Shields, J. (1966) 'Contributions of twin studies in perspectives
on schizophrenia' in Maher, B.A. (ed.) *Progress in Experimental Personality*
Research (Academic Press, New York)
Grotowski, J. (1969) *Towards a Poor Theatre* (Methuen, London)
Henderson, D. (1962) *Psychopathic States* (Norton, New York)
Hill, P., Murray, R. and Thorley, A. (1979) *Essentials of Postgraduate Psychiatry*
(Academic Press, London; Grune & Stratton, New York)
Holden, U. and Sinebruchow, A. (1978) 'Reality orientation therapy: a study
investigating the value of the therapy in elderly people', *Age & Ageing*, *7*, 83.
Holden, U. and Woods, R.T. (1982) *Reality Orientation* (Churchill Livingstone,
Edinburgh)
James, N. (1978) 'One way of working', *J. Brit. Assoc. Drmthpy*, *1, 4*, 17-20
——— (1979) 'Introduction to dramatherapy and the role of staff members
in a drama session' (Napsbury Hospital, St Albans)
Jaspers, K. (1963) General Psychopathology, 7th edn; (University of Chicago Press)
and translation by Hoenig, J. and Hamilton, M; (Manchester University Press)
Jennings, S. (1978) 'Dramatherapy: the anomalous profession', *J. Brit. Assoc.*
Drmthpy, *1, 4*, 1-6
——— (1982) 'Role, flexibility: a central concept for dramatherapy', Conference
proceedings (College of Art & Design, St Albans)
Johnstone, K. (1981) *Impro* (Eyre Methuen, London)
Jonstone, S. (1982) 'Recall' in *Reminiscence Theatre* (ed. G.E. Langley and B.
Kershaw), Theatre Paper No. 6 (Dartington College, Devon)
Jones, S. (1977) 'Teach the elderly' in *The Quality of Life of the Elderly in*
Residential Homes and Hospitals (Beth Johnson Foundation & Dept of Adult

Education, University of Keele)

—— (1982) 'The role of education in the long-stay ward' in *Conference Report: Quality of Life in Extended Care* (RCPsych., London)

—— (1983) 'Education and life in the continuing care ward' in *Care of the Long-stay Elderly Patient* (ed. M. Denham) (Croom Helm, London)

Jung, C.G. (1979) *Man and His Symbols* (Aldis Books, Jupiter Books)

Kaplan, G. (1961) *An Approach to Community Mental Health* (Grune and Stratton)

Kaplan, G. (1964) *Principles of Preventive Psychiatry* (Basic Books)

Kastenbaum, R. (1974) '. . . gone tomorrow', *Geriatrics* (Nov.), 29 (ii), 128-34

Kemp, M. (1978) 'Audiovisual reminiscence aids for elderly people, including the mentally frail' (DHSS, London)

Kennedy, A. (1959) 'Psychological factors in confusional states in the elderly', *Geront. Clin.*, *1*, 71-82

Klein, M. (1952) *Developments in Psychoanalysis* (Hogarth Press, London)

Koestler, A. (1964) *The Act of Creation* (Hutchinson, London)

Kuh, D. (1982) 'Evaluating service quality: key issues and concepts' in *Conference Report: Quality of Life in Extended Care* (RCPsych., London)

Laing, R.D. (1965) *The Divided Self* (Penguin)

Langley, D.M. (1979a) 'Psychodrama: the gentle art', *New Forum* (Autumn)

—— (1979b) 'Uncovering educational needs through psychodrama', *Apex: J. Brit. Institute Ment. Handicap*, *7, 1*, 26-7.

—— (1981) 'Dramatherapy in the training of psychiatric nurses', *J. Brit. Assoc. Drmthpy*, *5, 2*, 19-20

—— (1982) 'Theatre in therapy', Conference paper, Art & Dramatherapy (College of Art & Design, St Albans)

Langley, G.E. (1982) 'Quality of life in extended care' in *Conference Report: Quality of Life in Extended Care* (RCPsych., London)

Langley, G.E. and Corder, J.M. (1978) 'Workshop on the contribution of reminiscence theatre to reminiscence therapy with the elderly', Seminar report (Exe Vale Hospital, Exeter, Devon)

Langley, G.E. and Kershaw, B. (1982) *Reminiscence Theatre*, Theatre Paper No. 6 (Dartington College, Devon)

Lewis, C.N. (1971) 'Reminiscing and self-concept in old age', *J. Geront.*, *26, 2*, 240-3

Lyman, S.M. and Scott, M.B. (1975) *The Drama of Social Reality* (Oxford University Press, New York)

McMahon, A.W. and Rhudick, P.J. (1964) 'Reminiscing: adaptational significance in the aged' *Arch. Gen. Psych.*, 10, 292-8

Maslow, A.H. (1943) 'A theory of human motivation', *Psychol. Review, 50*, 370-96

Matthews, R. and Kemp, M. (1979) 'Rooms of the past strike a chord in the mentally infirm', *Geriatrics* (June), 37-41

Mian, I.M. (1982) 'Doctors, decor and diversity' in *Conference Report: Quality of Life in Extended Care* (RCPsych., London)

Miller, E. (1977) 'The management of dementia: a review of some possibilities', *Brit. J. Soc. Clin. Psychol.*, *16*, 77-83

Mitchell, A.R.K. (1982) 'Art and dramatherapy as part of a multidisciplinary team', Conference paper (College of Art & Design, St Albans)

Mueller, D.J. and Atlas, L. (1972) 'Resocialisation of regressed elderly residents: a behavioural management approach', *J. Gerontol.*, *27*, 390-2

Norris, A.D. (1982) 'The role of reminiscence in improving the quality of life in extended care wards' in *Conference Report: Quality of Life in Extended Care* (RCPsych., London)

Parlett, M. and Hamilton, D. (1977) 'Evaluation as illumination: a new approach to the study of innovatory programmes' in *Beyond the Numbers Game* (ed. D. Hamilton *et al.*) (Macmillan, New York and London)

Powley, D. (1980) 'Viva v Video', *J. Brit. Assoc. Drmthpy, 1 & 2*, 46-54

—— (1982) 'Images of power', *J. Brit. Assoc. Drmthpy, 5, 3 & 4*, 40-53

Priestley, P., McGuire, J., Flegg, D., Hemsley, V. & Welham, D. (1978) *Social Skills and Personal Problem Solving* (Tavistock, London)

Quiltich, H.R. (1974) 'Purposeful activity increased on a geriatric ward through programmed recreation', *J. Amer. Ger. Soc., 22*, 226-9

Rah, R.H., McKean, J.D. and McArthur, R.J. (1967) 'A longitudinal study of changes and illness patterns', *Journal of Psychosanatic Research* 10, 355.

Recall (1982) Part 1 – Childhood and the Great War; Part 2 – Youth & Living through the Thirties; Part 3 – The Second World War and a Different World (Help the Aged, Education Dept, London)

Reid, S. (1982) 'The role the arts can play' in *Conference Report: Quality of Life in Extended Care* (RCPsych., London)

Robinson, K. (1980) *Exploring Theatre and Education* (Heinemann, London)

Saxby, P. and Merchant, M. (1981) 'Reality orientation: a way forward', *Nursing Times* (Aug.), 1442-5

Scheff, T.J. (1966) *Being Mentally Ill: A Sociological Theory* (Aldine, Chicago)

Schneider, K. (1957) 'Primary and secondary symptoms in schizophrenia' in Hirch, S. and Shepherd, M. (eds.) *Themes and Variations in European Psychiatry* (John Wright, Bristol)

Scoble, S. (1978) 'Dramatherapy with psychotic adults', *J. Brit. Assoc. Drmthpy, 1, 4*, 13-16

Scott, P.D. (1960) 'The treatment of psychopathies', *Brit. Med. J., 1*, 1641-6

—— (1977) 'Assessing dangerousness in criminals', *Brit. J. Psychiat., 131*, 127-42

Segal, H. (1975) *Introduction to the Work of Melanie Klein* (Howarth Press, London)

Shuttleworth, R.E. (1977) 'Dramatherapy in a professional training group', *J. Brit. Assoc. Drmthpy, 1, 1*, 1-7

Simpson, S., Woods, R. and Britten, P. (1976) 'Depression and engagement in a residents' home for the elderly', *Behav. Res. & Thpy, 19*, 435-8

Southern, R. (1962) *The Seven Ages of the Theatre* (Faber, London)

Stanislavski, C. (1980) *An Actor Prepares* (Eyre Methuen, London)

Stylan, J.L. (1971) *The Dramatic Experience* (Cambridge University Press, Cambridge)

Sutherland, J.D. (1971) *Towards Community Mental Health* (Tavistock, London)

Swift, C. (1976) *The Job of Acting* (Harrap, London)

Szasz, T. (1974) *The Myth of Mental Illness* (Paladin Press/Granada Publishing, London)

Thorley, A. and Stern, R. (1979) 'Neurosis and personality disorder' in *Essentials of Postgraduate Psychiatry* (ed. R. Murray and P. Hill) (Academic Press, London)

Vaughan, C.E. and Leff, J.P. (1976) 'The influence of family and social factors on the course of psychiatric illness', *Brit. J. Psychiat., 129*, 125-37

Venables, P.H. (1966) 'The psychophysiological aspects of schizophrenia' *British Journal of Medical Psychology, 39*, 289.

Wagner, B. (1979) *Drama as a Learning Medium* (Hutchinson, London)

Ward, P. (1980) *Quality of Life in Residential Care* (Personal Social Services Council, London).

Way, B. (1967) *Developments through Drama* (Longman, London)

West, D.J. (1974) 'Editorial', *J. Psychol. Med., 4*, 1-3

Wing, J.K. (1973) 'Social and Familial Factors in the causation & Treatment of Schizophrenia'. in *Biochemistry and Mental Illness* (ed. Iverson.L.L. and Rose, S.P.R.) (London, The Biochemical Society)

Wing, J.K. (1977a) *Psychiatric Medicine* (ed. Usdin, G.) (Bruner Mazel, New York)
——— (1977b) 'Schizophrenia and its management in the community' (National Schizophrenia Fellowship, Surbiton, Surrey)

Witkin, R. (1982) Discussion in *Reminiscence Theatre* (ed. G.E. Langley and B. Kershaw), Theatre Paper No. 6 (Dartington College, Devon)

Woods, R.T. and Britten, P.G. (1977) 'Psychological approaches to the treatment of the elderly', *Age and Ageing, 6*, 104-12

Wright, J. (1978) 'A case for drama with institutionalised subnormal children', *J. Brit. Assoc. Drmthpy, 1, 3*, 9-12

Yon, K. (1979) *Word-music: Word-play*, Theatre Paper No. 4, 3rd series (Dartington College, Devon)

INDEX

actue admission wards 183-4
audio-visual aids 156-66
   art 156-8, 160-1
   drama 160-1
   music 158-61; *see also* Appendix II
   pictures/photographs/slides 162-3
   tape recorders 161-2
   video 163-6

British Association for Dramatherapists 175

clinical
   records 195-6
   responsibility 178
communication 16
concentration 16
   in schizophrenia 65

drama 9, 172-4, 203-4, 210, 215

elderly 39-53, 184-5
   game 43-5
   grouping of 40-2, 47-53
   mental disability 40
   movement 43
   music 42
   physical disability 39-40
   reality orientation 45
   reminiscence therapy 46-7
   role play 45-6
eye contact 33-4, 89, 113

games 23-38
   active 30-2
   children's 34-6
   cohesive 28-30
   eye contact 33-4
   introduction 30
   personal assessment 37-8
   quiet 32-3
   sense training 36-7
   trust 27-8
goals 17-19
   in rehabilitation 91
group
   cohesion 14, 83, 161-5

dynamics 166, 186, 206
experience 205-6
facilitator 191-2
formation 212-14

honesty 84-5
human needs 11, 180

liaison 199-200
long-stay patients 60-7, 184

management and dramatherapists
   178
mental health 173
motivation 17
movement 15
   in schizophrenia 62-5
   in social skills 122-6
   training in 208
music 158-61; *see also* Appendix II

neurosis 20-1, 185-6

occupational therapy 88, 193
organic brain disorder 21, 200-1

personal development 84, 181, 186
personality disorders 75-87
physical contact 89, 208-9
physiotherapy 88
prevention of disability 181-2, 200
professional development of dramatherapy 189
projection techniques 14
psychiatric services 176-8
psychodrama 19-20, 175, 185, 191,
   207-8
psychopathic personality 75-7
   causes of 76-7
   use of dramatherapy in 78-81
psychosis 20; *see also* schizophrenia

quality of life 180, 202

rehabilitation 88-95, 182-3
   duration of 92
   goals 91

pace of 92 2
relaxation 16, 84
remedial drama 175
reminiscence 142-55
    barriers to 144
    claimed effects of 143-4
    evaluation of 154
    further uses of 154-5
    techniques and variants of
        145-52; attitude therapy
        151; audio-visual aids 148;
        behaviourist techniques
        150-1; creative drama in
        147; other techniques 149-50;
        photography 148-9; psychiatric
        rehabilitation approach 152;
        reality orientation 150;
        role of education 151-2;
        theatre 146-7
    training of presenters 152-3
role play 96-111
    in staff training 108-10
    in therapy 102-3; fantasy
        and reality 103-5
role reversal 106
roles 96-102
    conflict 99
    function 101; see also
        rehabilitation

schizophrenia 54-74
    causes 55-6; dopamine theory
        55; double bind 56; family
        conflict 56; hereditary factor
        56; psychoanalytic 56
    explanation of 54-5;
        delusional mood theory 54;
        loss of ego boundaries 54-5;
        selective inattention 55;
        stress 55
    matters of disability 56-8;
        long stay 60-7; new
        chronic 59-60; recent onset
        58-9

relating in 65-6
uses of dramatherapy in 58-74;
    ambivalence 69-71;
    emotional stress 71-2;
    fantasy life 67-8; group
    selection 72; slowness 68-9;
    stimuli 68-9
selection of patients for drama-
    therapy 186-7, 200-1, 211
sensory perception and physical
    awareness 14
    in schizophrenia 62
simulation 106-7
social rehearsal see role play
social skills 83-4, 112-32, 165
    assertiveness training 127-32
    movement 122-6
    voice 115, 118; effective
        speech 119-22
specialist training 207-8
staff training and education 165-6,
    186, 196-9, 202-3

teaching and dramatherapy 190
team 192-5
    informal contact 194-5
    meeting 193-4
    membership of 192-3
techniques of dramatherapy 174-5,
    203-9
theatre 133-41, 215
    uses in therapy 134-41;
    audience involvement 135-7;
    entertainment 134-5; as group
    experience 137-40; reminiscence
    137; warm-up to personal work
    140-1
Theatre of Spontaneity 19, 175
therapy 11-13, 204-5
training of dramatherapists 175-6,
    203-9
trust 14
    exercises 24
    in personality disorders 79, 81
    in schizophrenia 60-1

For Product Safety Concerns and Information please contact our EU
representative GPSR@taylorandfrancis.com
Taylor & Francis Verlag GmbH, Kaufingerstraße 24, 80331 München, Germany